Grieving Days,
Healing Days

Grieving Days, Healing Days

J. Davis Mannino
Santa Rosa Junior College

Allyn and Bacon
Boston   London   Toronto   Sydney   Tokyo   Singapore

*Death and loss of love are called the great levelers.
Even power, status, eminence, achievement, or wealth
have much weight or influence in those crippling and
equalizing times when we find ourselves both victim
and survivor all in one and all at once. I know, for like
many, I've been there on both counts.*

*Alfred Lord Tennyson said, "Tis better to have loved
and lost than never to have loved at all," and I suspect
that's good advice.*

*And I am forever reminded of an elderly women whom
I met in a San Francisco park one warm sunny day in my
early years, a long time ago. She had just lost her husband
from a long bout of cancer. While we talked she cheerfully
noted: "Oh I'll see Herbie again. In fact I told him about
the time he was dying that I had sent the word up to heaven
that none of those women better be hanging around my
Herbie, cause I'd be coming for him soon enough. And
they best keep their hands off my husband too. Herbie
smiled and died that night. I'm sure glad I warned those
girlies."*

*She had one of those good laughs that's as close to crying
as you can get. And I noticed some of the gold fillings in
her teeth glistening in the sunlight.*

Contents

Chapter Three - What To Do: Understanding, Helping, and Caregiving

Chapter Four - Preparing For Death While Embracing Life

Chapter Seven - Course Organization: Assessment Tools and Strategies

Preface

How each gets through life is a piece of art, not a piece of cake.
Each day is a brush stroke, whose boldness is determined
in great measure by a belief in oneself, persistence, and
adequate change for the parking meter.

Allow me to soothe you. I have two secrets for you. By discussing death you will not invite it. The pit in your stomach, when the topic of death arises, is of society's making or from your over- or under-exposure to death. The flush of red in your face of cultural discomfort, we owe, for most of us, to our families. You may be surprised, though the wise ones are not, that when you discuss death, acknowledge death, you in fact do not invite death, but rather invite life! If I may rework an old myth: What discomforts and frightens Old Man Death more is your unwillingness to worry about him and your passion for living life fully today.

And so why is it we call it "death and dying?" Why not "dying and death" or better yet "dead and gone?" I have always wondered about this. When I was asked in 1989 to teach a course on death and dying, I was confused by the appearance of that phrase everywhere: in book titles, course titles, article titles and in day-to-day discussions. I'm wiser now. You get that way when you have the privilege of working with people who are dying. You see, death is a certainty, dying is not. Death comes in a flash. Dying is uncertain. Dying may linger, change daily, or cause frightening displays of whatever. As human beings, we are uneasy about uncertainty. That is why we have myths such as "Old Man Death." Where there is no truth, we build myths and call them truths. Death comes first in the phrase "death and dying" because we are more comfortable with the finality of death than we are with the process of dying. What we are less certain of seems to always follow last in conversation. So there, now I've shared two secrets with you. Happily, there are many more in this workbook. But let us first pull back "death's veil" and look ahead. Ooops, I'm sorry. Did that expression "death's veil" unnerve you? We'll desensitize you to all of this very soon.

Not long into the next century the United States will hit a milestone: More people will be over age 65 than under that age. These people will want to have control over how they age and how they die. Every semester my classes in death and dying are over-subscribed. The looks on student faces that first day range from horror to concealed anxiety. Yet it is they who choose to take a course in death and dying. One of the last great secrets of life: death. People, young and old, just want to know, want to have some control over their life and over their death. It is the ultimate consumerism. Why is this you say? Let us examine this thought.

We shroud death in euphemisms like "left us" and "passed on." Our society relegates the dying to somber and often emotionally careless hospital wards with code words like "oncology." We ridicule the elderly and costume ourselves in garish hair dyes, make-up, and expensive surgical procedures, all in hopes we might fool death into passing us by. And when we do discuss death, it is usually in sympathy cards which dare not even use the words death or dying. Death is romanticized in literature and the media by deathbed scenes where good-looking actors say good and sweet things and die emotionally stable and articulate moments before their death, still looking good. All this is in shocking contrast to what any caregiver will tell you.

Over two-thirds of Americans don't have legal wills. There is some macabre belief that to have a last will is to somehow rattle the cage of death to take note of us. We know very little of what to say to someone who is dying let alone actually help them. Most of us don't even know how to write a decent condolence letter. Often the best-case scenario is a delivered casserole dish--usually tuna! Few are able to discuss the death of a pet with a child, so there will be even less chance of success talking about grandma's death. Ignorance colors our fears and thus the quality of our lives. So much of our life is fearing death, that in the process, we never quite get to live life fully, appropriately, and in the manner we choose. Sadly, this legacy, in addition to a disputed material estate, is left behind to our children and survivors as well. There must be more. Surely, a life is meant to be enjoyed and not just endured.

This workbook is a hands-on way and method to understand death. It is designed to desensitize fears of death and dying and thus maximize life. It offers ways to learn, grow, and help yourself and help others better understand the processes of death and dying. It provides practical consumer-oriented exercises and activities. In short, this workbook has four goals. They are: (1) to desensitize fears of death and dying through hands-on use of exercises and activities, (2) to provide knowledge and scholarship in death education, (3) to provide tools to assist you and others in death and dying preparation, and (4) to awaken spiritual and philosophical issues so your life may become more fully actualized.

For many, a career in death and dying chooses you; you do not choose it. At least that's my take on how I find myself an educator and counselor in death education. I have worked with, loved, and lost over 400 clients, friends, and family who have all since died. The vast majority died of AIDS. It has been my perspective, and privileged view, to observe one marvelous point. If one wishes to understand the meaning of life, it will most assuredly be found in the words off the lips of those who are about to leave life. And so it is my pleasure to share with you some of the fruits of my fifteen professional years working with those who have lived, died, and journeyed on. Having been worthy of living, these now deceased persons are also worthy of being remembered. And this I do through the legacy of this book.

The workbook is comprised of over 135 exercises and activities. Everyone should find it helpful in teaching, training, and facilitating an education and an understanding of death and dying complete with all its processes. With few exceptions, most of the exercises and activities have been tried out on my students at Santa Rosa Junior College, where I have taught Death and Dying for over ten semesters. I jokingly tell my students the course is a dead-end one. Since 1982, I have worked as a consulting individual therapist and group therapist with several San Francisco programs which deal with death and dying issues. These organizations helped me to hone my skills in this important and under-recognized field. In addition to writing a monthly newspaper column on caregiving, I have been providing counseling and psychotherapy since 1968. I think I know the "business" of death and dying.

Generally speaking, when people are sick and dying, they let you know rather quickly if what you are doing is helpful or not. The result is "things in this book" work! As for which exercises and activities to use, that is up to you. My best advice is to simply become familiar with them all and choose as you see fit. A good mix will likely be the right stuff. I believe students will enjoy the workbook atmosphere as well as the journal-keeping and textbook note keeping sections in the back. You the student should complete and keep your workbook as a handy resource aide when death and dying issues occur in your life. There are many fine death education and gerontology textbooks on the current market. I have designed and developed this workbook to complement these top textbooks. You will find this list of *suggested textbooks and other selected readings* on page 229 of the workbook. I know this workbook will serve those distinguished authors and their readership well. This interactive workbook has been organized into seven chapters. Each chapter is comprised of related clusters of exercises and activities. Each chapter has a brief introduction. In the front of the workbook there is a pre-test to gauge your "beginning personal assessment base" and a post-test at the end to demonstrate your growth and development. You will find a useful *Active Journal-Keeping* section on page 246 to further explore and grow as you complete readings, exercises, and activities. It is also a wonderful place to reflect and ponder personal but related issues. The workbook has been three-hole punched with perforated "tear-out" pages for ease of evaluation and return by your instructor or facilitator. A convenient tear-out title page with place for student name is also provided. This sheet may be slipped into any three-hole binder which has a clear plastic pocket on its cover. This approach will allow you to develop a total "Loss Source" binder for other materials as you progress through your program. Keep it up-to-date and available for future reference. Before you begin use of this workbook, please be sure to review the wonderful tools available to you in chapter seven.

A note about exercise and activity layout: Each exercise has a well-thought-out formula. First, you will find an opening quote to sharpen your focus and get you thinking and feeling. Second, you will find an overview whose purpose is to provide a rationale and in most cases some particular education and scholarship on the topic. Third, there are clear directions for completing each exercise. Fourth, debriefing questions are provided to help facilitate and encourage maximum utilization and growth from each learning opportunity. I've tried to weave in a little topical philosophy for you to consider as well. Fifth, *endnotes* at the back of the workbook provide references and, in many cases, further comment and answers. Finally, an effort has been made to keep each exercise or activity focused, structured, and tight by limiting space to only what is absolutely necessary--in most cases, a couple of pages or less. Most exercises and activities may be completed individually, though they have been designed with an interactive approach of working with others in mind. I have had students, clients, and workshop participants complete the workbook entirely on their own as an independent or personal growth project. Within each chapter, exercises are arranged by logical flow and growth-building. I know you will enjoy and find the workbook helpful.

If we have the courage to face and accept our own mortality and our own death, then we, our children, and those who follow behind us will better be able to have the courage to embrace and live life. I wish you success in learning about and understanding this important topic. I hope to hear from you with additional ideas about how to improve *Grieving Days, Healing Days*. In closing, I wish you a full, happy, and long journey through this life and beyond.

Dr. J. Davis Mannino

The Russian River
and San Francisco

Acknowledgments & Dedication

I am most appreciative of the many professional colleagues, friends, and students who assisted me in the development of *Grieving Days, Healing Days*. I would like to thank a few by name. They include Linda Bacci and Don Ross of Face-to-Face for their dedication to HIV-related community education programs; Carleen Madsen, Michael Montgomery, Eileen Bunning, and Robert Jones of Home Hospice of Sonoma County; Patricia Daniels and the entire Daniels clan at Daniels' Chapel of the Roses Funeral Home; Steve Vossbrink of Santa Rosa Memorial Park Cemetery; and the Sonoma County Coroner's Office, especially Sgt. Tom Siebie of the Sonoma County Sheriff's Department. I want to acknowledge the San Francisco AIDS Foundation, the Shanti Project, and the AIDS Health Project as well. I thank my colleagues at Santa Rosa Junior College, especially Rene' Peron, Caryl Emrys-Peron, Dianne Smith, Foley Benson, Joe Simons, Jean Simons, Jan Francis, Marilyn Milligan, Georgia Barrows, Brenda Collins, and Ricardo Joseph for testing of earlier drafts of this book in his death and dying classes. Special thanks to Reta Kyle, Lori Derum, Cate Whitlock, and Susan St. Clair for their friendship and kind "support services" over the years. I would like to acknowledge my associates at Allyn and Bacon Publishers, especially Susan Badger (now President of Wadsworth Publishing), Sean Wakely, Carolyn Merrill, and Jennifer Normandin. I am particularly indebted to the students of my death and dying classes, who over the last five years provided me with the setting for developing and testing many of the materials found in this workbook. Finally, I wish to acknowledge the kind personal support from close friends Damon Jacobs, Jonathan F. King, Peter Gettner, Sasha Czamanski, Monty Broughton, and Mr. and Mrs. Edwin S. Sarsfield.

I wish to particularly single out Dr. Carla Sofka, School of Social Welfare, State University of New York at Albany, who provided a critical review of the manuscript. In great measure, any success of this book will be due to her dedicated and caring review.

This workbook is dedicated to the hundreds of patients, friends, colleagues, and family members I have had the privilege of knowing and working with and who have all since died of AIDS. It has come to be my perspective that if you wish to know the meaning of life, you will find it in the words off the lips of those about to leave life. *Ars moriendi is ars vivendi*

Pre-Test

The reports of my death are greatly exaggerated!

Mark Twain

⇒ **Overview**

The purpose of this pre-test is to gauge your beginning *Personal level of information* about some of the major issues in death education. Don't feel embarrassed if you find you have little knowledge about many of the statements below. That's why you are taking this death education course and using this interactive workbook. There are some blank spaces at the end should your instructor or facilitator wish additional item statements to be included in this pre-test. Be sure to write them in before you begin. A similar post-test is at the end of this workbook. Complete the post-test <u>at the end</u> of this course, workshop, or semester. You'll be pleased with your growth! You may wish to compare your findings in a small group. What are your strengths and weaknesses? Develop a list of growth areas to work on. Enjoy your learning.

⇒ **Directions**

Using the following five-point scale, indicate your level of agreement or disagreement with each statement. Total your score for each statement and divide by the total number of statements (40). This is your knowledge level score.

Strongly Disagree	Disagree	Neutral	Agree	Strongly Agree
1	2	3	4	5

_____ 1. I am not uneasy thinking about death.

_____ 2. I feel able to discuss issues of death, dying, and bereavement with myself and others.

_____ 3. I feel able to face and accept my own death.

_____ 4. It is important to prepare for death in myself and with others I love.

_____ 5. I am knowledgeable in helping others face issues surrounding death.

_____ 6. I understand reasons for suicide.

_____ 7. I could actively help someone who is feeling suicidal.

_____ 8. I would be able to work with someone who is terminally ill.

I understand the function and utilization of the following:

9. _____ Hospital resources	11. _____ Spiritual resources
10. _____ Chaplaincy services	12. _____ Funeral homes

13. _____	Nursing homes	16. _____	Cemeteries
14. _____	Coroner's office	17. _____	Hospice programs
15. _____	Probate attorney	18. _____	Rituals

_____ 19. I understand many of the various community self-help and support programs available for people dealing with dying, death, grief, and bereavement.

_____ 20. I am knowledgeable about the issues of patient biomedical ethics.

_____ 21. I am knowledgeable about organ donor programs and transplantation programs.

_____ 22. I am knowledgeable concerning issues about "the right to die," advanced directives, living wills, and patient self-determination.

_____ 23. I understand what my particular fears of death are.

_____ 24. I understand how culture in general and my culture in particular responds to death with rituals.

_____ 25. I could hold discussions with a dying person.

_____ 26. I understand how AIDS is transmitted and other facts about AIDS.

_____ 27. I could be helpful in assessing how serious a suicide threat is.

_____ 28. I understand issues of death due to violence and natural disaster.

_____ 29. I would be helpful to someone who has lost a pet.

_____ 30. I could plan a funeral.

_____ 31. I could assist someone who is grieving a death.

_____ 32. I am able to discuss death with children.

_____ 33. I know how to write a condolence letter and how to choose and write a sympathy card.

_____ 34. I understand how our society views death and how the media portrays death.

_____ 35. I understand what an "out-of-body" experience is.

_____ 36. I have an understanding of afterlife issues.

_____ 37. I have developed philosophical and/or spiritual values.

_____ 38. I understand some of the processes of dying.

_____ 39. I understand some of the processes of mourning.

_____ 40. I am familiar with issues surrounding aging as it relates to death and dying.

_____ 41. _____

_____ 42. _____

_____ 43. _____

_____ 44. _____

Next Edition Update
Grieving Days, Healing Days

Have a Good Activity That Should Be in This Book?
Send It in and You Will Get Credit in the Next Edition!

To: Dr. J. Davis Mannino
      Post Office Box 14031
      San Francisco, CA 94114-0031
      Fax: (707) 869-0628 or email psychdavis@aol.com

1. _____   Davis, I think the following needs to be changed in your next edition.

_____

_____

_____

_____

_____

2. _____   Davis, I think an exercise regarding the following needs to be in your next edition.

_____

_____

_____

3. _____   Davis, I have attached a copy of a suggested activity I think should be in the next edition. I understand that by signing my name below I grant permanent and free permission to use the attached exercise and that I am the said author of the exercise. I understand further that the exercise may be modified and that I will be acknowledged as the author at the bottom of the exercise.

Name: _____

Signature: _____

Address: _____

_____

Phone/Fax/email: _____

1

Death:

You, Culture, and Society

Solomon Grundy,
Born on a Monday,
Christened on Tuesday,
Married on Wednesday,
Took ill on Thursday,
Worse on Friday,
Died on Saturday,
Buried on Sunday:
This is the end
Of Solomon Grundy

Anonymous
Old English Childhood Tale

Chapter 1

Death: You, Culture, and Society

I remember clearly going to my father one day in my youth with news that a friend of the family had died. My father paused a moment and asked, "Did he die with the aid of a doctor at his side?" I thought it an odd question but nonetheless replied: "No, he died at home, Daddy." "Well, good," my father said with a smile cutting across his chiseled Italian chin, "at least he died peacefully." It was just the way my dad was, irreverent to things he or anyone else had no control over. And no one has control over death. Humor is an icebreaker in the cold, sometimes harsh realities of life. That was my culture, that was my exposure to death. Among the tight New York Italian immigrant families and neighborhoods I grew up in, humor, booze, cigarettes, and food were what funerals were all about. You drank and smoked so you could handle the awkward stress of wailing Italian widows and other relatives. You ate and talked and reminisced, and smoked and ate some more. At the wake you told funny stories about the deceased often while leaning on the coffin itself. You lit candles in church and you passed envelopes filled with money to the all-in-black Italian widows. There were always just widows, as I remembered, never any widowers. That made sense too. Italian immigrant men worked hard, drank hard, smoked hard, and ate hard. They rarely made old bones, rarely lived a long life. That was my culture, that was my life. It was New York City Italian just-the-way-it-was life and death. No more, no less.

How we first learn about death follows us through life like fingerprints. So for better or worse, any study and exploration of death should first begin with us. It is important for us to examine the relationship between ourselves, our culture, and our society with that of death and all the subtleties that come with such an examination. That is why this chapter is entitled "Death: You, Culture, and Society." I believe it a fair assertion that to enjoy life, to live a fuller more meaningful life, requires that we accept our mortality. It is not a selfish perspective to want to live a happier, fuller life. Unless we are able to embrace ourselves in a loving manner, there is little chance for much overflow into the embracing of others in our lives and in our society. A world of peace, love, and harmony does indeed begin first within each of us.

So what are your fears, doubts, concerns, anxieties, hopes, and questions about death? What were your first encounters? How did you first come to hold these thoughts, values, and attitudes about death? In this chapter of exercises you will look back, reflect upon yourselves, search for answers, and reconstruct a road map, if you will, of how you came to see yourself and death.

There are some practical reasons for accepting the challenge to examine issues surrounding death. You will have a more effective life. You will better be able to plan your future, complete a will, make decisions about organ donation, discuss with your loved ones issues of funeral plans, life insurance, and probate--to name a few areas where you stand to gain. You will, in fact, become better in the business of living. That's good!

My hope for you, as you work your way through this exciting chapter, is to accomplish what the wise ones have; that is, to be able to look death in the eye, blink if you wish, and both chuckle. Carpe diem.

Death and Dying - A Semester-Long Watch

Man is the only animal that finds,
his own existence a problem he has to solve,
and from which he cannot escape.
In the same sense man is the only animal
who knows he must die.

Erich Fromm

Student Name: _____   Date: _____

⇒ **Overview and Directions**

During our journey together as we study the important issues of dying, death, and bereavement, keep in mind the following eight questions. (1) What is the impact of death in other cultures? (2) What insights from presentations, guest speakers, and field trips did you gain? (3) What death-related issues with children, adults, aging, and AIDS came to the surface? (4) What did you learn about risk-taking behaviors? (5) How has your awareness of choices regarding funerals, rituals, caregiving options, bio-medical ethics, advance directives, and legal issues grown? (6) What did you learn about your fear of death? (7) How have your relationships with others changed? and (8) How has your personal understanding of the "precious precariousness of life" been enhanced? This is a semester-long exercise, during which you will build upon "factual and personal" growth.

Throughout the course keep an ongoing journal in the back of the workbook which addresses these eight questions. (See page 246.) This activity may be collected and reviewed by your instructor. This is a very important growth activity, so be sure to devote enough time to it. Use whatever space you need and feel free to photocopy and add more journal pages to your workbook. Allow yourself to be thoughtful and candid.

_____

_____

_____

_____

_____

_____

_____

_____

_____

_____

_____

_____

_____

_____

Living with Death and Dying

A dying man needs to die,
as a sleepy man needs to sleep,
and there comes a time when it is wrong,
as well as useless, to resist.

Stewart Alsop

⇒ **Overview**

The purpose of this activity is to provide you with a global focus regarding material to be covered in this course. The following questions will keep you tuned to some of the significant issues to be covered in your examination of death, dying, losses, and grief.

⇒ **Directions and Debriefing**

The following are questions to ask yourself and examine throughout this death education course. As we start our journey in the study of death and dying, think about its various perspectives. Take time to assess the areas that seem of particular value to you in this course. (1) Debrief what you have learned at the end of the course by using the Active Journal section located at the back of the workbook. (2) Do you feel you have learned much in these areas? You may wish to inventory your cumulative learning in an essay.

1. What insights develop from examining death from the viewpoint of different cultures?

2. What insights developed from field trips, guest presentations, and media viewings?

3. How do insights gained from examining death and childhood relate to your own death experiences as a child or adult?

4. What are some of your own risk-taking behaviors? What aspects of your lifestyle involve risking death?

5. What choices would you make regarding funeral ritual, terminal care, life-sustaining medical technologies, advance directives, and legal issues? What have you learned that can be helpful to you as a survivor of others' deaths?

6. What are you learning about yourself while confronting your own mortality and inevitable death?

7. What have you noted from studying death and dying, in terms of how this study engages both the cognitive faculties and the emotional faculties?

8. How has your awareness of death affected your relationships with others?

9. Does an awareness of "the precious precariousness of life" prompt a greater sensitivity towards your own needs, the needs of others, and a greater compassion for all?

10. How has your personal journey into death and dying had a rippling effect, extending outward to those around you, to your community, and to the global community at large?

11. What types of spiritual, philosophical, or intellectual thoughts, insights, or awakenings are occurring?

12. In what areas are you learning to better assist those in the midst of dying, death, and loss?

Death Images and You

The tragedy of life is
what dies inside a man while he lives.

Albert Schweitzer

⇒ **Overview**

I have a friend who plays the same golf course three or more times a week. Whenever he plays golf with business associates, he always wins. He must be good you say? Not at all, and he'd be the first to agree with me. He just knows that particular golf course like the back of his hand and thus generally always has a good performance. The same is true of any subject matter. If you practice with it again and again, you'll become good at it. An excellent method of learning, and learning more efficiently, is to peruse or review a textbook in advance of reading it. This proven familiarization technique will give you the upper hand for better performance, much like my buddy who plays golf all the time.

Additionally, reviewing your study materials will help you gather up your thoughts, feelings, and attitudes towards the subject matter being covered. This is most important in death education where the tendency is to deny and not to confront thoughts, feelings, attitudes, and emotions. Set the groundwork for your study of death education properly.

⇒ **Directions and Debriefing**

Individually or in group, as time allows, review your textbook and any other assigned reading materials, paying special attention to photographs, graphs, poems, quotes, drawings, and other such visual aids. Note chapter headings and subtitles. Think about your own life and how it relates to the images brought to mind by your review. Be prepared to discuss the following. (1) What were your observations from this exercise? (2) Do you find you now have a better feel for the topic to be covered? (3) What emotions, thoughts, attitudes, and feelings surfaced as you reviewed your textbook?

1. Which images are the most provocative to you?

2. What thoughts and feelings are provoked in you? In your group?

3. In which areas of death and dying do you have little or no information?

4. In which areas do you have more knowledge and information?

5. In which areas would you like to have more information?

6. If your were re-designing your textbook, or other reading materials, how might you do so? What areas not covered would you cover? How so? List improvements.

7. After reviewing photographs or other visual aids in your textbook, select two visual aids which elicited the most significant response. If this is a group activity, discuss similarities and differences among individual reactions. Use your new skills to review this workbook!

Color of Death

Ah, grief and sadness!
The fishing-line trembles
in the Autumn breeze.

Buson

⇒ **Overview**

Many of our fears regarding death are triggered by things, events, times of the year, people, smells, and even the color of the night sky. Our fears are often represented by symbols and clusters of symbols which represent death and our lack of control over this inevitable event. We sometimes "shake, rattle, and roll" with anger at our fragile mortality and our "we'll be gone like the wind" eventuality. In this exercise, examine your death hair-trigger fears using free association for the following open-ended statements. Discover what your fragile moments during the year and at other times are.

⇒ **Directions and Debriefing**

In this exercise examine your death triggers--your death bullets. Let your mind go and free-associate responses to the following. Be as candid as possible. Discuss findings in group. (1) Make a list of interesting patterns you discover. (2) How might you develop strategies for dealing with stressful times and periods of the year which represent loss in your life? Complete the "Color of Life" exercise that follows.

1. Death brings to mind thoughts of: _____

_____

2. Death brings to mind the color (s): _____

3. Death brings to mind the smell (s): _____

4. The time of day I think of when I think of death is: _____

5. Death brings to mind thoughts of weather which is: _____

6. Death brings to mind the following place or places: _____

7. The season that comes to mind when I think about death is: _____

8. The person or persons that come to mind when I think about death are: _____

_____

9. The animal(s) I think of when I think of death are: _____

10. The flower I think of when death comes to mind is: _____

11. The spiritual/philosophical thoughts that come to mind when I think about death are:

_____

_____

Color of Life

The earth and ocean seem
To sleep in one another's arms, and dream
Of waves, flowers, clouds, woods, rocks,
And all that we
Read in their smiles, and call reality.

Percy Bysshe Shelley

⇒ **Directions and Debriefing**

In the previous exercise we saw how fears regarding death are triggered by things, events, times of the year, people, smells, and even colors. Now let's do the same exercise thinking about <u>life</u> and not about death. Let your mind go and free-associate responses to the following. Try and be candid. Keep in mind that life and death are attitudes and clusters of symbols which we use to represent life and death in our minds. Might some of these attitudes and symbols be wrong in the way you "color" life?

1. Life brings to mind thoughts of: _____

   _____

2. Life brings to mind the color(s): _____

3. Life brings to mind the smell(s): _____

4. The time of day I think of when I think of life is: _____

5. Life brings to mind thoughts of weather which is: _____

6. Life brings to mind the following place or places: _____

7. The season that comes to mind when I think about life is: _____

8. The person or persons that come to mind when I think about life are: _____

   _____

9. The animal(s) I think of when I think of life are: _____

10. The flower I think of when life comes to mind is: _____

11. The spiritual/philosophical thoughts that come to mind when I think about life are:

   _____

   _____

Notes: Use this section to compare what you learned from completing the Color of Death (previous page) and the Color of Life exercises. How have these two exercises affected your attitudes on death and dying? _____

_____

_____

My doctor told me I should go out with women my own age.
I told him women my own age were all dead!

George Burns, age 100

⇒ **Overview**

Since the beginning of the century life expectancy has increased by a third. Males born in 1992 may expect to live until age 72.3 and females may expect to live until age 79.1. That's the good news. The bad news is that the "grim reaper's clock still ticks!" In 1992 a record 2.2 million deaths were registered in the United States. That's over 6,027 deaths per day. The following table[1] shows your life expectancy by birth year. The table also shows differences for both men and women. You can figure out your remaining years, on average, by subtracting your current age from your life expectancy age.

⇒ **Directions and Debriefing**

Review the table below and consider the following questions. (1) With time running out, what might you be doing differently? (2) What are your fears and what are your concerns as your "life clock ticks down?" (3) How does one maximize life? (4) What are your thoughts about the "quality of life" versus the "quantity of life?" (5) What age did your grandparents live to? (6) What age do you want to live to? (7) Do you have a "feeling" about when you will die? What is that based on? (8) What might you do to "assure" that you live longer and "beat the odds?" (9) Why do you suppose women live longer than men? (10) What negative risk factors might hasten your death? (11) What positive health factors might lengthen your life?

Birth Year	All Races Both Sexes	Male	Female
1992	75.8	72.3	79.1
1991	75.5	72.0	78.9
1990	75.4	71.8	78.8
1985	74.7	71.1	78.2
1980	73.7	70.0	77.4
1975	72.6	68.8	76.6
1970	70.8	67.1	74.7
1960	69.7	66.6	73.1
1950	68.2	65.6	71.1
1940	62.9	60.8	65.2

Assessing Your Life Expectancy

And our hearts like muffled drums,
are beating funeral marches to the grave.

Henry Wadsworth Longfellow

⇒ **Overview**

Shaking his head with an ain't-no-big-deal-look-on-his-face, a dying cancer patient whom I worked with and admired said: "Like a change of clothes, that's all, like a change of clothes, death is." Cool and somber right to the end, this patient was most clear about how much life expectancy he had left when he said: "Not much!" We humans are presumably the only living creatures who know they will die at some point in time. How does that affect and shape your actions, beliefs, and behaviors in life? How do these contribute to your expectancy of life? Will you live long or will you live short? In a sense, how do you load the dice?

Life expectancy, as a term, is defined as the average lifespan in years for persons born in the same calendar year. For the average American, life expectancy has increased from 47 years in 1900 to around 75.8 years for someone born in 1992.[2] Most of this increase is due to cleaner water, healthier food, shelter, and better medical care. But other factors affect death as well. Special occasions, such as holy days, birthdays, and important events can help determine death. Some people literally die when they're ready, when their special event has come and gone.[3] Both Thomas Jefferson and John Adams died on July 4th in 1826. Mark Twain died on the eve of Halley's Comet arriving, a date he predicted he would die on. Place of death affects life expectancy too. Death rates are higher in Africa than in North America. Higher infant mortality and lower life expectancy due to poor quality of life are the culprits there. Longevity and life expectancy are influenced by the important variables of sex, marital status, ethnic background, and personal differences such as diet, exercise, temperament, personality, and heredity. Women live longer than men because men are more prone to abuse their bodies with alcohol and drugs, to smoke, to engage in violence, to harbor emotions and stress, and to have poor social support systems in place. As women enter the workplace and take on roles and lifestyles similar to those of men, their life expectancy becomes similar to that of men. In other words: less! One wonders if there a price for equality in our society? What factors affect long life?

⇒ **Directions and Debriefing**

The following questionnaire is for older adults. Younger students should "anticipate what your life might be in the future" when answering questions 9, 10, 11, 13, and 14. The questionnaire provides a rough estimate and points to the inevitability of dying. It identifies some specific ways of increasing your chances of living a longer life. Obviously, not all factors are accounted for here, but the major factors which account for a person's life expectancy are. (1) Share your findings in class. (2) How did you "add up?" (3) What are some of your thoughts about this exercise? (4) How might you improve your life? (5) How do you feel about your score? (6) Were there any surprises? (7) To what extent do people have control over life and death in themselves and others? (8) How do you account for self-destructive behavior in yourself and others? Do you have any new goals?

13

Life Expectancy Questionnaire[4]

_____ 1. Start with 72[5].

_____ 2. Subtract 3 if you are male; add 4 if you are female.

_____ 3. Subtract 2 if you live in an urban area with over 2 million people.

_____ 4. Add 2 if you live in a town of under 10,000 or on a farm.

_____ 5. Add 2 if any of your grandparents lived to age 85.

_____ 6. Add 6 if all four of your grandparents lived to age 80.

_____ 7. Subtract 4 if either parent died of a stroke or a heart attack before age 50.

_____ 8. Subtract 3 if either of your parents or a brother or sister under 50 has (or had) a heart condition, cancer, or has had diabetes since childhood.

_____ 9. Subtract 2 if your earn over $50,000 a year.

_____ 10. Add 1 if you finished college; add 2 more if you have a graduate or professional degree.

_____ 11. Add 3 if you are 65 or over and still working.

_____ 12. Add 5 if you live with a spouse or friend. Subtract 1 for every 10 years you have lived alone since age 25.

_____ 13. Subtract 3 if you work behind a desk.

_____ 14. Add 3 if your work requires regular, heavy physical labor.

_____ 15. Add 4 if you exercise strenuously five times a week for at least half an hour. Add 2 if you exercise strenuously two or three times a week.

_____ 16. Subtract 4 if you sleep more than 10 hours each night.

_____ 17. Subtract 3 if you are intense, aggressive, easily angered.

_____ 18. Add 3 if you are easygoing and relaxed.

_____ 19. Add 1 if you are happy. Subtract 2 if you are unhappy.

_____ 20. Subtract 1 if you have had a speeding ticket in the past year.

Source: From Aiken, Lewis R. _Dying, Death, and Bereavement._ © 1994 by Allyn and Bacon. Reprinted by permission.

Fear   death?
To feel the fog in my throat,
the mist in my face.

Robert Browning

⇒ **Overview**

There are many shades of loss in our life and many fears regarding death, dying, and these losses. Use the following exercise to help you explore these various kinds and types of losses. You may wish to use this exercise in conjunction with the "Death Anxiety Scale" on page 18 in this chapter and with the "Fears in a Dying Person's Life" exercise found on page 93 in chapter four.

⇒ **Directions and Debriefing**

Individually, or in a small group, try and categorize your personal fears and fearful experiences regarding loss and death. Develop a list of these fears. Identify those related to death. Discuss how these fears prevent the individual and society from living life to the fullest. Come up with specific examples from your own life about how fear has hampered your living life more fully. Other losses to consider include: (1) dissolution and divorce, (2) war and violence, (3) lifespan and generational losses, (4) stigma and disenfranchisement, (5) mental functioning losses, and (5) losses from natural disasters.

15

I Am Afraid of Dying!

No man can be ignorant that he must die,
nor be sure that he may not this very day.

Cicero

⇒ **Overview**

I once told a colleague of mine that I was taking my psychology of death and dying class to the cemetery for a field trip. Wide-eyed with open mouth, he snapped: "I wouldn't be caught dead there!" Jokingly I asked my colleague where, then, did he want to be placed when he was dead, since he didn't want to be "caught dead" in a cemetery. His uneasy smile gave way to bewilderment and silence. On another occasion, while taking an evening class on a field trip to a funeral home, the night sky broke into terrific rain and thunder while we were at the funeral home. Halfway through the presentation and tour our gracious host summoned us all to the coffin display room, where to my total surprise was a birthday cake complete with candles ablaze. It was my birthday. How they found out I don't know. What a sight! With the night sky flashing and crackling with lightening, rain, and thunder, there we all were, leaning on shiny new coffins eating birthday cake and drinking coffee. No one would ever forget that night, I am certain. It is a story told often at the college where I teach. What a "death-defying" night indeed!

Death in and of itself has no meaning except for what each of us gives it. And what each of us usually gives death is fear. Death anxiety or death fear seems to rise out of ignorance rather than fact. So why does death have such a bad reputation? Americans of all ages have been taught to systematically fear death. There are ghosts and goblins, bogeymen and skeletons, and horror movies and Halloween. Anything to do with death is to be avoided at all costs. The American way of dying is a negative mindset. By avoiding situations involving death, we soon begin to ascribe to death a dishonest view that it is more terrible, more frightening, more scary, and therefore more avoidable. On field trip experiences, my students are constantly commenting about how ordinary the county morgue really is. Facts often dispel fears. Often what you get differs from what you fear.

Some death fears are provoked by proximity. That is, you've seen someone die in an auto accident, you've seen someone drown, you've seen someone shot and killed, or you've seen a suicide. Proximity to the experience can lessen fears. But such events are uncommon to most people. So what it comes down to is this: Death is what we charge it with emotionally. Michael Lemming describes eight basic death fear types. (1) dependency, (2) pain in the dying process, (3) indignity in the dying process, (4) isolation, separation, and rejection (often part of the dying process), (5) leaving loved ones behind, (6) afterlife concerns, (7) the finality of death and, (8) the fate of body remains.[6]

Exactly how fearful are Americans about death? Many "self-report" scales, such as Templer's *Death Anxiety Scale* (found on page 18), have been used extensively and seem to show a low-to-moderate anxiety level. A 1991 Gallup Poll found three out of four adults did not fear death.[7] How accurate these findings are is still subject to much debate and discussion. How would you have answered that question?

16

Directions and Debriefing

This exercise is designed to help you recognize and confront your death fears. Identify your sources of death anxiety and fear by responding to each statement. To the left of each statement write in Yes, No, or Maybe to describe your fear level. (1) Break into small groups and discuss your responses. (2) Were there some common fears? (3) Were you surprised by your fears? (4) How might you manage these fears? Develop some strategies with the class. (5) What might be some positive results of not fearing death? (6) What might be some negative results of not fearing death? (7) How might you desensitize your fears of death and issues of mortality? As a class, develop some strategies for dealing with your fears, getting your life to work better, and becoming a fuller and healthier person.

I am afraid of:

1. _____ a lingering death.

2. _____ a sudden and violent death.

3. _____ accidental death.

4. _____ being helpless and having to depend on others.

5. _____ the pain associated with dying.

6. _____ death because I don't know what happens after death.

7. _____ death from a disaster.

8. _____ dying alone.

9. _____ dying before I am ready to die.

10. _____ having a heart attack or dying of cancer.

11. _____ leaving behind those who count on me most.

12. _____ leaving behind, sad and hurt, those who love me.

13. _____ losing control over my body.

14. _____ losing my ability to think and feel.

15. _____ losing those I love.

16. _____ being murdered.

17. _____ not having time to amend my sins or wrongdoings.

18. _____ nothingness.

19. _____ punishment after death.

20. _____ sudden death.

17

Death Anxiety Scale [8]

The fear of death is more to be dreaded than death itself.

Titus Livius

⇒ **Overview**

"The only thing we have to fear is fear itself," said Franklin Roosevelt in 1933 as the Great Depression swept through America. Might the same be said of death? Upon close examination might you find it is not death we fear, but rather the fear itself? It is an absolute truth that each of us is entitled to one life and one death. How does fear haunt us and keep us from living that life? What are your fears? Are you afraid of spiders? Are you afraid of airplanes? Do you fear death? dying? pain? This exercise will help you look at and examine some of your fears. As Thoreau said back in 1851, "Nothing is so much to be feared as fear." In other words, the monster that haunts us, many times, is nothing more than the fear of ourselves. When we face ourselves and face our fear, this fear begins to dissipate. Fear may be the number one obstacle keeping us from fuller lives.

⇒ **Directions and Debriefing**

During reflective time or in group, respond to the following statements. Circle T if the statement is true of you. Mark F if the statement is false of you. Complete all statements. You must choose. There is no right, wrong, or average response. This exercise will give you some insight into your feelings and anxieties about your own sense of mortality. See endnote #8 in the back of the workbook for scale responses and commentary.

T	F	1.	I am very much afraid to die.
T	F	2.	The thought of death seldom enters my mind.
T	F	3.	It doesn't make me nervous when people talk about death.
T	F	4.	I dread to think about having to have an operation.
T	F	5.	I am not at all afraid to die.
T	F	6.	I am not particularly afraid of getting cancer or AIDS.
T	F	7.	The thought of death never bothers me.
T	F	8.	I am often distressed by the way time flies so rapidly.
T	F	9.	I fear dying a painful death.
T	F	10.	The subject of life after death troubles me greatly.
T	F	11.	I am really scared of having a heart attack.
T	F	12.	I often think about how short life really is.
T	F	13.	I shudder when I hear people talking about World War III.
T	F	14.	The sight of a dead body is horrifying to me.
T	F	15.	I feel that the future holds nothing for me to fear.

Death and Dying - Spirit and Soul

Leaves have their time to fall,
and flowers to wither at the northwind's breath,
And stars to set--but all,
Thou hast all seasons for thine own, O Death!

The Hour of Death
Felicia Dorothea Hemans

⇒ **Overview**

A client of mine called in total despair. As a gay man, he had watched all of his friends die of AIDS. He not only was alive but was also free of the HIV virus which causes AIDS. So why his despair? So why his troubling call to me? Doctors had just told him he had incurable leukemia. "There was nothing more we can do," the doctors said. Just because we escape one close call or one fatal disease doesn't mean others aren't still lurking in the shadows. After all, life is a fatal disease. It will eventually get us all. But there is more than just death and dying of the flesh and bones. There is also death and dying of the spirit and soul. What other kinds of "death-like" events are human beings also experiencing during the course of their lives? This exercise will help you realize that there is more to death than just death of the flesh and more to life than just being alive. Put on your "reflective hat" and ponder.

⇒ **Directions and Debriefing**

We experience many losses in a lifetime. The losses most commonly acknowledged are those involving a death. However, the most common losses are those related to changes or transitions that may happen once or many times. On the following page is a "Loss History Checklist." Place a check by the losses you have experienced. When you have completed this checklist, consider the following debriefing questions.

(1) How do these conditions in life steal away our hopes and dreams and ultimately our very life? (2) Were you surprised by how many losses other than death you have experienced? What is the condition of your spirit and soul? (3) How might we all contribute to humanizing life a little bit more for all of us? (4) Did any of the checklist items have particular meaning to you? Which ones? Why? Are there other checklist items you might have included? (5) When finished, consider your thoughts about this exercise.

Notes _____

_____

_____

_____

_____

_____

_____

_____

_____

_____

_____

Loss History Checklist*

A. Losses through <u>death</u> of:

_____ biological mother	_____ biological father	_____ adopted mother
_____ adopted father	_____ foster mother(s)	_____ foster father(s)
_____ child(ren)	_____ grandparents	_____ husband/wife
_____ grandchild(ren)	_____ companion/lover	_____ other relative(s)
_____ brothers	_____ sisters	_____ friend(s)
_____ pet(s)	_____ counselor/therapist	_____ support person(s)

Other(s)? Describe. _____

_____

B. <u>Relationship losses</u> that did not involve death include:

_____ my own divorce	_____ my own separation(s)
_____ divorce of parents	_____ separation of parents
_____ loss of boyfriend/girlfriend	_____ loss of co-worker(s)
_____ loss of neighbors	_____ loss of doctor(s)
_____ loss of contact with parents	_____ loss of counselor/therapist
_____ loss of contact with children	_____ unable to have children
_____ loss of contact with brothers/sisters	_____ loss of custody of children
_____ loss of contact with friends	

Other(s)? Describe. _____

_____

C. <u>Other losses</u> such as:

_____ loss of home/residence	_____ loss of support services	_____ unable to walk/be active
_____ being homeless	_____ loss of identity	_____ abuse (all forms)
_____ loss of job	_____ loss of potential	_____ loss of independence
_____ loss of ability to work	_____ loss of control	_____ loss of freedom
_____ loss of physical health	_____ loss of time/years	_____ loss of dreams
_____ loss of vision/hearing	_____ loss of purpose in life	_____ loss of goals
_____ loss of sexuality	_____ loss of personhood	_____ loss of spirituality/faith
_____ loss of trust	_____ loss of neighborhood	_____ loss of safety
_____ loss of childhood/innocence	_____ loss of country (refugee)	_____ loss of security
_____ loss of comfort	_____ loss of possessions	_____ loss of privacy
_____ loss of sense of humor	_____ loss of money/income	_____ loss of confidence
_____ loss of self-esteem	_____ bad accident or fire	_____ loss of respect
_____ loss of life as it was	_____ loss of hope	_____ other?

Other(s)? Describe. _____

_____

Source: "Loss History Checklist," by Dr. Carla Sofka. School of Social Welfare, University at Albany, New York. © 1996. Do not reproduce without permission.

A Dead-End Exercise

Grow old with me!
The best is yet to be.
The last of life,
For which the first was made

Robert Browning

⇒ **Overview**

While riding a subway in New York City a long time ago, I overheard two young guys talking. I'll never forget their conversation. It struck me as so very odd then, and even more so now in retrospect. "I'm dead-serious," this guy said to the other, "she was drop-dead gorgeous. There she was dead-ahead walking towards me while I sat killing time. She was a dead-ringer for Janis Joplin [a 1970s music legend who died of a drug overdose]; you know I've been dying to meet her." The other guy responded kind of laughing, "Why would she want to meet a dead-end, deadbeat guy like you?" They both laughed and the first guy concluded with, "Wow, this conversation is dead, dead in the water!"

These two college students' whole conversation was filled with death words and idioms. Though death really wasn't the subject matter, you still received the message from their conversation that death was ever-present, didn't you? We lace death as a descriptor throughout much of our everyday language. Death has impact on our lives and so too does death impact our everyday language usage. Death is never really far from our consciousness, is it? It is interesting to note that when we do mean to use the words death and dying, we don't, and when we don't mean to use the words death and dying, we do. For example, we're more comfortable using euphemisms such as "passed on" or "gone" when what we mean is died or dead. But when we don't mean death and dying, we feel free to use them like in my college student example above. The message here for us to learn is simply awareness. If we can become more aware and understanding of death, perhaps we might become more able to live as people.

⇒ **Directions and Debriefing**

Examine these common death-related expressions used in non-death situations. Be careful not to mix up euphemisms for death with death-related expressions used in non-death situations. (See "Euphemisms for Death" on page 22.) (1) How might our awareness of death affect how we live our lives? (2) What unconscious motivations of death and dying do you suppose hamper our living more fully in the "now?" (3) What would people's lives be like if we had no fear of death? (4) If we had no death at all?

body of death	dead serious	dead-ahead	deadbeat
dead end	deadhead	dead-end career	drop dead
dead-end course	dying to get out of here	dead from the neck up	dying to meet you
dead personality	graveyard shift	dead reckoning	killing time
dead-right	political suicide	dead-ringer	scared to death
deadweight	talk to death	to die for	to my dying day

_____   _____   _____   _____

Euphemisms for Death

It is nothing to die;
it is frightful not to live.

Victor Hugo

⇒ **Overview**

As humans beings our fear of death and dying shows clearly in the hundreds of euphemisms we have for death in our own English language. The English language is not alone, for every language and every culture have their own list of euphemisms for death. It is as if we don't call it death, it won't be death, it won't be so. It seems no one wants to use the "D" word. You need only look to sympathy cards to see proof! They almost never use the word dead or death in their flowery prose. When the late President Kennedy was assassinated in 1963, I remember watching a television announcer say: "He now belongs to the ages." In other words, President Kennedy had died. This announcer did not want to use the "D" word.

⇒ **Directions and Debriefing**

In this exercise, name euphemisms for death you are familiar with; for example, "dead as a doornail" and "gone with the wind." Try to determine their usage and meaning. Try and relate them to context, culture, and society. Point out usage in language such as the expressions, "We lost him" or "He passed on." <u>After</u> you have developed your list of euphemisms, compare your list with the list of euphemisms on the following page. Note both serious and humorous usage in language and separate by harsh and gentle expressions. See if you can come up with some cross-cultural examples as well. Get used to using the "D" word.

1. _____

2. _____

3. _____

4. _____

5. _____

6. _____

7. _____

8. _____

9. _____

10. _____

11. _____

12. _____

13. _____

14. _____

15. _____

16. _____

17. _____

18. _____

19. _____

20. _____

21. _____

22. _____

23. _____

24. _____

Euphemisms for Death in American English Language

A long sleep
Angels carried them away
Annihilated
Ashes to ashes
Asleep in Christ
At river's end
Back to the molecules
Belongs to the ages now
Beyond the great divide
Bit the dust
Bought the farm
Breathed their last
Brought down the curtain
Burnin' in hell
Called home
Came to an end
Cashed in
Changed their form
Checked out
Consumed
Croaked
Crossed over Jordan
Curtains
Dead as a door nail
Departed
Departed this life
Dodge City
Down glory's road
Dropped the body
Ended his/her days
Ended it all
Eternal rest
Expired
Feeling no pain
Fertilizer now
Found everlasting peace
Gave it up
Gave up the ghost
God took 'em
Gone but not forgotten
Gone fishin'
Gone home
Gone to heaven
Gone with the wind
Goner
Got mertelized
Got on with it
Heard the trumpet call
History now
In cyberspace

In God's hands
In the arms of God
In the great beyond
In the spirit
Is no more
Just pooped out
Kicked the bucket
Laid to rest
Left this world
Left us
Liquidated
Lost/Lost it
Lost on the table
Lost the race
Made the change
Met their maker
Moved on down the line
No longer with us
Nothing but kitty litter now
On the heavenly shores
On the other side
Out of their misery
Passed on/away
Perished
Pushing up daisies
Ran out of gas
Ran out of time
Resting in peace
Retired
Returned to dust
Reunited with those gone before us
Rode into the sunset
Rubbed out
Signed off
Six feet under
Snuffed
Succumbed
Terminated
That was all she wrote
Their time was up
Transcended
Translated into glory
Was done in
Was taken
Was taken by the "grim reaper"
Wasted
Went on to glory
Went out like a light
Went to their eternal reward
With the angels

With the big mainframe now
With the force
Withered away
Wormmeat
Zapped
Zittzed
Called to a final reward
Shakin' hands with the devil
Living in box city
Lying in State
Gone over
Went to a new life
Napping in dirt
Offed themselves
Ate it
At rest
Final rest
Bit the big one
Sleeping
Is in a better place
Roadkill

Cultural Customs of Death

In the long run we are all dead.

John Maynard Keynes

⇒ **Overview**

It is as certain as the moon ups and the sun downs that death is universal. What is not universal is how each of us responds to it. Death elicits responses which are molded by our attitudes, values, and beliefs. They are uniquely ours, because each of us derives from a culture. Whether it be the prevailing culture or a smaller subculture, our vision and our world view are colored by our culture. I come from an Italian family. My culture treats and responds to death differently than someone from a Jewish or Hispanic or other particular religious background. The beauty of examining different cultures is we better learn to understand our own culture and our own world. My hope is you will spend time with your reading materials and instructor examining cultural issues in death and dying.

⇒ **Directions and Debriefing**

In group compare and contrast aspects of your culture, or another culture you are familiar with, regarding death and dying rituals. Use your textbook for guidance. Discuss the following questions in class. Prepare for a lively discussion. Try to examine your own personal culture and compare it with another culture of your choice.

1. What culture have you chosen to examine? Describe some beliefs and practices.

_____

_____

_____

2. What aspects of these practices did you like? dislike? Why?

_____

_____

_____

3. Describe how the disposition of body remains is handled. Explain some of these tasks.

_____

_____

_____

4. What are some death rituals and customs? Give examples (i.e., burial ceremonies).

_____

_____

5. What are some of the cultural beliefs concerning afterlife? religion? spirits?

_____

_____

Customs, Culture, and Death

Turn up the lights,
I don't want to go home in the dark!

O'Henry

⇒ **Overview**

Nothing affects our understanding, our fears, or our beliefs about death and dying more than the culture we are from and the religion we practice. For example, in Mexico, "El Dia de los Muertos," or "Day of the Dead," not only celebrates family members who are dead but even pokes fun at some of the silliness of death and dying rituals and practices. Among some American Indian tribes, the name of the deceased is never mentioned because to do so would anger the spirits. In some African cultures, death is not complete until a funeral of "great standing" has occurred, sometimes years later, after a family has gathered and saved up enough money to carry out the funeral in the prescribed manner.

⇒ **Directions and Debriefing**

In group develop a list of death customs you and your family have participated in or heard about. Use as your frame of reference both your culture and your religion. When you return together as a class, be prepared to compare and contrast customs you have participated in with those of other cultures described in your readings. (1) What are the purposes of these customs and beliefs? (2) How do these customs and practices fit into the larger society? (3) How does this exercise make unfamiliar practices seem less bizarre, less unfamiliar, and less exotic? (4) Which customs and practices might you like used at your own death ritual? (5) About which customs do you want learn more?

Notes: _____

_____

_____

_____

_____

_____

_____

_____

_____

_____

_____

_____

_____

_____

_____

_____

Collage on Death

To every thing there is a season,
and a time to every purpose under the heaven:
A time to be born, and a time to die;
A time to weep, and a time to laugh;
A time to mourn, and a time to dance.

Ecclesiastes

⇒ **Overview**

The visual arts have long depicted the fear, sadness, and precarious uncertainty of death, dying, and loss. Many an artist has been driven to seek refuge in a visual medium as a reprieve from the powerful emotional charge of loss. And equally so, many a patron of the arts has sought solace in the commissioned works of artists. Throughout history no subject has had more representations than death. Whether in classical mythology or in the great religious texts, one may find the visual arts serving as gatekeepers to the heart and soul of our very questioning existence. Death knows no cultural boundaries. Whether it be the art of Native Americans, African Bush tribes, or on the tombs of ancient Egyptians, the themes, if not the actual stories, are often the same: birth, life, demise, and death. Western civilization is filled with images of death. No angle of death has been left untouched, it would seem, from an artist's rendering.

Art is a timeless medication for easing the pain of loss and an age-old therapy for the countless moments in life when loss may seem all but unbearable to us. Art therapy has long been used for processing suffering, pain, and loss. "One day at a time, keep busy," was often the advice I heard while growing up around loss, death, and grief issues. Whether you work the ceramic wheel, sculpt, paint on canvas, or work the shutter of a camera, art is an excellent form of expression for dealing with loss. Hands-on involvement with the visual arts can provide us a better examination and understanding of our thoughts and of our fears about death and dying. Use the following exercise to familiarize yourself with the visual arts. How might they help you manage some of life's losses in your life?

⇒ **Directions**

For this exercise you will need scissors, some glue, heavy duty butcher-type paper, coloring pencils or crayons, and several colorful magazines. The goal of this exercise is to examine life and death through the medium of a collage. Cut and trim as many clippings as are associated with life, dying, and death. You may write in words and phrases, but they are to be kept to a minimum. Remember, the accent in this exercise is on the visual! Take careful note of how you represent life and death in your collage. Consider the following: (1) What was difficult and easy in constructing your collage? (2) Did you show a strong distinction between life and death or did they blur? (3) Be prepared to explain your collage, and thus some of your current attitudes about life and death. (4) What insights did you gain? (5) As an alternative, assign one group the task of constructing one group collage. What issues developed in trying to reach "collage consensus?" (6) How might art therapy be helpful for someone dying or experiencing loss?

26

Death in the News

The lightning said to the oak tree:
Stand aside, or take what is coming to you!

Sufi tale

⇒ **Overview**

"Elvis Presley can't be dead, I just saw him on television!" The mass media has a way of blurring and numbing our view of reality and death. Death touches our lives from a dozen poignant and matter-of-fact angles each day. "Oklahoma City Bombing--Hundreds Dead!" "Firefighter lost fighting fire!" "Police officer killed in drug war crossfire!" These are common headlines in our local newspapers. Technology brings death right into our homes. From the early days of the Vietnam War to the Challenger space shuttle disaster of 1986 to the "blow-by-blow" battle play of the Desert Storm war in Iraq, death is in our faces, up-close and personal. Death arrives on our doorsteps personally and impersonally day in and day out. Most recently it has been the horrid bloodshed in Bosnia. Late Soviet Union dictator Josef Stalin once observed: "A single death is tragedy, while a million deaths is a statistic."

Our view of death is sanitized, coded, and isolated in our society. We don't have the firsthand experience we need to place a "face" on death, to personalize death. As long as death is a statistic, we don't have to feel any emotion. Early each semester, in my death and dying classes, I ask students if any of them have had any experience with death that class day. Almost all say no, thinking I'm talking about immediate family. All have forgotten or chosen to "selectively omit" the dozen or so discussions of death which occurred on that day and for that matter each day of the year. We all tend to forget the newspaper accounts of death, the magazines, the books, the movies, the television, the radio, the readings, the personal accounts, and even the sights around us: accidents, shootings, and sundry killings of animals and otherwise. Death is everywhere, whether we choose to see it or not see it. Death is much more than a death notice or an obituary. This exercise will bring home this point.

⇒ **Directions and Debriefing**

One activity to help increase our awareness of death and dying and enhance our understanding of the power of the media in fashioning our attitudes towards death and dying is to examine the type and kinds of articles found in our local newspaper. Such an activity will assist in sensitizing and formulating a deeper level of empathy for anyone who has loved someone who has died. Also, understanding different ways people die allows us to better develop helpful strategies for survivors, and maybe even for preventing some deaths.

Review a major daily newspaper. Inventory or cut out different articles on death. Take one of the most impersonal articles and rewrite the article by personalizing and adding a "face" to that impersonal death. Be prepared to read in class the impersonal article and the rewritten version. (1) What are your thoughts about how we desensitize ourselves to death? (2) How does the media shape our images? (3) Why might it be important to not be too desensitized to death? (4) Is society truly preoccupied with death? Or does the media tend to focus on death-related news events because they are considered newsworthy, placing the topic in front of a typically death-denying society? (5) Clip your article to this page.

27

*It is impossible to experience
one's death objectively and
still carry a tune.*

Woody Allen

⇒ **Overview**

The media's view of issues related to death permeates our society to the core. Therefore, the media is an important source for understanding society's view of death. This exercise will help you better understand death through an examination of the media.

⇒ **Directions and Debriefing**

Over the next week or so, select art, photographs, and magazine and newspaper clippings which show and discuss death and dying. Bring in your favorite choices. Submissions will be collected and distributed randomly in class. In group discuss your thoughts and feelings from these images. Bring your selections to class and prepare to discuss the following.

1. What specifically about each image caught your attention or triggered an emotional response in you?

_____

_____

2. What themes and topics regarding death and dying were found in the media?

_____

_____

3. What values, attitudes, and behaviors from culture and society are "commented upon" in the media?

_____

_____

4. Relate the above to lyrics in music and dialogue found in movies and television regarding death and dying.

_____

5. How difficult was it to find cartoons and humor in the media regarding death?

_____

_____

6. Compare the various images and gauge how different groups responded to them and how they compare to you.

_____

Television and Death

He can't be dead, I just saw him on television!

⇒ **Overview**

Perhaps no medium is more responsible for our understanding and misunderstanding of death and dying than television. Cartoons characters get run over by steamrollers, and their deaths are reversed with no serious consequences to their bodily functions. Then, their slapstick comedy routine returns in the blink of an eye. A good example of this is "The Itchy and Scratchy Show" from the Simpsons TV show--a cartoon show within a cartoon show. Moving from imagination to reality, the vivid scenes of the war in Vietnam told us too well that war was indeed hell complete with body bags, body counts, and on-the-scene coverage of "instant death."

People have always been mesmerized by life and death hanging in the balance, only a breath and TV remote control away. The medical, police, and emergency-type shows which are filling our airways these days are great examples of how television portrays death and dying. For television, death is a time of contrition. Good must prevail! The guilty confess on their deathbed and on cue. The wrongfully accused are cleared moments before they die with their loved ones in attendance. Death seems to come timely and forthrightly. There is something in our society's psyche which says all wrongs must be righted and justice and truth prevail, if not in life, certainly no later than prime-time death time. What does this all say about our sense of truth and fair play? Why are we always waiting and expecting the condemned killer to confess and apologize for their atrocities just moments before their execution? Why is it we expect the record to be set straight at death time? What is it about morality and death we hold so sacred?

⇒ **Directions and Debriefing**

For this exercise watch several different medical, police or emergency-type programs on television, paying special attention to how terminally ill patients, their doctors, nurses, other caregivers, family, and friends are shown and portrayed. Another method is to watch the evening news. Be prepared to discuss the following questions in class.

1. How do fictional television show portrayals of death and dying differ from evening news accounts?

2. What were the patient ages, sex, and economic levels in the shows you watched?

3. What were the personalities like? Were there differences in "good guys" versus "bad guys?"

4. How did family and medical staff treat these TV show patients?

5. How was death presented? Realistically? Any stereotypes? Cultural issues?

6. What were some of the causes of these television deaths?

7. Were the deaths similar or different from your own experience with and perspectives of death?

8. What values, morals, and ideals were expressed in these deaths? Humor? Euphemisms used?

9. Which shows did you find most realistic? Most unrealistic? Fun to watch?

Deathbed Media Scenes

And I looked, and beheld a pale horse:
and his name that sat on him was Death.

Revelations

⇒ **Overview**

Deathbed scenes have been stylized and idealized throughout human history. The young American Indian brave summons his companions to battle with the chant "It is a good day to die!" The godfather blesses his family one last time. The biblical sinner renounces his ways and embraces Christ while nailed to a cross. The Japanese kamikaze pilot aims his plane into an American aircraft carrier. The frontier marshal who is hit with a fatal bullet as his guns blaze away at cowboy criminals while the sun sets in the backdrop.

The two greatest sources of romanticized deathbed scenes come from literature and television.[9] Most of us are familiar with some or many literary deathbed scenes. So let's talk about television. TV has always depicted deathbed scenes as though they were a farewell performance for the dying actor. The romanticized portrait of the dying person is generally one of happy and gentle kindness. The dying person looks and talks well right up to the moment of death--something that, in fact, rarely happens. The words are always loving, forgiving, and mostly sweet-sounding. What most healthcare professionals and caregivers will tell you is that people generally die in death as they were in life. If they were grumpy, angry, and persnickety sorts, they'll go out that way too. If they were easy going, gentle sorts they'll go out that way as well. If a person was unable to self-actualize in life, it is unlikely they will accomplish it at dying time. After all, dying is a fairly time-consuming process, not conducive for getting one's life together. That is not to say there are not exceptions and profound transformations during the dying process, but the script is fairly predictable based on one's life to date. Death is a time for honesty. And dying can be a process by which to achieve that honesty.

⇒ **Directions and Debriefing**

In this exercise focus on deathbed scenes you've read about in literature and seen in the "pop-death" media. (1) Come up with your own list. What did you find? (2) Why have these fantasies developed in the arts and in our society? (3) What do you believe you might find in real deathbed scenes? (4) What are some of your fears and anxieties about your own deathbed scene? (5) What do you think your actual deathbed scene will be? (6) Will you even die in bed or will it be in an accident, murder, or other tragedy? (7) We've heard the expression "the good death." What, in fact, does the good death actually mean to you? What would a good death and a good deathbed scene be for you? (8) Is there anything we can do to assure a good death or good deathbed scene? Explain yourself.

As a continuation of this exercise ask yourself: Will you die at home or in some other institution? Will you die of old age or in your prime? Will you die quickly or slowly? Will you have those you love around you or be away from them? Will you remain alert to the end or in a drugged stupor? Will you die in pain or free of pain? Nobody really knows the answers to these questions, do they? But what are your speculations?

Humor and Death

I'm not afraid of dying.
I just don't want to be there
when it happens!

Woody Allen

⇒ **Overview**

Where I grew up there was a funeral parlor which sponsored a large advertising billboard along a stretch of highway notorious for accidents. The sign read: "Don't drink and drive! We'd rather wait. Mulheny's Funeral Parlor." And then there is the gravestone with a simple begrudging comment carved in stone: "I told you I was sick!" A colleague of mine tells the story of his late father Bill, who kept his sense of humor right to the end. Bill, old and tired, arrived at the hospital after a long decline in health. Death was only a short ways off. The attending nurse, while holding Bill's hand, offered: "You can let go Bill, it's OK to let go. You can go now, just follow the white light." After several minutes of being told to "to go, let go," Bill opened one twinkling eye and said: "OK, but only if you come with me!"[10] Even during the worst of times some people rise to the occasion as though it was the best of times. My late brother Gary was one such example. Isolated in a distant hospital wing, dying of AIDS, and only 33 years old, he was nearing death when I flew in from San Francisco to be with him in New York. When I got to his dying bedside and asked how he was doing he replied: "Well, it's not a 'Macy's White Flower' sale day." The cartoon on the following page pokes fun as well at that last great taboo: discussion of death. At the beginning of each semester I introduce my course to my bewildered students as a "dead-end course." Humor, and the laughter from it, is a great icebreaker.

What do all these different examples of death humor have in common? They are all methods of dealing with the fragile veil separating life from death and with our whispering uneasiness of this simple knowledge. Death humor is as varied as the town we live in or the culture we come from. In Mexico death is celebrated in a yearly national fiesta know as *El Dia de los Muertos*--Day of the Dead. Death is satirized with humorous candy skulls and coffins. Children playfully dance with skeletons and eat bread made in the shape of bones. Death itself is made fun of in almost defiant fashion while the deceased relatives are given renewed respect and encouragement to return back and rejoin families for dinner. Places of respect are set at the dinner table and food served to the returning spirits. As you perhaps now know, humor is a way of neutralizing the nail-biting and pit-in-the stomach feelings that death brings about in most of us; the uneasiness of the unfamiliar. Emotionally speaking, our options are quite limited. We either shut up and shut down or open up and speak up. Humor is the great equalizer in a society which discourages breaking down the long established taboo of discussing death.

⇒ **Directions and Debriefing**

During the next week or so, select a cartoon or other media expression which deals with death in a humorous fashion and manner. Paste a copy of your submission below. Be sure to credit its source, creator, date, etc. (1) Why did you choose the humor you did? (2) Bring examples to share in class. (3) Explore how humor is useful in stressful situations.

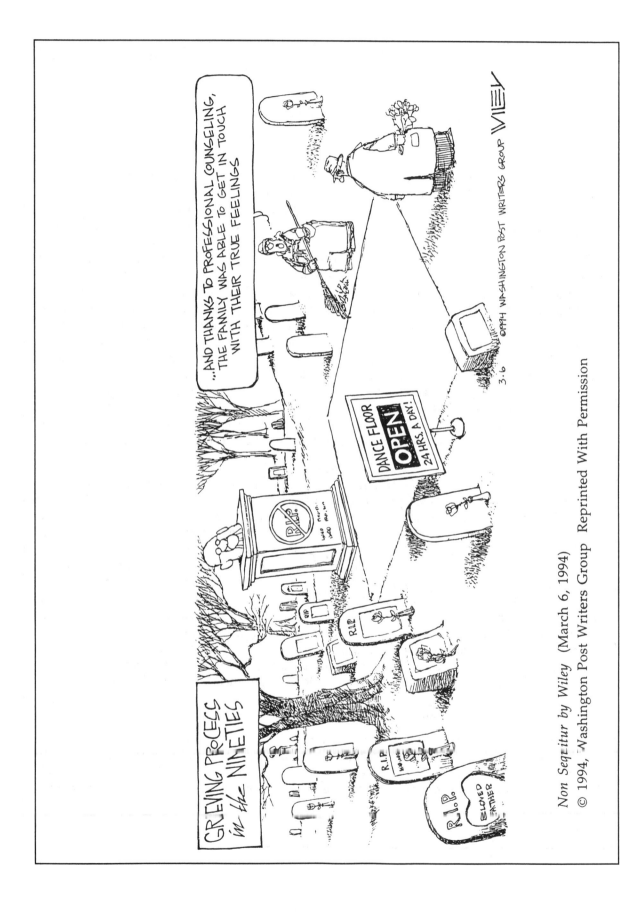

Non Sequitur by Wiley (March 6, 1994)
© 1994, Washington Post Writers Group Reprinted With Permission

Paste your humor selection from the media on this page.
Be sure to see the cartoons in this workbook on pages 1, 32, 242, and 245!

Filling Out Your Own Death Certificate

But at my back I always hear
Time's winged chariot hurrying near;
And yonder all before us lie
Deserts of vast eternity.

Andrew Marvell

⇒ **Overview**

Nothing so symbolizes death more than a death certificate! It is legal assurance of fact that someone is indeed dead. The death certificate is such a potent symbol that when one is mistakenly filled out for a person who is in fact not dead, the occurrence may often make the local radio and TV news stations. This exercise provides an opportunity to review a death certificate and to actually fill one out on yourself! The exercise will take you "up-close and personal" to your own sense of mortality and death. Death certificates are important documents required for release of pension and life insurance funds to survivors and in wills and probate matters. So there is educational and consumer value in becoming familiar with them. Additionally, you will not have such an opportunity again, at least in this life, to fill out you own death certificate! The next time your name is on a death certificate, you'll be dead! So enjoy the novelty.

⇒ **Directions and Debriefing**

Complete the following standard California* death certificate as you see fit. Be somber. Be humorous. Be realistic. The choice is yours. This is one of the best exercises for desensitizing some of the societal fears and personal fears about death and dying that we might harbor. When done, be prepared to discuss your responses, feelings, and thoughts. This document is often very bureaucratic in nature and difficult to complete. Your instructor or facilitator may need to explain what some of the information requests mean on the death certificate form. Be sure to fill in all the blanks.

Consider the following as you complete this exercise. (1) Which information asked for was personally difficult for you? (2) Which questions dealt with lifestyle risk factors that you currently face? (For example, death from cancer due to smoking, etc.) (3) You may want to address some of the issues this exercise brings to the surface in your Active Journal Keeping section. (4) Consider individually, in group, or in class your reactions to completing this activity. (5) Why did you fill out your death certificate the way you did?

_____

_____

_____

_____

_____

_____

*To get a copy of the death certificate used in your state, contact your local county or state health department.

34

CERTIFICATE OF DEATH
STATE OF CALIFORNIA
USE BLACK INK ONLY

STATE FILE NUMBER | LOCAL REGISTRATION DISTRICT AND CERTIFICATE NUMBER

DECEDENT PERSONAL DATA

1A. NAME OF DECEDENT—FIRST (GIVEN) | 1B. MIDDLE | 1C. LAST (FAMILY) | 2A. DATE OF DEATH—MO., DAY, YR. | 2B. HOUR | 3. SEX

4. RACE | 5. HISPANIC—SPECIFY | YES | NO | 6. DATE OF BIRTH—MO., DAY, YR | 7. AGE IN YEARS | IF UNDER 1 YEAR — MONTHS | DAYS | IF UNDER 24 HOURS — HOURS | MINUTES

8. STATE OF BIRTH | 9. CITIZEN OF WHAT COUNTRY | 10A. FULL NAME OF FATHER | 10B. STATE OF BIRTH | 11A. FULL MAIDEN NAME OF MOTHER | 11B. STATE OF BIRTH

12. MILITARY SERVICE | 19 ___ To 19 ___ | NONE | 13. SOCIAL SECURITY NO. | 14. MARITAL STATUS | 15. NAME OF SURVIVING SPOUSE (IF WIFE, ENTER MAIDEN NAME)

16A. USUAL OCCUPATION | 16B. USUAL KIND OF BUSINESS OR INDUSTRY | 16C. USUAL EMPLOYER | 16D. YEARS IN OCCUPATION | 17. EDUCATION—YEARS COMPLETED

USUAL RESIDENCE

18A. RESIDENCE—STREET AND NUMBER OR LOCATION | 18B. CITY | 18C. ZIP CODE

18D. COUNTY | 18E. NUMBER OF YEARS IN THIS COUNTY | 18F. STATE OR FOREIGN COUNTRY

20. NAME, RELATIONSHIP, MAILING ADDRESS AND ZIP CODE OF INFORMANT

PLACE OF DEATH

19A. PLACE OF DEATH | 19B. IF HOSPITAL, SPECIFY ONE: IP, ER/OP, DOA | 19C. COUNTY

19D. STREET ADDRESS—STREET AND NUMBER OR LOCATION | 19E. CITY

CAUSE OF DEATH

21. DEATH WAS CAUSED BY: (ENTER ONLY ONE CAUSE PER LINE FOR A, B, AND C) | TIME INTERVAL BETWEEN ONSET AND DEATH

IMMEDIATE CAUSE (A)

DUE TO (B)

DUE TO (C)

22. WAS DEATH REPORTED TO CORONER | REFERRAL NUMBER | YES | NO

23. WAS BIOPSY PERFORMED | YES | NO

24A. WAS AUTOPSY PERFORMED | YES | NO

24B. WAS IT USED IN DETERMINING CAUSE OF DEATH | YES | NO

25. OTHER SIGNIFICANT CONDITIONS CONTRIBUTING TO DEATH BUT NOT RELATED TO CAUSE GIVEN IN 21 | 26. WAS OPERATION PERFORMED FOR ANY CONDITION IN ITEM 21 OR 25. IF YES, LIST TYPE OF OPERATION AND DATE.

PHYSICIAN'S CERTIFICATION

27A. I CERTIFY THAT TO THE BEST OF MY KNOWLEDGE DEATH OCCURRED AT THE HOUR, DATE AND PLACE STATED FROM THE CAUSES STATED. | DECEDENT ATTENDED SINCE | DECEDENT LAST SEEN ALIVE MONTH, DAY, YEAR

27B. SIGNATURE AND DEGREE OR TITLE OF CERTIFIER | 27C. CERTIFIER'S LICENSE NUMBER | 27D. DATE SIGNED

27E. TYPE ATTENDING PHYSICIAN'S NAME AND ADDRESS

CORONER'S USE ONLY

28A. I CERTIFY THAT IN MY OPINION DEATH OCCURRED AT THE HOUR, DATE AND PLACE STATED FROM THE CAUSES STATED. | 28B. DATE SIGNED

28A. SIGNATURE AND TITLE OF CORONER OR DEPUTY CORONER

29. MANNER OF DEATH—specify one: natural, accident, suicide, homicide, pending investigation or could not be determined | 30A. PLACE OF INJURY | 30B. INJURY AT WORK | YES | NO | 30C. DATE OF INJURY MONTH, DAY, YEAR | 31. HOUR

32. LOCATION (STREET AND NUMBER OR LOCATION AND CITY) | 33. DESCRIBE HOW INJURY OCCURRED (EVENTS WHICH RESULTED IN INJURY)

FUNERAL DIRECTOR AND LOCAL REGISTRAR

34A. DISPOSITION(S) | 34B. PLACE OF FINAL DISPOSITION | 34C. DATE MO. DAY. YR. | 35A. SIGNATURE OF EMBALMER | 35B. LICENSE NO.

36A. NAME OF FUNERAL DIRECTOR (OR PERSON ACTING AS SUCH) | 36B. LICENSE NO. | 37. SIGNATURE OF LOCAL REGISTRAR | 38. REGISTRATION DATE

STATE REGISTRAR

A. | B. | C. | D. | E. | F. | CENSUS TRACT

MAKE NO ERASURES, WHITEOUTS, OR OTHER ALTERATIONS

VS-11 (REV. 7-92)

2

Young Losses:

Infants, Children, and Adolescents

And when he shall die
take him
and cut him out in little stars
and he will make the face of heaven
so fine
that all the world
will be in love with the night
and pay no worship
to the garish sun.

William Shakespeare
Romeo and Juliet

An eight-year-old child just told by her parents that "grandma has left us" responds, "But won't she need her socks? They're still all in her bedroom." Children bring a simple and blessed logic of their own to death, dying, and loss, don't they?

The study of death and dying with children and adolescents is not new. The father of the American Psychological Association, G. Stanley Hall, studied the topic in 1904.[11] Hungarian psychologist Maria Nagy studied the topic in 1948.[12] She found three age-related stages children go through as they learn to process and understand death. First, children learn death is a form of separation, followed by death is an escapable fact, and finally they settle into understanding that death is final and irreversible. The fact that discussion of death and children seems to go unnoticed in our prevailing society is more a reflection of how our society views death. If it is something to be hid and not discussed in general, then children in particular will be "protected" from seeing and discussing death at all. This is a shame as studies show children are very aware of the death and dying process.[13] Whether they are included or not included, death colors and affects them throughout their lives. Culture affects children as well. In a recent study, children's thoughts on death were compared in Sweden and America. The thoughts of American children depicted violent causes for death (violence in our society and on TV may account for this), whereas in Sweden, children's thoughts included more cultural symbols, such as crosses, churches, and cemeteries. [14]

"You're a dead dude, man. I zapped you," I heard a four-year-old say as his Nintendo game consumed just a hint of a whisper of his energy level. It all comes down to one basic fact: children, even the youngest, think about death. Whether it be from early childhood experiences with the death of a pet or the death of daddy, children soon process death in various ways. Death is in the songs and rhymes of play and in the rough-and-tumble day-to-day of childhood. Fairy tales are spiked with images of death and yesterday's games are often reflections of the death of the times. For example, the song and game "Ring-Around-the-Rosie" reflected the harsh realities of the plague years of fourteenth-century Europe. "Rosies" referred to the red and black spots of the disease visible on the skin and "all fall down" referred to dying.[15] Today's children are no less involved in games of death as evident in the cyberspace games of computer animation. A child's understanding of death is a developmental one. Accordingly, how we discuss death with a child must be in a context that recognizes their developmental stage. And that is sometimes no simple task.

This chapter examines many facets of death and the young. You will explore "discussing death" with children to how children "process" issues surrounding death. You will examine memories and attitudes in your own childhood. You will explore "drawing death" to discussing infant losses. From storytelling to myth-writing, opportunities are abundant for examining the whys and hows and therefores of childhood, death, and you. Finally and most amazingly of all, you will hopefully learn some of the secrets of childhood resiliency that allow children to spring back happily from the depths of loss--something we adults seem less able to do. And that's a "super cool idea, dude," as the young kids today say!

Childhood Memories of Death

The hospital, which is on the way to McDonald's,
is the place people go on their way to heaven.

nine-year-old girl

⇒ **Overview**

Listening to others share memories of loss in their lives sometimes opens up memories of loss in our own lives. Memories long past are often perceived as safer than dealing with current feelings of death in our here and now. A review of past memories, feelings, and experiences surrounding death may also affect the way we see our present. This coloring has a strong influence on how we live our lives. Resolution of these losses and repressed memories can contribute to a higher level of well-being. Life's best lesson is to remember not to forget life's past lessons.

⇒ **Directions and Debriefing**

In group, discuss and compare your earliest childhood memories of death using the following questions. Keep the above comments in mind as you discuss the following questions, and also consider how repression of stressful events in our lives might hinder our quality of life. Consider what you would teach children about death and dying. Be as candid as possible.

1. What are some of your earliest childhood memories, feelings, and experiences surrounding sickness, dying, and death?

2. Who did these experiences involve? Family? Friend? Pet? Neighbor? Sibling?

3. What do you recall most vividly and least vividly?

4. How did your family handle the loss?

5. What did you learn of sickness, dying, and death from friends?

6. What kinds of children's games did you play relative to death and dying?

7. Was death explained to you? If so, how? Whom did you go to for help and care?

8. Were you ever seriously ill or near death? Has someone close to you died?

9. Have you ever killed living things? animals? people? during military service? in self-defense? What are your thoughts and feelings about these killings now?

10. Are there aspects of your life today which carry emotional scars or other "psychological baggage" from your early childhood memories, feelings, and experiences of death and dying ?

11. What other questions might you ask or encourage others to explore in this exercise? What have you learned from this exercise about your own death attitudes?

12. Based on this exercise, what do you suppose we adults might do to better assist children and adolescents in: (1) dealing with death, (2) exploring death, and (3) examining their own feelings and experiences?

Drawing Death

Between grief and nothing, I will take grief.

William Faulkner

⇒ **Overview**

Forget as you may, death is not easily forgotten! Sometimes we tend to repress that which is sad and hurtful in our lives. Our first losses, those first deaths in our lives, are all such events we may hide away in the back reaches of our mind like movie house stubs in blue jean pockets. Sometimes memories of death remain forever vivid in our minds. They follow us along like a hungry and stray puppy, longing for care and resolution.

⇒ **Directions and Debriefing**

For this exercise you will need to bring in a box of crayons or coloring pencils and some drawing paper. In group think back to any childhood memory of death. Who was your first loss, your first death? Was it a grandparent? Was it a pet? Was it a parent or a sibling? Was it the next-door kid you used to play with? As a group, guide yourselves into recalling details using all your senses of touch, smell, sight, and sound. Try and recall who, what, where, and when. Defer to your dreams, think back to your youth. With these memories as a backdrop, draw a picture of that death.

After completing your drawing, prepare for a lively discussion. The key is not to be timid. Take some risks and express yourself. Use signs and symbols to represent your thoughts as you experiment in drawing death. Above all, have some fun. Tempted as you might be, as in childhood, please don't eat your crayons!

During this exercise, consider your feelings and emotions from these questions and guidelines. (1) What feelings surface? (2) What fears surface? (3) Are you frustrated trying to draw death? (4) What is the frustration level for others, such as for children? (5) Try and draw using your non-dominant hand. The task is toughened, isn't it? (6) List some of the obstacles children and adults must overcome in dealing with death. Have patience, take time, and grow! (7) What were some of the happy and hopeful moments and memories which came to mind as you were drawing? Perhaps knowing the suffering was over for the special person or animal in your life is a good enough memory. (8) Use the space below to draw some universal symbols of death, such as a "skull and cross bones."

Child Expert

"Who killed Cock Robin?"
"I" said the sparrow,
"With my bow and arrow, I killed Cock Robin"
"Who saw him die?"
"I" said the fly,
"With my little eye, I saw him die."

Who Killed Cock Robin?
Mother Goose Nursery Rhymes --Anonymous

⇒ **Overview**

The purpose of this exercise is have you learn and then compare the various theoretical models for how children process and develop an understanding of death. It is suggested that the theories of Freud, Erikson, Piaget, and Nagy be explored and considered.

⇒ **Directions**

This exercise requires four groups. Each assigned group is to consider themselves as Freudian, Eriksonian, Piagetian, or Nagy child experts. Spend an appropriate amount of time discussing the most important elements of your particular school of thought. Your chosen theories should directly apply to how children understand and process an understanding of death and dying. Each group should be prepared to explain, in their own words, how their model relates to children's comprehension of death. This assignment may be assigned in advance to enable you to research these theorists.

Almost all textbooks have some reasonable coverage of of these theorists, but I would recommend the following primary sources for discussion of their theories. For the purist, you might look at Freud, S. (1959). Mourning and melancholia, *Collected Papers*, vol. 4. New York: Basic Books, pp. 152-170; Nagy, M. H. (1948). The child's view of death. *Journal of Genetic Psychology*, 73, 3-27; Erikson, E. (1950). *Childhood and Society*. New York: W.W. Norton; Pulaski, M. A. S. (1980) *Understanding Piaget: An Introduction to Children's Cognitive Development*. New York: Harper and Row; Gruber, H. E. and Voneche, J. J. (Eds.) (1977). *The Essential Piaget*. New York: Basic Books.

⇒ **Debriefing**

(1) What are the major similarities and differences between these theories? (2) Which theory do you like best? Why? (3) Can you relate to any of these theories from your own experiences in learning about death? (4) How might these theories be used to facilitate and help children learn about death? Which theory do you suppose would be best to use if you were to write a children's book on loss? (5) What does "attachment theory" say about children and their responses to death?

*A note about the nursery rhyme which opens this exercise. The rhymes of Mother Goose originated in French as Contes de ma mere l' oye (Mother Goose Tales ,1697) by Charles Perrault (1628-1703) The tales were first translated in 1729, as *Mother Goose's Melody* in 1781 by Robert Samber, and published in London by John Newbery (1713-1767), who originated the publication of children's books. There are other versions of the rhymes, such as *Gammer Gurton's Garland* (1784), which also included older rhymes of English origin.

Writing a Death Myth for a Child

If it is convenient that there be gods,
and, as it is convenient, let us believe there are.

Albius Tibullus

⇒ **Overview**

It is the human experience to provide certainty where uncertainty lies. What we do not know for sure we weave into a fabric of often colorful myths which, in short time, take on truth. Myths are filled with symbolism. We as humans like our patterns of truth as long as we have woven them. This exercise should be introduced with a discussion of the origin, purpose, and use of mythology in understanding and explaining death. The purpose of this exercise is to understand how myths affect our thinking and our everyday lives concerning death. It is a wonderful cross-cultural experience as well. Students are encouraged to bring in myths from other cultures to share. Remember that they should address how children are exposed to death through the use of myths.

⇒ **Directions and Debriefing**

Write a myth about death suitable for a child in middle-childhood. For example, you might use the theories of Freud, Piaget, or Erikson as a guide. Myths written from the perspective of different cultures would enrich this experience greatly. The myth should be your sole creation, double-spaced, typed, and fill a full sheet of paper. An option may be to collect the myths and read them aloud. In one of my small classes, we bound them into a booklet so all the "merry myth-makers" could have a copy. The following are questions for you to consider.

1. What difficulties did you encounter in completing this exercise?

2. How did you choose your symbols? the story line? characters? setting?

3. Did you construct a myth which adhered to your views on death?

4. Did you incorporate anything related to who you are or your own experience into your myth?

5. What were your thoughts after hearing readings from the other myths?

6. Was there common symbolism regarding death in the myths that were read?

7. Did some of the myths capture the flavor of your "woven truths" (things you hold to be absolute truths)?

8. Try out some of the myths with children, yours or others. Report back to class.

9. Were these myths read suitable for middle-childhood kids? others? who?

10. Do the myths appeal to the child in you? What are the universal messages?

Children, Death, and "The Bog"

In Flanders fields the poppies blow
Between the crosses, row on row.

John McCrae

⇒ **Overview**

Discussing death with a child is serious business. How this topic is approached and handled can have lifelong repercussions for how children manage issues of death as adults. The following selection is from a popular horror novel. It contains a description of a child's response to death. This exercise[16] will help you formalize and apply your learnings to date.

⇒ **Directions**

Read the excerpt from Michael Talbot's "The Bog"[17] and respond to the following questions. Discuss your findings in class, and prepare responses to the debriefing questions at the end of the excerpt.

1. Which euphemism does the father use when describing what happened to Ben? Underline each appearance in the excerpt.

2. Pick another euphemism and substitute it for the one used in the story excerpt. How does the excerpt read now? What other substitutions can you could up with?

3. Using Piaget's model of cognitive development, identify the developmental phase that is presumed in the father's explanation.

4. What age range might you suspect is associated with this developmental phase?

5. What are some of the characteristics of this phase?

6. What message is the parent communicating about death in this story?

7. Based on your text readings and class discussion, what do you think about the parent's communication skills? Use specific examples to identify the elements you find appropriate as well as the elements you find inadequate or inappropriate.

8. Given the child in this story is a survivor from a high-grief death, identify several possible benefits to this child from this conversation with his father.

9. Do you find such instances where fictional characters talk with children about death are unusual in contemporary novels?

10. What "expert advice" might you give the author if you knew, in fact, the child was only five years old?

11. What are your thoughts about the dialogue at the point where the child is crying and the father intervenes?

Excerpt from "The Bog"

Tuck wiped the tears from his eyes as he pondered this. "Daddy?"

"Yes, Tuck?"

"Are we still going to move?"

"Not for the time being. Maybe in a little while."

Tuck fiddled with a button on his shirt. "I'm glad we didn't leave," he returned. "You know why?"

"Why?"

"Because that would have meant that we were leaving Ben behind." After this remark Tuck continued to fumble distractedly with his shirt button, gazing meditatively off into space. David drew in his breath, grateful at least that Tuck had not phrased the remark in the form of a question, and hugged his son tighter. Nonetheless, a moment later David noticed that Tuck's expression had taken on a darker cast, and as he continued to stare off into the distance some inner voice seemed to be speaking to him, prodding him with things he found painful.

"Daddy?"

"Yes, Tuck?"

"Is Ben ever coming back?"

David closed his eyes as he embraced his son tighter still. It was the question he had been dreading. As long as he himself had been ignorant of Ben's fate it had been easy to be evasive, to postpone confronting the matter. But now that he knew the truth he was left in a quandary. The last thing in the world he wanted to do was tell Tuck the truth, for he feared it would send Tuck even further into his ever-increasing depressions. But after what he had said about Mrs. Comfrey he felt he had no right to lie. He took a deep breath.

"No, Tuck. Ben isn't coming back."

Tuck remained absolutely motionless, absorbing the information with no visible sign of distress.

"Why not?" he asked.

David took another deep breath. "Do you know how every fall the flowers die and the leaves fall off the trees? Do you know why they do that?"

Tuck shook his head in the negative. "Cause winter's coming?" he offered tentatively.

"Partly because the winter's coming," David returned. "But partly because they have to make room for the new flowers and leaves. You see, that's the way nature works. Everything has a beginning and an end. If it didn't the world would become stagnant, like a bucket of water that you just let sit and sit. Can you imagine what the world would be like if everything lasted forever? Just think about it. Every bee that ever lived, every tree and every person would still be here, and what a crowded place it would be. The only problem is that it's painful when things we love go away. We miss them and that's okay. But what's not okay is to think that it's bad that things have to go away, because it's not bad. It's a very important thing. It's what allows new flowers to grow, and new leaves to replace the old, and the world to renew itself."

"And Ben went away?"

"Yes, Ben went away."

Text of pg. 192-194 from *The Bog* by Michael Talbot. Copyright © 1986 by Michael Talbot. By permission of William Morrow and Company, Inc.

"Where did he go?"

"To heaven," David replied.

Tuck's lower lip started to quiver. "But why did he have to go to heaven?"

"Because it was his time to go."

A large tear rolled down Tuck's cheek and hit David's arm, and he gave his son another reassuring hug. "Hey, now, I don't want you to be upset about this. I told you the truth about Ben because I don't want you to be afraid when things have to go to heaven. Too many people in this world spend too much time being afraid of that, and it's just silly. When something goes to heaven it's a scary thing, and it's a painful thing. But you've got to be brave about it. Things don't go to heaven very often, but when they do, you've got to face it like a man."

Tuck wiped the tear from his eye. "I've got to have moxie, huh, Dad?"

David smiled. He had forgotten about that. "Yes, Tuck. You've got to have moxie."

⇒ **Debriefing**

(1) How was death discussed with you as a child? Explain. (2) Would you be able to discuss death with a child? Explain. (3) What are the key points to remember when discussing death with a child? (4) Should students receive education about how to discuss death with children? with adults? If you were developing a curriculum, what would you include? What would be most important to teach about death and dying?

_____

_____

_____

_____

_____

_____

_____

_____

_____

_____

_____

_____

_____

_____

_____

_____

_____

The Dos and Don'ts of Discussing Death and Dying with Children

Afterlife is where good people go. You know, like Heaven.
The other people, the bad ones, go where it's hot all the time,
like in Florida. "

nine-year-old girl.

⇒ **Overview**

Everyone seems to agree, children and youth are special. Their needs are special as well. One of the greatest needs is to be loved, to feel secure, and to have a sense they have some mastery over their quickly developing lives. Children want to be like adults as much as we adults want them to become *good* adults. Accordingly, children and youth must be included in the processes of life, and that includes death as well. Obviously, we must provide for and protect them, but we should never lie, coverup, or hide from children the everyday facts of life. Death and dying is a sensitive area for children and youth. We must take into account their developmental ages, and how we choose our words when discussing this topic with them. No matter how well-meaning, dishonesty in our discussions of death and dying can contribute greatly to how modest or how full their lives are later. The following tips will help in providing some guidelines.

⇒ **Directions and Debriefing**

For each "tip[18]" below, explain what you think is meant by the tip. Develop some good examples of what to say and some equally bad examples of what not to say. First develop some scenarios to practice on. For example, how might these tips be used with a five-year-old who has lost a pet or a 12-year-old whose grandmother has just died this morning. You will find a brief discussion of each tip in endnote 19 in the Endnotes section of the workbook.[19] Consider the following questions. (1) As a child, how was death and dying discussed in your home? Explain. (2) Do you think children can be harmed by lack of candor, or too much candor, in discussing death and dying? Explain. (3) In growing up, do you think you were helped or harmed from the manner in which death and dying was discussed by your parents? Explain. (4) In class develop a list of the best "dos and don'ts" for each tip.

1. Be direct and honest in discussing death. _____
_____
_____
_____

2. Share facts about health, sickness, and dying early on. _____
_____
_____
_____

3. Explain the facts of death in general. _____
_____

_____

_____

4. Explain the facts of a particular death. _____

_____

_____

_____

5. Don't use euphemisms. _____

_____

_____

_____

6. Pace out information in manageable doses for children to understand. _____

_____

_____

_____

7. Use honesty when discussing god and spirituality issues. _____

_____

_____

_____

8. Involve children and youth in death rituals. _____

_____

_____

_____

9. Provide opportunities for children to express their grief. _____

_____

_____

_____

10. Maintain helpful resources at home and know community resources. _____

_____

_____

_____

_____

_____

Storytelling Death to Children

Men fear death, as children fear to go in the dark;
and as that natural fear in children is increased with tales,
so is the other.

Francis Bacon

⇒ **Overview**

"Now I lay me down to sleep. If I cry before I wake, pray the Lord my soul to keep." My younger brother never did get that line in our bedtime prayers right. We were always correcting him. "Gary," my mother would say, "It's 'if I *die* before I wake'." "Oh!" my brother would say with a never-ending look of confusion upon his face. For children, death is a perplexing occurrence. It never quite adds up, it never quite seems to make sense. For that matter, does death ever make total sense to anyone at any stage of life? For adults asked to explain death to a child in a sensitive manner, a formidable task lies ahead. This exercise will help you carry out this often tough but necessary task in life.

⇒ **Directions and Debriefing**

The purpose of this exercise is: (1) to look at children's books and stories on death and dying and then read them aloud in class, noting developmental differences as presented in the light of Erik Erikson's eight stages of psychosocial development, (2) to sensitize you to the developmental nature of death concepts in children and adolescents, (3) to allow exercise participants a "safe haven" for exploring and looking at their own early childhood memories of death, and (4) to be wiser and of real help when called upon (or having volunteered) to explain this most universal of events to the young. After all, it was Erik Erikson who said: "If we have the courage to face our own death, our children will have the courage to live their own lives."

This exercise is best begun by looking at some "death milestones" in our own early lives. What was your earliest experience with death as a child? Was it a pet? loss of a grandparent? parent? What did you learn about death from family members? How did peers and friends mold your thoughts and experiences? What were your memories and thoughts about killing living things? hunting? stepping on bugs? maybe worse things, huh? Who did you turn to for help and guidance? How did you as a child explain and rationalize death in your young mind?

When it comes time to read your storybook or story tale, be prepared to comment on these three concepts: (1) the irreversible-reversible factor in children's understanding of death, (2) any universal symbols in the story line, (3) developmental issues as they relate to Erikson, and (4) how we might provide a caring and supportive environment to the child or youth who has recently experienced a loss of something significantly loved by them. This can be animate or inanimate in nature.

You may wish to write a reaction paper for this exercise so as to provide closure and to consolidate your learning and wisdom.

47

Mother: "Honey, why did you tear out the page about bullfrog?
seven-year-old son: "I didn't want bullfrog to die."

⇒ **Overview**

As pertains to the above quote, how stunningly marvelous of a child to think that by plucking out the page of a storybook he can help his animate hero escape death, that death is reversible. In another couple of years, this child will understand he could not have kept bullfrog from his appointed fate with death. He will further learn he has ruined a perfectly good book! Children learn about death in the games they play and stories they read.[20] How they also learn is often a family affair, with this process being a developmental one. For every thousand ways a child experiences his first death, there are two thousand ways a child is influenced by such a death throughout his life.

Death enters the realm of childhood and adolescence in many ways. There is the death of parents, death of siblings, death of pets, death of grandparents, and death of other family members down the often long chain of relatives and in-laws. Children lose classmates and friends to sickness and chance. There are accidents and suicides, violence and war. There are many possible and types of losses in young people's lives. Fortunately there are excellent books to guide us helpfully through most of these circumstances. Many of the better books concerning particular losses are often written by someone who has been down that particular road of loss. This is good, as truth is often found at the source.

⇒ **Directions and Debriefing**

Visit a local bookstore (if you want to buy some) or library and select a cross-section of children's books which address some aspect of death. Select books for different developmental levels and ages of childhood. Bring these books to class. Break into groups and discuss them. Read sections from the books and then pass them around among other members and groups. At the end of this exercise you will find a list of books for children. Questions to consider during and after this exercise include:

1.   What developmental age group would be helped most by your book? Why?

2.   How is death presented? Was there a particular cultural or societal perspective used? Did your book deal with any cross-cultural issues?

3.   When and how would your book be useful?

4.   How important are the pictures and/or illustrations?

5.   What other tools and techniques might be helpful for a child experiencing loss?

6.   What general themes do most of the books seem to have in common, if any?

7.   Have you ever used such a book with a child before? If so, how did he or she respond? Was the book and experience useful?

8.   If you were to write a children's book on some aspect of death and dying, what might you do differently? What topics still need to be addressed in children's books?

48

⇒ **Overview**

The following is a fairly comprehensive listing of books for children concerning life-threatening illness, death, dying, loss, and bereavement.[21] At the right you will find three heading codes. EC stands for early childhood and includes ages 3-8. MC stands for middle childhood and includes ages 9-12. LC/A stands for late childhood and adolescence and includes ages 13 and above. In addition to showing which age group the book is best for, you will also find, for some books, additional coding in place of the "x." This coding includes: c=cross-cultural significance, ad=AIDS orientation, ca=Asian orientation, caa= African-American orientation, ch=Hispanic orientation, cn=Native American Orientation, p=pet orientation, r=religious orientation and w=war orientation. I believe this coding will be helpful in selecting a book that is right for you. Use this list with the exercise "Children's Books on Death and Dying," which precedes this exercise on page 45.

	EC	MC	LC/A
Abells, C. B. (1986). *The Children We Remember*. New York: Greenwillow.		cw	c
Agee, J. (1959). *A Death in the Family*. New York: Avon.			x
Bach, A. (1980). *Waiting for Johnny Miracle*. New York: Harper & Row.			x
Bach, R. (1970). *Jonathan Livingston Seagull*. New York: Macmillan.			x
Bauer, M. D. (1986). *On My Honor*. New York: Clarion.		x	
Berger, T. (1971). *I Have Feelings*. New York: Human Sciences Press.	x		
Bonnet, S. (1974). *About Death*. New York: Stein, Walker.	x		
Breebaart, J. & Breebaart, P. (1993). *When I Die, Will I Get Better?* New York: Peter Bedrick Books.	x	x	
Brown, M. W. (1965). *The Dead Bird*. Glenview, IL: Scott Foresman.	x		
Bunting, E. (1982). *The happy funeral*. New York: Harper & Row.		ca	ca
Bunting, E. (1990). *The Wall*. New York: Clarion Books.		w	w
Bunting. E. (1985). *Face at the Edge of the World*. New York: Clarion Books.		caa	caa
Carlson, N. (1970). *The Half-Sisters*. New York: Harper & Row.		x	
Carrick, C. (1976). *The Accident*. Illustrations by Donald Carrick. New York: Seabury/Clarion.	p	p	
Clifton, L. (1983). *Everett Anderson's Good-bye*. Illustrated by Ann Grifalconi. New York: Holt, Rinehart and Winston.	caa	caa	
Coerr, E. (1977). *Sadako and the Thousand Paper Cranes*. Illustrations by Ronald Himler. New York: Putnam.	cw/a		
Cohen, M. (1984). *Jim's Dog Muffins*. Illustrations by Lillian Hoban. New York: Greenwillow-William Morrow.	p	p	
Corley, E. (1973). *Tell Me About Death, Tell Me About Funerals*. Illustrations by Philip Pecorado. Santa Clara, CA: Grammatical Sciences.		x	
De Paola, T. (1973). *Nana Upstairs and Nana Downstairs*. New York: Putnam's Sons.	x	x	
DeVries, P. (1961). *Blood of the Lamb*. Boston: Little, Brown.			x
Erdman, L. (1973). *A Bluebird Will Do*. New York: Dodd, Mead.		x	
Farley, C. (1975). *The Garden is Doing Fine*. New York: Atheneum.		x	
Fassler, J. (1971). *My Grandpa Died Today*. New York: Behavioral Publications.	x		
Foreman, M. (1994). *War Game*. New York: Arcade.		w	w
Gaes, J. (1987). *My Book for Kids with Cancer: A Child's Autobiography of Hope*. Aberdeen, SD: Melius and Peterson.		x	x

	EC	MC	LC/A
Garcia, R. (1986). *My Aunt Otilia's Spirits/ Los Espiritus de Mi Tia Otilia*. San Francisco: Children's Book Press.	ch	ch	
Gerstein, M. (1987). *The Mountains of Tibet*. New York: Harper & Row.		ca	ca
Girion, B. (1979). *A Tangle of Roots*. New York: Charles Scribner's Sons.		x	x
Graeber, C. (1982). *Mustard*. Illustrations by Donna Diamond. New York: Macmillan.	p	p	
Greene, C. C. (1979). *Beat the Turtle Drum*. New York: Dell.			x
Greenfield, E. (1993). *Nathanial Talking*. New York: Black Butterfly Children's Group.		caa	caa
Greenlee, S. (1992). *When Someone Dies*. Illustrated by Bill Draft. Atlanta: Peachtree.		x	
Grollman, E. (1991). *Talking About Death: A Dialogue Between Parent and Child*. 3d ed. Boston: Beacon Press.	x	x	
Harris, A. (1965). *Why Did He Die?* Minneapolis: Lerner Publications.		x	
Hogan, B. (1983). *My Grandmother Died*. Illustrations by Nancy Munger. Nashville: Abingdon.	x		
Holden, D. L. (1989). *Gran-gran's Best Trick: A Story of Children Who Have Lost Someone They Love*. Illustrated by Michael Chesworth. New York: Magination Press.	x	x	
Hoyt-Goldsmith, D. (1994). *Day of the Dead: A Mexican-American Celebration*. Photographs by Lawrence Migdae. New York: Holiday House.	ch	ch	
Hunter, M. (1974). *A Sound of Chariots*. New York: Harper & Row.		x	
Irwin, H. (1988). *So Long at the Fair*. New York: McElderry-Macmillan.			x
Jordan M. (1989). *Losing Uncle Tim*. Niles, IL.: Albert Whitman.		ad	ad
Kantrowitz, M. (1973). *When Violent Died*. New York: Parents Magazine Press.	x		
Kerr, M. E. (1986). *Night Kites*. New York: Harper & Row.		ad	ad
Klein, N. (1974). *Sunshine*. New York: Avon.			x
Krementz, J. (1981). *How It Feels when a Parent Dies*. New York: Alfred A. Knopf.		x	
Krementz, J. (1991). *How It Feels to Fight for Your Life*. New York: Simon & Schuster.		x	x
L'Engle, M. (1980). *A Ring of Endless Light*. New York: Farrar, Straus & Giroux.			x
L'Engle, M. (1980). *The Summer of the Great-grandmother*. New York: Seabury.			x
Landcaster, M. (1985). *Hang Tough*. New York: Paulist Press.		x	
Leder, J. M. (1989). *Dead Serious: A Book for Teenagers About Teen Suicide*. New York: Avon.			x
Lee, V. (1972). *The Magic Moth*. Boston: Houghton Mifflin.			x
LeShan, E. (1976). *Learning to Say Goodbye: When a Parent Dies*. New York: Macmillan.		x	
London, J. (1994). *Liplap's Wish*. Illustrated by Sylvia Long. San Francisco: Chronicle Books.	x	x	
Lorenzo, C. L. (1974). *Mama's Ghosts*. New York: Harper & Row.		x	
Marcus, L. S. (1994). *Lifelines: A Poetry Anthology Patterned on the Stages of Life*. New York: Dutton.		x	
Mazer, N. F. (1987). *After the Rain*. New York: William Morrow.			x
McLendon, G. H. (1982). *My Brother Joey Died*. Photographs by H. Kelman. New York: Simon & Schuster.		x	
McNamara, J. W. (1994). *My Mom is Dying: A Child's Diary*. Illustrated by David LaRochelle. Minneapolis: Augsburg Fortress.			
Miles, M. (1971). *Annie and the Old One*. Illustrations by Peter Parnall. Boston: Little, Brown.		cn	
Mills, J. C. (1993). *Gentle Willow: A Story for Children about Dying*. Illustrated by Michael Chesworth. New York: Magination Press.		x	
Mills, J. C. (1993). *Little Tree: A Story for Children with Serious Medical Problems*. Illustrated by Michael Chesworth. New York: Magination Press.		x	
Mobley, J. (1979). *The Star Husband*. Illustrations by Anna Vojtech. New York: Doubleday.		cn	
Moutoussany-Ashe, J. (1993). *Daddy and Me*. New York: Alfred A. Knopf.	ca	ca	
Myers, W. D. (1988). *Fallen Angels*. New York: Scholastic.			w
Nystrom, C. (1992). *What Happens When We Die*. Illustrated by Eira Reeves. Chicago: Moody Press.		r	

Reference	EC	MC	LC/A
Nystrom, C. (1994). *Emma Says Goodbye: A Child's Guide to Bereavement*. Illustrated by Annable Large. Elgin, IL: Lion Publishing.	r	r	
Olander, J. & Greenberg, M. H. (1978). *Time of Passage*. New York: Taplinger.			x
Old, W. C. (1995). *Stacy had a Little Sister*. Illustrated by Judith Friedman. Morton Grove, IL: Albert Whitman.	x	x	
Orgel, D. (1970). *The Mulberry Music*. New York: Harper & Row.		x	
Porte, B. A. (1985). *Harry's Mom*. Illustrations by Yossi Abolafia. New York: Greenwillow-William Morrow.	x		
Quinlan, P. (1994*)*. *Tiger Flowers*. Illustrations by Janet Wilson. New York: Dial/Penguin.	ad		
Rofes, E. E. (1985). *The Kids Book About Death and Dying: By and for Kids*. Boston: Little, Brown.	p	p	
Rogers, F. (1988). *When a Pet Dies*. New York: G. P. Putnams's sons.	x		
Shector, B. (1973). *Across the Meadow*. New York: Doubleday.	x		
Shott, J. (1988). *The House Across the Street*. Nashville: Winston-Derek.		x	x
Simmonds, P. (1987). *Fred*. New York: Alfred A. Knopf.		p	
Simons, N. (1986).*The Saddest Time*. Illustrated by Jacqueline Rogers. Morton Grove, IL: Albert Whitman.	x	x	
Slaughter, C. H. (1994). *The Dirty War*. New York: Walker.		cw	cw
Smith, A. W. (1986). *Sister in the Shadow*. New York: Atheneum.			x
Smith, D. B. (1973). *A Taste of Blackberries*. New York: Crowell.		x	
Stein, S. B. (1974) *About Dying: An Open Family Book for Parents and Children Together*. New York: Walker.	x	x	
Stull, E. (1964). *My Turtle Died Today*. New York: Holt, Rinehart & Winston.	p		
Teakle-Barnes, H. (1993). *My Daddy Died: Supporting Young Children in Grief*. San Francisco: HarperCollins.	x	x	
Tressalt, A. (1971). *The Dead Tree*. New York: Parents Magazine Press.	x		
van den Berg, M. (1994). *The Three Birds: A Story for Children About the Loss of a Loved One*. Illustrations by Sandra Ireland. New York: Magination Press.	x		
Varley, S. (1984). *Badger's Parting Gifts*. New York: Lothrop.	p	p	
Viorst, J. (1971). *The Tenth Good Thing About Barney*. New York: Atheneum.	p	p	
Walker, A. (1988). *To Hell with Dying*. Illustrated by Catherine Deeter. New York: Harcourt Brace Jovanovich.		caa	
Warburg, S. (1969). *Growing Time*. Boston: Houghton Mifflin.	x		
Watts, R. (1975). *Straight Talk About Death with Young People*. Philadelphia: Westminster.	x		
White, E. B. (1952). *Charlotte's Web*. New York: Harper & Row.	x		
Yukio, T. (1988). *Faithful Elephants: A True Story of Animals, People, and War*. Boston: Houghton Mifflin.		cw	cw
Zolotow, C. (1974). *My Grandson Lew*. New York: Harper & Row.	x		

Added:

Reference	EC	MC	LC/A
Nobisso, J. (1989). *Grandpa Loved*. Illustrated by Maureen Hyde. San Diego, CA: The Green Tiger Press, Inc.	x	x	
Nobisso, J. (1990). *Grandpa's Scrapbook* Illustrated by Maureen Hyde. San Diego, CA: The Green Tiger Press, Inc.	x	x	
Schulz, C. (1990). *Why, Charlie Brown, Why: A Story About What Happens when a Friend Is Very Ill*. New York: Topper Books.	x	x	
Brandenberg, F. (1990). *I Wish I Was Sick, Too*. Illustrated by Aliki. New York: Mulberry.	x	x	

Oh such a loss, is the child not yet born!

⇒ **Overview**

The importance of saying "hello" before saying "good-bye" is an important factor in counseling parents, grandparents, siblings, and others in loss associated with infant deaths. Miscarriages, stillbirths, neonatal deaths, SIDS (Sudden Infant Death Syndrome), abortion, and even infertility are areas of special concern for caregivers.

One of the complicating factors for miscarriages is that there is often no tangible evidence. Often, with miscarriages, the pregnancy may not even have been announced to some family members and friends. Such parents-to-be face the additional difficulty of experiencing a loss that others may not even be aware has occurred. Another issue is how to deliver the news of this sad event to family members and friends.[22]

The following exercise will deepen your awareness of one often unspoken yet tragic area of loss: stillbirths. As you complete this exercise, think how you might assist someone grieving such a loss.

⇒ **Directions and Debriefing**

Use this exercise[23] in class or group. Discuss the importance of the following in infant deaths caused by stillbirth and, where appropriate, other infant losses. (1) What is the value of each for parents and caregivers? (2) Have you had or been near an infant death in your life? (3) What was it like emotionally for you and the deceased infant's mother and father? (4) How might your assistance differ for a miscarriage, SIDS, abortion or other pre- or postnatal loss?

1. Naming the baby

2. Describing the baby

3. Holding the baby

4. Spending time alone with baby

5. Keeping mementos (ID bracelet, hair lock, pictures, birth certificate, baby's footprints)

6. Sharing details (length, weight, eyes, special noted features)

7. Discussing autopsy findings

8. Funeral and/or memorial services

9. Grief recovery support groups for:

   a. Loss and grief
   b. Personal prenatal care guilt

c. "Did we do enough?" and "did we do harm?"

d. "Did we cause the death?"

10. Providing literature on loss and grief

11. Hospitals:

    a. Do not abandon mother at this time of loss

    b. Provide nonviable fetus delivery areas

    c. Acknowledge these losses

    d. Treat dead fetus respectfully

    e. Include father

12. Abortion has particular pitfalls:

    a. Moral issues

    b. Guilt and concern over abortion decision

    c. Ambivalence

    d. Prior emotional issues

    e. Bonding issues related to later trimester abortions

    f. Pain issues

    g. Fetal malformation, "imperfect child"

13. Depression and Support Systems

    a. Postpartum depression (more intense in failed births)

    b. Lack of support systems for grieving parents

    c. Mental health issues

Notes: _____

_____

_____

_____

_____

_____

_____

_____

_____

Source: From "Stillbirth," by S. H. Hutchins, in *Parental Loss of a Child* (pp. 129-144), edited by T. A. Rando, 1986. Champaign, IL: Research Press. Copyright 1986 by T. A. Rando. Adapted by permission.

Childhood Attitudes on Aging, Death, and Dying

Oh, write of me, not died in bitter pains,
but emigrated to another star!

Helen Hunt Jackson

⇒ **Overview**

Though they enter this world a "tabula rasa" or blank slate to use John Locke's words, they soon fill it. Children, like sponges, absorb everything around them from their environment. They mirror many of the attitudes and values of their parents and friends. Children live and breathe to be adults. They copy and pretend and fantasize the rules that we adults play. And so it is too with death and dying. They soon observe sorrow and loss as well as grief and bereavement. Though, depending upon their age, they may not understand much if any of this "thing about death and dying," they soon learn it is a serious time, a tenuous time at best. From tears in their mother's eyes at grandma's bed to the long ride in the fancy black cars to a cemetery, children's attitudes about death and dying are rooted early on in their childhood.

⇒ **Directions and Debriefing**

For this exercise interview a child of middle childhood (7-12). Discuss their attitudes toward aging and death and dying by using the following questions. First be sure you have parental permission and have briefed the child's parents as to what your interview is all about. It is also prudent to remind you to exercise caution when discussing death with a child, as they may become easily distressed. If discomfort arises, halt, and speak with their parent(s).

For this exercise to work well you will need some paper and drawing materials. Interview the child in an easygoing but non-distracting setting such as after lunch or before dinner or during some other quiet study time. Be sensitive and gentle in your interview with the child. Progress slowly and allow lots of time for the child to respond. The questions about death work best while the child is drawing, as it allows them to channel any uneasiness about the questions into the drawing. Sometimes it may take awhile for the child to formulate an answer, so you might move along with your questioning and return later to an earlier question. Based on prior experiences, some children have much to say while others little. Don't go into the interview with any expectations and be light and airy. Have some fun. Paraphrase the following questions as time and need dictate. Prepare to discuss your results.

1. Do you know any real old favorite people?

2. What are some of the things you like most about your favorite person?

3. Can you draw a picture of your favorite person playing a game that you like also?

4. Has anything or anyone you liked or loved died? Can you tell me about it?

5. Have you ever had a pet die? What was that all about? Tell me.

6. What happens when people die?

7. When these people die do you get to see them again? When and how? Can you tell me?

8. How old do you think you will live to be?

Dying is a very dull, dreary affair.
And my advice to you is to have nothing
whatever to do with it.

W. Somerset Maugham

⇒ **Overview**

I remember very clearly a story about a child who was very angry with God. His mother had told him that the reason Daddy had died was "God took him." The child, with tears in his eyes, replied: "Well, God can't be a very nice person to take my daddy." We must choose our words carefully and above all be honest with children about death and dying. Whether it be loss of a pet or loss of a family member, children need to be included in the process of death and dying when it involves their feelings, their loves, and their attachments. But what do you say to a child, and more importantly how do you say it? How much does a child comprehend about death and dying? These are some of the important and fair questions that adults might ask concerning death, dying, and loss as pertains to children.

The better textbooks on death education discuss the importance of understanding where children are developmentally and cognitively in their mental, emotional, and physical development. (See *Suggested Textbooks and Other Selected Readings* list on page 229.) As mentioned earlier, Sigmund Freud, Erik Erikson, Jean Piaget, and Maria Nagy are theorists often referred to when discussing death and dying issues with children in developmental terms.[24] (See the suggested reading list for these theorists located on page 40.)

⇒ **Directions and Debriefing**

This exercise assumes the reader has: (1) reviewed the relevant theoretical frameworks of the above theorists as they relate to children and adolescents regarding death and dying issues and (2) has had additional discussions and done additional readings regarding issues of death, dying, and loss with children and adolescents.

In small groups decide upon age-appropriate, accurate, and emotionally helpful responses to the following commonly asked questions and commonly mentioned statements by children and adolescents regarding the death or illness of someone significant to them. In the vignettes where there is a death, assume that the death was recent. Some of the vignettes used work from the angle that the person referred to is in the hospital with a life-threatening illness or other emergency. How does that change your responses?

1. A nine-year-old girl asks her mother during a visit to the hospital to visit her father, "Where is Daddy's hair? Why is he so skinny? Why don't we feed him more?"

2. A five-year-old boy asks his father, "Can I die and be with Grandpa?"

3. Two eight-year-old twins ask their mother at the cemetery, "Will I see Daddy again?"

4. A fourteen-year-old asks his grandfather, "Why was Dad so tired that he said he couldn't go on living any longer?"

5. A four-year-old asks, "Where is dead?"

6. A seven-year-old girl asks, "What happens when you die? How do you know if you go to heaven or hell?"

7. An eight-year-old boy asks, "Mommy died and didn't say good-bye to me. Why? Was I bad?"

8. A seven-year-old girl states, "I never want to go to the hospital, you only die there."

9. A four-year-old states, "Only bad guys get killed, right? My daddy is good. He won't die at the hospital."

10. A twelve-year-old boy states, "I feel like dying myself. I'll never get over Peter's death." (best friend)

11. A twelve-year-old girl whose 13-year-old girlfriend died in an automobile accident asks her mother and father at the dinner table, "What did Grandma mean by only the good die young?"

12. A six-year-old is crying because his father told him his cat was so sick they had to "put him to sleep." Now the child is afraid to sleep and even more afraid of becoming sick. How would you counsel him?

⇒ **Debriefing**

(1) What were your thoughts and feelings concerning this exercise? (2) How does having an understanding of developmental milestones in child growth and development assist parents and others in helping children understand issues of death, dying, and loss? (3) Have you ever had to counsel a child who has experienced a loss? If so, what did you say and do? What might you do differently in light of your new knowledge? (4) What types of school educational programs do you think would be helpful for children in learning about death, dying, and loss? (5) Is there a particular book for children on death and dying you have read and liked? As a reference, use the list provided on pages 49-51. (6) What types of play activities might be helpful for children in processing loss and grief? (7) In what ways have your childhood experiences with death influenced you?

⇒ Notes: _____

_____

_____

_____

_____

_____

_____

_____

_____

_____

_____

_____

_____

Humanity shows itself in all its intellectual
splendor during this tender age,
as the sun shows itself at dawn...

Maria Montessori

⇒ **Overview**

One of the great difficulties for growing children is learning how to communicate. This task is no less difficult for adults when the topic and discussion are about death. I know of a story where parents, when asked by their 7-year-old son why his best friend had died in an auto accident, replied: "God chose to take him." Their young son took a deep moment and with tears streaming down his eyes said, "Well, that was not very nice of him. I don't want God as my friend anymore." Helping children work through loss is a sensitive task, one, that done right or wrong, may well affect the child all his life.

Children are less familiar with death than were previous generations. Death has become less visible, less public, and less a topic of conversation. Though there is more openness, children are typically the last to know. In our desire to spare children suffering, we in fact seal within them a lifelong sense of anxiousness. How much should children be told about death? How should we tell them? How do we choose our words so their meanings are understood? These questions are the challenge for parents who find themselves face-to-face with the inquisitive child who wants to know why Buster the cat died or why grandma is no longer at home.

The television cartoon character who is run over by a steamroller only to jump up and play again is consistent in logic for the child under the age of 4 who views death as reversible. Nagy (1948)[25], in a well-respected study, found that children's conception of death comes about in three stages. In the first stage between 3-5 years of age, children do not distinguish between death and separation. In the second stage, between 5-9 years of age, children view death as irreversible but avoidable. And in the third stage, children over 10 begin to understand death is real, inevitable, and irreversible. Other factors such as culture and locale affect children as well. Other researchers such as Erik Erikson and Jean Piaget also believe an understanding of death develops as children enter new stages of human development. Erikson's theory of human development uses seven psychosocial stages of development and suggests death is most relative to the stage the child is in. For example, a child who loses a parent while an infant proceeds along in his or her development handicapped.[26] Another great theorist, Piaget, is long recognized as an authority on children. His cognitive or intellectual development theory suggests all children go through four sequential and precise stages of development. How quickly each child enters a period or stage varies, however. For example, children 2-7 years of age enter a stage Piaget calls "preoperational." In this second of four developmental stages, children use magical thinking and fantasy reasoning, which are then woven into some realistic thinking about "why things die."[27] What these theorists all have in common is an understanding that any discussion of death is shaped and colored by the developmental age and stage a child is in. It is therefore very important for adults working with children to have an understanding of child development.

⇒ **Directions and Debriefing**

The development of language, emotions, and intellect do not all mesh in neat patterns. An effective approach for communicating with children who are experiencing a loss is through interactive play: art, games, toys, etc. The following "Child's Loss Puzzle" is a fun and soothing method of helping children formulate thoughts and articulate feelings concerning the loss of a living being they loved that is either animal or human. Test out this puzzle with another adult so as to get the "hang of it." Then use it with a child of late middle-childhood or older. The puzzle should work well with children age ten and up. Younger children may need adult guidance with some of the words.

The following words are located at various angles within the puzzle: *love, remembrance, sadness, loss, death, pain, remorse, memory, lonely, hurt, afraid, miss, feelings, anger, mourn, god, torn, eternal, heaven, sorry, nice, hope, child, grief, play, holy, fun, save, favors, and nature.* These words were chosen as they are descriptive emotive words from which a child can build mental pictures and then share feelings. They are prompting props for getting in touch with feelings. The task is to locate as many words in the puzzle as possible, and have the child choose which of the words best expresses his feelings about a loss. The adult should then coach the child to explain more fully. The activity is excellent for bringing out feelings and developing closure. One can add words to the puzzle which have additional meaning, such as an animal's or person's name.

(1) What were your impressions of this activity? (2) How did it work for adults? for children? (3) What have you learned about communicating loss with children? How much do you understand about child development? (4) What are some of the other advantages of having an understanding of child development? (5) What would you have done differently in any discussions you might have had with children in the past on death? (6) What will you do in the future when this topic with a child comes up?

A Child's Loss Puzzle

R	E	M	E	M	B	R	A	N	C	E	P
E	L	O	N	E	L	Y	N	E	V	O	L
G	R	I	E	F	O	X	G	O	D	X	A
R	E	M	O	R	S	E	E	H	O	L	Y
E	H	O	P	E	S	N	R	U	O	M	X
T	O	R	N	E	T	E	R	N	A	L	X
S	A	D	N	E	S	S	O	R	R	Y	X
H	E	A	V	E	N	M	E	M	O	R	Y
X	H	U	R	T	G	R	I	E	F	O	M
N	A	T	U	R	E	F	A	V	O	R	S
U	C	H	I	L	D	X	P	A	I	N	O
F	E	E	L	I	N	G	S	S	S	I	M

50

3

What To Do:

Understanding, Helping, and Caregiving

...for you must go
and I must die.
But come ye back
when summer's in the meadow,
or when the valley's hushed and
white with snow.
For I'll be here
in sunshine and in shadow.
Oh Danny boy...
I love you so.

Irish Folksong

Chapter 3

What To Do: Understanding, Helping, and Caregiving

There was an uneasiness in the air as death was at hand, just a short time away. The doctors and nurses had all agreed Tim had little time left, maybe a couple of days or maybe a couple of hours. As his therapist, I noted Tim didn't seem resigned to die. But no one bothered to ask him. One nurse indicated to me that the patient was in the acceptance stage, a reference to Kübler-Ross's stages of dying. He had been in and out of the hospital several times the last couple of years with leukemia. What everyone failed to recognize, however, was that it was Tim's call at dying--not ours. Tim hated hospitals, hated hospital food, and generally wasn't very fond of medical staff. By the next day he felt well enough to get up, check out, and drive home--all against medical advice. Tim left a note on his bed the morning he snuck out. The note read: "You guys better get a life, I got one!" Some months later Tim died at home on his turf, and on his terms.

How we are in life is generally how we are in death. As for the stages of dying or stages of mourning, my best suggestion is to leave them to the stage actors. Tim's "deathbed scene" was performed much the way he performed his life--with a keen sense of humor. Throughout our lives, death, dying, bereavement, grief, loss, and sorrow--fill in your own words--will spring up like seasonal flowers. We often have little choice but to arrange them as best we may. The message of this chapter is for us all to learn to take our cues from those we care for, and not force them into those neat little packages so readily available in death education.

More than one in 10 Americans--13% of the population--is over age 65. That translates into 33 million seniors in America today. Many are affected by our perceptions of their worth. For this reason any discussion of death and dying must also include a discussion of aging.

This chapter offers an opportunity to advance and enhance your knowledge base and skills. When you complete this chapter you should be better able to understand, to help, and to plan when, to quote an old expression, "death comes knocking at your door."

The flow of this chapter is designed to take you through a discussion of issues related to aging, death-related occupations, risk-taking behaviors, and discussion starters and role-play surrounding death education issues. The chapter moves deeper into stress, burnout, and the many dimensions of caregiving. As with all the chapters, you will find "morals and values" development exercises as well. The primary focus is the learning of how to take care of others and yourself. The chapter finishes up with exercises on working with "grief and unfinished business," often areas of concerns for caregivers, the dying, and the bereaved.

In essence, this chapter is not only about surviving loss, but also preparing for loss in both ourselves and others we care for. We don't have to embrace death, but we should be able to meet the challenges that death presents in our lives. If we do it right, we flourish and evolve into happier, healthier, and heartier persons. In a nutshell, we're talking about acquiring the "right stuff," so as to make both life and death work for us. If we blend that "stuff" correctly, it should be enough to get us through this life and halfway through the next--all with a bit of a perky smile!

One thing is certain and the rest is lies:
The flower that once has bloomed forever dies.

Edward FitzGerald

Overview

Stereotypes are generalized beliefs or opinions based on individual experience. They are generally irrational thinking at best. Stereotyping and labeling seem to fulfill a human need to structure, compartmentalize, and organize situations in order to minimize ambiguity and to clarify where we stand in relation to others. Though some stereotypes are positive, most are negative. Stereotyped impressions regarding older individuals which are based on singular traits, such as age, show a lack of understanding, education, and fair play.[28] What are your thoughts and stereotypes concerning the aged? Tip: Make a list writing down whatever comes to mind about the aged. In other words, free-associate.

⇒ Directions and Debriefing

For this exercise[29] think of three words that come to mind when thinking of someone for each of the decades listed. Take about 15 minutes to complete the form. Next place an "E" next to the age span decade that was easiest for you and an "H" next to the age span decade for which it was hardest to think of three descriptors. Tally the E's and H's. Be prepared to discuss your results. Compare and contrast descriptors for each age span decade and prepare for a discussion in the context of myths and stereotypes about the various age segments of human development. (1) Sharpen your focus and prepare for a discussion of issues surrounding aging and the elderly. (2) What were your thoughts about this exercise? (3) What did you learn? (4) Were you surprised at any of your myths and stereotypes?

Lifespan Development

Decade

00 - 09	_____	_____	_____
10 - 19	_____	_____	_____
20 - 29	_____	_____	_____
30 - 39	_____	_____	_____
40 - 49	_____	_____	_____
50 - 59	_____	_____	_____
60 - 69	_____	_____	_____
70 - 79	_____	_____	_____
80 - 89	_____	_____	_____
90 - 99	_____	_____	_____

Ageism and Stereotypes

On his ninetieth birthday the British House of Lords
held a special session to honor Sir Winston Churchill.
As he descended the stairs, one member said to another,
"They say he's getting senile." Churchill stopped, turned and said,
"They also say he's deaf!"

⇒ **Overview**

One of the fastest growing fields in psychology is *behavioral gerontology*, the study of psychological aspects of aging and the elderly. At the beginning of this century about 3 percent of the U.S. population was over age 65. Today the figure is 13%, and by the year 2030 nearly 25% of the U.S. population will be over age 65. In fact, more people will be over age 65 than under age 20, a dramatic reversal.[30]

Our society values growth, strength, and physical appearance and worships youthfulness. To many the enemy is "getting old," a process marked by signs of decline and weakness. Many fear getting old worse than death itself. Ageism, or prejudice against older people, is prevalent in our society, which further perpetuates the problem.

Many myths about sex drive, loss of vision, hearing, and overall stamina are based more on folklore than sound empirical evidence. For example, there is the myth that "you can't teach an old dog new tricks." In other words, the elderly can't learn new tasks or use new technological tools. Computers are a good example. The fact is that the elderly can and do learn new tasks and can learn to use new tools such as computers. Research has shown that while it is true the elderly may not learn as quickly as younger people, they more than make up for it by their ability to see the whole picture, to utilize their wisdom and global viewpoint--an ability often lacking in younger learners. Secondly, if teaching and training techniques are varied, their ability to learn is enhanced further.

⇒ **Directions and Debriefing**

In a society that values youth and views aging as the enemy, is it any wonder that many older Americans perpetuate themselves into roles of living "half-dead" lives? For this exercise reflect and respond to the following statements and directions.

1. What comes to mind when you hear the words "old," "aged," and "elderly?" What negative and positive thoughts surface? List both types.

_____

_____

_____

2. What stereotypes comes to mind when you think about the elderly driving, using computers, and at check-out counters?

_____

_____

_____

3. What are the origins of these stereotypes?

_____

_____

_____

4. Can you recall stories or anecdotes that contradict these stereotypes?

_____

_____

_____

5. Bring in pictures of the elderly from magazines and newspapers. Include in your selection of picture clippings those that depict older people engaged in both positive and stereotypical activities. Which pictures seemed to be more prevalent?

_____

_____

_____

6. What methods do people use to try and hide their true age and improve their looks?

_____

_____

_____

7. How does the media deal with aging? What strategies do advertisers use to "win" over the elderly? How do the media and advertising contribute to stereotyping?

_____

_____

_____

8. How do stereotypes about the elderly affect your perceptions and thoughts about death and dying?

_____

_____

_____

_____

9. Prepare to discuss what you have learned about ageism and stereotyping of the elderly.

_____

_____

_____

Death is Ageless!

Old saying

⇒ **Overview**

It's better to be "over the hill than under it," I heard my 96-year-old grandmother say once upon a time. She was always busy with things to do. I guess you could say she was in the habit of living. In fact, these days the old are living so long they have created a second summer for themselves. Since 1900, the life expectancy of the average American has increased from 47 years to 74 years. At the end of World War II, only 8% of the population was over 65. Today, more than one in ten Americans, or 13% of the population, is over age 65. That translates into 33 million seniors over age 65 in America today.[31] By the year 2030 it is likely to be 25%. That would translate into over 100 million older Americans. Centenarians, those over age 100, has tripled since 1980. Today there are also 52,000 people over the age of 100 in America.

In a well-written book by Cambridge University historian Thomas R. Cole entitled *The Journey of Life: A Cultural History of Aging in America* (Cambridge University Press, 1992), Cole notes that during the last couple of hundred years the social and biomedical sciences have looked upon old age as simply "an engineering problem to be solved or at least ameliorated." Cole takes the position that by reducing old age to a problem, science has impoverished it. Science has robbed old age of the rich symbolism and purpose it has had throughout most of our history. Old age doesn't seem to stand for anything anymore. It is empty, purposeless, void of meaning. This is most unfortunate, as Cole quickly notes, because we are spiritual animals; we need our meaning in life no less than we need our sustenance and health. As Michael Norman notes in a fine article in *The New York Times* entitled "Are People Living Too Long?", the elderly are enjoying a second summer in their lives. It is a period from age 65 to 85 where the wishes and dreams of retirement can come into fruition, though they still generally follow the same patterns seen in earlier adult life. This work-retirement pattern is dictated by the institutions of family, school, work, church, government, and culture. The activities of retirement revolve around these institutions much as they did in earlier life. According to Norman, this second summer begins to sour in the lives of the "oldest old," those over age 85. For the oldest old, it is a time marked by what gerontologists call the dreadful D's--decline, deterioration, dependency, and death. For the oldest old, second summer soon changes to winter with all the harshness that entails. For many of the very old it becomes a time of dependency, and that's the bogeyman in our society. Norman says our society despises dependency and along with it people who are old, weak, and vulnerable. Along with the despise comes the howl from the experts, fiscal planners, and bioethicists who all seem to worry aloud about resources, means, and expenditures. And therein lies the dilemma. We have so sold society on the virtues of independence that we have made it impossible for people to be dependent. We are forcing our most elderly from what Erik Erikson called the "willful mastery" of life into the "existential dread" of life. Somewhere along this uncharted road we, as compassionate human beings, will need to embrace dependency among our most elderly with joy and care and respect for time well spent during their earlier lives. And yes, we will also need to continue searching for the meaning in this longevity. For surely, as Carl

Jung wrote, no one would grow to be 70 or 80 years old if this longevity had no meaning for the species.

As the above discussion would indicate, growing old is not without its pitfalls. Many of today's elderly are affected by a term we call "ageism." *Ageism* is a term for prejudice against the elderly. Prejudice and discrimination against the elderly limit their opportunities. We need to raise the social status of elders in our society by expanding their roles and addressing their needs. For many elders, the golden years have turned into the lost lonely years. Part of the problem is how those younger perceive those older. It all boils down to how our attitudes and stereotypes develop into prejudicial thoughts and discriminatory actions. It makes good sense to work now to provide meaning and respect for those in their elder years because, soon enough, they will be our years.

Before beginning, take a moment and consider all the positive encounters you have had with older adults. What types of volunteer programs and other positive endeavors do we find seniors involved in today? How have such programs as the American Association of Retired Persons (AARP) and others helped contribute to happier, healthier, and more active seniors?

⇒ **Directions and Debriefing**

Examine some of your perceptions regarding aging. Choose true or false for each of the following statements.[32] Consider younger as under 65 and older as over age 65. Discuss your responses. See endnote 32 in the back of the workbook for correct responses. Consider the following questions. (1) Do you want to grow old? (2) What are your fears of aging? (3) How might our attitudes about aging affect our fears about death? (4) How might you assure yourself a long, happy, full, and active life? (5) Were you surprised by the answers? (6) How did your "attitude" compare with the answers? (7) What you have learned? Reflect on this.

T   F   1.   Older people are more likely than younger people to attend church.

T   F   2.   Older people are more cautious and less likely to make risky decisions as young people might.

T   F   3.   As people age, they tend to become more alike.

T   F   4.   Older people have more difficulty than younger people in adapting to a changing environment.

T   F   5.   A decrease in life satisfaction is usually experienced by older people.

T   F   6.   The majority of people over 65 live in nursing-home type institutions and settings.

T   F   7.   Mental disorders occur more frequently in older people than in younger people.

T   F   8.   Depression is more common in older people than in younger people.

T   F   9.   Decreasing intelligence, as measured by IQ tests and other measures of cognitive functions, is one of the inevitable changes that occur with aging.

T   F   10. Aging of the brain leads the way for deterioration of other bodily systems and functions.

T   F   11. The suicide rate is higher for the elderly than for younger people.

T   F   12. Alzheimer's Disease affects nearly 50% of the elderly between the ages of 65 and 75.

65

Brainstorm Death-Related Occupations

Often the test of courage is not to die but to live!

Conte Vittorio Alfieri

⇒ **Overview**

We've all heard the expressions "He has a killer job" or "Her job's deadly" or "She's in a dead-end career." But some jobs are not only deadly; they actually <u>deal</u> with the dead. Generally speaking, there are only a handful of vocational fields which minister to the dying, the dead, and the grieving. They, for the most part, divide into three groups. (1) For the dying, health-related professions include medicine, nursing, and long-term institutional care. (2) For the dead, professions include mortuary sciences and cemetery management. (3) For the grieving, mental health and spiritual professions include social work, counseling, and chaplaincy services. In some professions there is overlap.

⇒ **Directions and Debriefing**

The following professions and careers often deal with death and dying. (1) Add some of your own job suggestions which have high contact with death. (2) Briefly describe what might be the best and worse aspects of each job's contact with death, dying, and grief. (3) Which job might you be willing to work at? (4) Interview someone in any of these positions and ask them how they manage stress? How do they manage death in their everyday jobs? (5) What do they do to "unwind" from the day-to-day stress of their work?

1. AIDS Drug Researcher	16. Physician
2. Ambulance Driver	17. Police/Highway Patrol Officer
3. Bereavement Counselor	18. Probate Attorney
4. City or County Coroner	19. Psychologist or Therapist
5. Clergy	20. Suicide Prevention Counselor
6. Crematorium Operator	21. Undertaker
7. Crime Scene Criminalist	22. _____
8. EMT/Paramedic	23. _____
9. Fire Fighter	24. _____
10. Forensic Pathologist	25. _____
11. Grave Digger	26. _____
12. Infectious Disease Officer	27. _____
13. Monument Designer/Engraver	28. _____
14. Nurse	29. _____
15. Organ Donor Worker	30. _____

High-Risk Vocations and High-Risk Avocations

Die when I may. I want it said of me by those who knew me best,
that I always plucked a thistle and planted a flower where
I thought a flower would grow.

Abraham Lincoln

⇒ **Overview**

I remember switching through the television channels one day and noticed channel after channel had adventuresome people involved in high-risk activities. They included everything from skydiving and to mountain-climbing to police riding in high-speed-hot-pursuit in their police cruisers to football players crashing heads on the line of scrimmage. Why do we take such risks in our lives? Why is it we choose to face death so often up close and personal? Why do we have such a range of risk-taking behaviors? Activities such as smoking, drinking, drugs, and speeding in our automobiles, though for pleasure, all seem to welcome and encourage death. Other risk-taking behaviors seem to come with the job such as in police work, fire protection, test-pilot work or from the work of those brave souls who work the electrical power lines during storms. How about stress? One government report cited that the best predictor of a long life was satisfaction with your job.[33] The following exercise looks at your risk-taking behavior in work and play. How often do you, through your risk-taking behavior, seem to be beckoning death to come by for a visit?

⇒ **Directions and Debriefing**

The following exercise examines risk-taking behaviors in employment, leisure, and in life generally. In group list high-risk vocations (work) and high-risk avocations (pleasure). Which of those vocations and avocations are you involved in or would like to do? Rank the items on a scale of 1 to 5 with 1 least and 5 most attractive. (1) Evaluate your items in terms of risk-taking behavior. (2) Prepare to discuss your life and the risks you and others take. (3) How do risks affect our thoughts and actions about death? (4) Do you have risk-taking behavior? If so, were you aware of it prior to this exercise? Is this behavior something you wish to change? If so, how might you bring this change about?

Vocations:	Avocations:
1.	1.
2.	2.
3.	3.
4.	4.
5.	5.
6.	6.
7.	7.
8.	8.

Risk of Living

⇒ **Overview**

There's a line in a Woody Allen movie which puts the health consciousness phenomenon in perspective. Allen says: "Someday medicine is going to discover that the secret to long life is cigarettes and Hershey candy bars." Allen's comments aside, there are few guarantees in life for a long life. We can try and attempt to do the right things. Keeping risks to a minimum is tough work. We can attempt living and working in only nurturing environments. We can try and eat the right foods and watch our weight. We all try and seek out employment that is meaningful and seek out play that is fun and not too harmful or risk-intensive. We strive to foster nurturing relationships and hope to find time for exercise, rest, and leisure. We know safe sex is a must, yet some of us fail to follow through with precaution. We often find ourselves driving out of the way to avoid dangerous and otherwise violent situations. That's life, isn't it?

If you think about it all, it's all quite enough to make you drink, something else which we must do only in moderation. What were the results of your last physical? If you had one at all, your cholesterol was probably too high. Taking responsibility for our actions is tiring at best; besides, being fatigued is bad for our immune system, leaving us susceptible to illness and disease. With all the above said, the best advice still seems to be what our grandparents told us: everything in moderation. Research seems to be proving that as well. The following exercise looks at the risks of living.

⇒ **Directions and Debriefing**

The following exercise examines risks to our health by looking at what we do and don't do with our lives. Review the following risk factors and evaluate yourself in relationship to them. How might you live a longer, healthier, and more enjoyable life? Read each of the risk factors and place a check mark next to the yes or no response if it represents something you do and use in your life or do not do and use in your life. Keep in mind these factors include both negative and positive risk factors. When you are through, review your findings. (1) Were you surprised at your risks, both positive and negative? (2) Develop a plan which includes a timeline for making changes in your life that reduces your risks of living. (3) What were some of the major risks shared by others in your class? (4) Were many of your negative risks somewhat offset by positive factors? If so, which ones?

Factors	Yes	No
Abuse Alcohol		
Abuse Drugs		
Alone		
Annual Physical Exams		

Factors	Yes	No

Dangerous Hobbies
Dangerous Work
Depressed
Destructive Relationships
Domestic Violence in Home
Drive Aggressively
Drive Under the Influence
Eat Junk Food
Enjoy Pets
Exercise
Regular Dental Checkups
Follow Medical Directions
Good Health Care
Overweight
Personal Growth Outlets
Quality Time
Reading Regularly
Smoke
Under High Stress
Unkind or Abusive
Unsafe Sex Practices
Use Seat Belts

Notes: _____

_____

_____

_____

_____

_____

_____

_____

_____

_____

_____

_____

_____

_____

_____

_____

Opinions and Beliefs

To conquer fear is the beginning of wisdom.

Bertrand Russell

⇒ **Overview**

To understand the issues of death and dying, as in life itself, requires developing opinions and beliefs. Having beliefs and opinions in place provides order and allows you to choose how you live your life. Any good therapist will tell you that much of the emotional charge to any fear is a result, in part, of not having examined that fear closely. When fear is examined, the emotional charge begins to dissipate quickly. There is nothing to really fear but fear itself. Fear gets in the way of a full and rational life.

⇒ **Directions and Debriefing**

The purpose of this exercise is to assist you in formulating and developing beliefs and opinions which ultimately help you to identify and desensitize your fear of death and dying. Such an approach may better help you actualize your life by providing you choice in how you live life. In the space provided respond to the following statements by indicating whether you: (SA) Strongly Agree, (A) Agree, (U) Undecided, (D) Disagree or (SD) Strongly Disagree. (1) In group, discuss your responses and prepare to discuss them in full class. (2) Did this exercise help you identify a fear(s)? (3) Did this exercise help you desensitize some of your fears? (4) What are strategies you might use? (5) Which of the statements below had particular meaning to you? Why?

1. _____ A child or adolescent should not be told they have a life-threatening illness when there is a strong possibility of death.

2. _____ Death that occurs suddenly is preferable to all concerned over a lingering degenerative disease.

3. _____ Having the knowledge that you are dying can lead to new opportunities to communicate those matters that are important to family, friends, and others.

4. _____ I would want to know if I had a life-threatening illness or was dying.

5. _____ Knowing one is dying can allow for making the most of what time remains.

6. _____ One needs to consider how much to tell a person about their terminal illness. If you tell too much, a person may begin to lose the will to live.

7. _____ Only family members should tell a person they have either a life-threatening or terminal disease.

8. _____ Pain, which is hard to manage, is the toughest aspect of a terminal condition.

9. _____ Telling a family member they have a life-threatening disease is not a responsibility I could handle.

10. _____ Telling or not telling a person they have a terminal illness is a physician's decision.

Problem is Terminal

Talk is cheap, it takes money to buy whiskey.
Death is a cinch, it's the dying part that's dreary.

Paul, AIDS patient

⇒ **Overview**

Paul went to his doctor's office with a bad case of flu. He came out with a diagnosis of AIDS. It was early 1982, as I recollect. Experts didn't call it AIDS yet. They didn't even know how to diagnose this disease, as there was no HIV antibody test yet. But we in the San Francisco health-care professions had already seen enough cases to know that this disease, whatever it was, was cruel, destructive, and quick at killing. Over the next all-too brief-months, I watched Paul, age 25, deal with all the issues and show all the reactions typical for some dying persons.[34] His losses began to add up quickly. Loss of control, independence, productivity, security, cognitive abilities, predictability, pleasure, plans, dreams, hopes, possessions, surroundings, self and identity meanings, and finally his very life. I watched Paul deal with painful physical symptoms and painful emotional issues. Feelings of ambivalence, anger, jealousy, and a sense of being cheated flooded his thoughts and his conversations. In the end, Paul did die peacefully and in harmony. But that is a story for another time. What this exercise is all about is coping with the worst news now. This activity will prepare you for the worst so you can live your best.

⇒ **Directions**

This activity is for small groups of three to four persons. Role-play that you have just received a diagnosis of a terminal disease. Your instructor will assign you a terminal disease (lung or bone cancer, AIDS, liver disease, heart disease, viral infection, leukemia, brain tumor, etc.). You still feel relatively fine, though somewhat ill and not fully yourself. Your physician has referred you to a support group of other early-stage terminally ill patients. In your support group choose a facilitator from among yourselves. In group discuss your illness and related issues, and help address the issues of others concerning their impending deaths. At regular intervals of 5-10 minutes, your instructor will call out a month. If the month announced is the month you actually have a birthday in, you die. All twelve months in the calendar year will be called at random intervals in this fashion. When you die go to the front of the room and stand quietly, observing how your former group continues to interact without you. Continue until all the months have been called and all have died.

⇒ **Debriefing**

Consider the following questions during and after this activity. (1) What were some of your initial thoughts upon hearing of your terminal diagnosis and specific disease? (2) What were some of the first concerns you had? (3) In terms of group process, what were some of your reactions in relationship to others in the group? Did you note any emotional and physical changes such as fear and stomach upset? (4) How might you prioritize any "time you have left?" (5) Which people in your life are you most concerned about? What are these concerns? (6) Which affairs do you need to "get in order" first? (7) What advance directives do you want in place? (8) Did you have thoughts or discussions about your actual dying? your death? body disposition? Did you have any thoughts about afterlife during this activity? Share your other thoughts in class. (9) How might you help others in such a sad and powerful situation?

71

...death hath ten thousand several doors
for men to make their exits.

John Webster
The Duchess of Malfi, 1612

⇒ **Overview**

Jeanne Calment of France celebrated a special birthday February 21, 1996. She turned 120. As the oldest known and documented living human being, she was beseiged by media and news reporters. One reporter asked a simple question: "Ms. Calment, what sort of future do you anticipate having?" Without hesitation she replied: "A very short one!" Clearly, Ms. Calment is the consummate reality tester. And so it is with those who are dying. As assuredly as the moon ups and the sun downs, they know.

But how does one talk about dying with someone who is dying or whose death is perhaps at hand? The easy answer is: honestly. Society is reluctant to discuss death and dying. Family, friends, caregivers, and usually the dying themselves prefer that the topic not be brought up. This is politeness at its worst. There is this pervasive belief that if we don't talk about death it will go away. It does not. During the 1960s, research showed that as many as two-thirds of physicians were reluctant to tell their patients about their terminal illness.[35] By the late 1970s this had changed to where over 90% of physicians told their patients about their terminal condition.[36] This is good since, generally speaking, the dying know it. But many caregivers and most of society still play the charade. But why? To communicate adequately with the dying requires some basic information about some basic questions. Many of us just don't have that information. How informed is the dying person about their illness? What is the illness or disease in question? What is the sophistication level of the person and their age? There are vast differences between a 70-year-old and a 15-year-old, so the above questions must also be in a context. Knowledge and care is crucial in being with and helping the dying.

Though there is no right way to be with or talk with someone who is dying, the following guidelines will be useful for communicating and being helpful to someone who is dying.

1. Accept death as a natural process of living. It is all right to talk about death and dying. Talk about the illness. Call it what it is. If it's AIDS, call it AIDS. Share your frustration, confusion, and your feelings. Be honest with your feelings.

2. Encourage the dying to make each day special through your actions, your faith, and your love. Work with them to make it so. Flowers, a poem, a visit by a child all help to make a day special.

3. Deal with the dying in the now. "How are you feeling today?" "What are they doing to make you feel comfortable?" "I have this short story I'd like to read to you, if you would like me to."

4. Listen. Simply being there and being attentively quiet often provides the dying with the necessary "timing" to consider discussing their dying or their situation with you. Quiet provides the trust to explore the human experience. On the other hand, it is quite all right to ask the dying if they want to talk about their thoughts, and if so, let them know you are more than willing to listen.

5. Don't trivialize or moralize a dying person's situation by saying things like "Oh, you'll live until a 100," "Oh, I'm sure you'll outlive us all," or "Don't be so pessimistic." It is the dying's right to either discuss or not discuss their condition, and if they do to expect honesty.

72

6. Don't lie. If a dying person asks if they are dying and you know, tell them what you know and what you think.

7. Talk with the dying about what they want to talk about. Listen, be genuine, and be compassionate. Keep the focus on the person, not on yourself.

8. Be available to the person and take an interest in their comfort, pain management and maintaining their bodily dignity. Assist them in maintaining their independence.

9. Touch, hold, hug, kiss and be more than just a physical presence.

10. Encourage emotions, feelings, and crying. Assure the dying person of their appropriateness.

11. Provide some concrete help. Offer to help the dying person write a letter to someone, read to them, or feed them. If they are at home, offer to stop by regularly or offer to help them clean up or bathe. Give of yourself in some real and helpful manner. Assist in facilitating interactions with family or friends.

12. Encourage a dying person to explore faith in a higher being or in the meaning of life if these discussions come up. Share your honest thoughts on the subject if asked.

The above guidelines can result in positive consequences. In addition to your own personal growth and development, you may develop stronger faith. Your sense of empathy and compassion will be enhanced. And, importantly, your sense of love for yourself and others, together with a sharp awareness of the precious precariousness of life, will be assured. It has been my perspective that working with the dying is a privilege filled with positive opportunity.

⇒ **Directions and Debriefing**

Individually or in group role-play a hospital visit to a close friend who is dying. Apply the knowledge and information you have gathered from your instructor, textbook and other readings, class discussions, group work, and the above discussion and guidelines. Brainstorm and develop strategies for communicating with your close friend who is dying. Put to work what you have learned. Questions to consider: (1) What will you do when the time really arrives for you to be with someone who is dying? You may wish to present your strategies and findings in an essay format for future reference. The Active Journal Keeping section at the end of the workbook is an excellent location for your thoughts. (2) If you were dying, what would you want? How would you want to be treated by family, friends, and professional staff? List some of your concerns. (3) Why is it, do you suppose, Americans have such little skill in the area of helping someone who is dying? (4) What types of education programs are needed in our communities? (5) What were your thoughts and feelings from this exercise? (6) Do you feel more capable now than prior to this exercise? If so, why? If not, why not? (7) What other questions came up?

Notes: _____

_____

_____

Caregiving to Death

Time goes, you say. Ah no!
Alas, time stays, we go.

Austin Dobson

⇒ **Overview**

Like fog rolling in at night over a sleepy town, it happens slowly over time. You are providing primary care for someone who is dying or has a life-threatening illness. You begin providing more and more care for someone's everyday needs. Slowly over time, sometimes before you even realize it, you are "caregiving to death." In other words you are "killing yourself," in the process of caring for someone else. You are helping to preserve a quality of life for one at the expense of your own quality of life. As the cared person loses more and more independence, you begin to assume more and more responsibility. Independent tasks like bathing turn into a shared task, and shared tasks such as shopping now turn solely into your task. Slowly you find yourself becoming a caretaker and less a caregiver. One way of preventing "caregiver burnout" is to spread the caregiver tasks among others. Equally important is to keep the person being cared for involved in his own care for as long as is practical. Good caregivers keep sight of their own needs and take good care of themselves so as to provide better care for others.

⇒ **Directions and Debriefing**

Review the following list of common roles caregivers often fulfill. In group or class discuss them. Prioritize which ones might best be performed by you, the caregiver, and which might best be served by other support and caring persons. In other words, which roles do you fill and which roles do you delegate? What are some other roles not listed? Put a "P" next to those roles which might be appropriate for you to provide as a caregiver. Place a "D" next to those roles best delegated to others. Suggest other types of support people who might also best perform some of these other roles. In group or class discuss your findings.

_____ Attorney	_____ Nurse's Aide
_____ Baby-sitter	_____ Nutritionist
_____ Bookkeeper	_____ Paramedic
_____ Case Manager	_____ Personal Attendant
_____ Chauffeur	_____ Personal Valet
_____ Chef	_____ Pet-sitter
_____ Companion	_____ Pharmacist
_____ Confidant	_____ Psychologist
_____ Counselor	_____ Secretary
_____ Doctor	_____ Social Director
_____ Finance Manager	_____ Social Worker
_____ Friend	_____ Spiritual Advisor
_____ Gardener	_____ _____
_____ Health Care Manager	_____ _____
_____ Housekeeper	_____ _____
_____ Maintenance Person	_____ _____
_____ Massage Therapist	_____ _____

Student Stress Scale

⇒ **Overview**

There's a story about a man walking along a riverbank. He notices a man drowning, so he jumps in and saves him. Just as he has resolved this ordeal, another person screams for help. So our hero rescues him from the river. As he is about to leave, fatigued and overwhelmed, yet another person screams for help. This time our hero yells to a person standing along the river's bank to jump in and rescue this third victim. "Where are you going?" the stranger yells to our hero. "I'm going upstream to see who's throwing all these people in the river." To me, the point of this story is simple. The stress of life will overwhelm us if we don't take charge in thoughtful and meaningful ways.

Stress is no stranger to any of us. We experience it in our work, in our lives, and with those we love and care for and about. Stress is the flip side of challenge and the root cause of burnout. There are two components to stress. The *stressors* are the stimuli that affect us and *stress* is how we respond to these stimuli. In other words, do we meet the challenge in a positive manner or succumb in frustration and pain? Another important component is self-esteem, or the reputation we acquire with ourselves.[37] We spend much time trying to preserve and enhance our self-esteem. Stress can lower it. When this happens, we back away or attempt to counter the imbalance. Caregiving situations challenge us with stress and attack our self-esteem. Though stress can be positive, you, like most, probably report negative stress situations with family, co-workers, bosses, patients, and other life interactions. Stress is impersonal. It doesn't attack us because the stressors don't like us. It occurs, for the most part, because we don't like ourselves. We blame ourselves and allow the relationship we have with ourselves to deteriorate.

As the story above indicates, we must choose interventions in life. We must take action! The real struggle, however, is to make these interventions proactive rather than reactive. The secret is to take charge. You can do this in many ways. You can learn to set limits. You can break situations down into manageable compartmentalized components. You can prepare for stressful situations in much the way you would prepare for a hiking trip by planning and packing well. In our case that means developing good workable strategies to be used against stressful situations. You can view stress not as a threat but as a challenge to be met with optimism rather than with fear. You can choose your commitments in life carefully and take control rather than be controlled. You can learn communication skills and how to exercise, relax, and meditate. These are all proven stress-busters. As the father of stress research, Hans Selye advised to learn to know yourself. Are you a turtle or a racehorse? Learn to take care of yourself. Develop social support networks you can love and trust.[38] But before any of the above will really make any sense to you, you must first learn to assess the stressors in your life. Use the following *Student Stress Scale* as a beginning tool to understand stress in your life. Remember, it represents life stress factors which have occurred within the last year. Be thoughtful in responding.

⇒ Directions

The *Student Stress Scale*[39] (LCU) represents an adaptation of researchers Homes and Rahe's *Social   Readjustment Rating Scale*[40]. Check off each life event which has occurred in your life within the last year.

Life Event	Life-Change Units
____ Death of a close family member	100
____ Death of a close friend	73
____ Divorce between parents	65
____ Jail term	63
____ Major personal injury or illness	63
____ Marriage	58
____ Being fired from job	50
____ Failing an important course	47
____ Change in the health of a family member	45
____ Pregnancy	45
____ Sex problems	44
____ Serious argument with close friend	40
____ Change in financial status	39
____ Change of major	39
____ Trouble with parents	39
____ New girl or boyfriend	38
____ Increased workload at school	37
____ Outstanding personal achievement	36
____ First quarter/semester in college	35
____ Change in living condition	31
____ Serious argument with instructor	30
____ Lower grades than expected	29
____ Change in sleeping habits	29
____ Change in social activities	29
____ Change in eating habits	28
____ Chronic car trouble	26
____ Change in number of family get-togethers	26
____ Too many missed classes	25
____ Change of college	24
____ Dropping more than one class	23
____ Minor traffic violations	20

⇒ Debriefing

Add up your total. Each life event has a score that represents the amount of readjustment a person has to make in life as a result of this change. People with scores of 300 or higher have a high health risk. People scoring between 150 and 300 points have about a 50-50 chance of serious health change within two years. People scoring below 150 have a 1-in-3 chance of serious health change. (1) What was your score for the last year _____? (2) Were you surprised? (3) Do you better understand what stress is? (4) Which stressors do you have control over? What are some of your "daily hassles" in need of management? (5) If you were caregiving, how might you manage stress? (6) What changes do you need to make in your life? (7) What score would you give "fear of death?" Is fear a stressor?

*It is sweet to mingle tears with tears;
griefs, where they wound in solitude,
wound more deeply.*

Seneca

⇒ **Overview**

We've all been stressed out. It's just part of the human condition in life called "being hassled." Concern over stress dates back to Hippocrates.[41] (460-377 b.c.) Canadian scientist Hans Selye is considered by many to be the founder of modern stress research. Selye developed a concept in stress research called the General Adaptation Syndrome, or GAS for short.[42] His theory simply states there are three phases to stress. When a person suffers physical or emotional trauma, an <u>alarm</u> reaction occurs. The heart rate zooms; changes in blood pressure and direction occur; and you feel the surge of shock, fear, and apprehension. In phase two you meet the challenge through <u>resistance.</u> That is, both your mind and body begin to mobilize and address this alarming challenge. Your body turns out hormones while your mind sorts and chooses strategies to effectively address the stress. If stress persists, you may deplete your energy reserves and enter the third phase, called <u>exhaustion.</u>

Persistent hassles and stress over time can lead to the condition of mental, physical, and emotional exhaustion called burnout.[43] Teachers, nurses, social workers, police officers, and caregivers are notable examples where stress and burnout are of real concern. The term burnout has become a buzzword, so loosely used that anything from traffic jams to headaches are sometimes seen as signs of burnout. Despite its loose definition and overuse at times, there is consensus that burnout is a very real phenomenon with important implications for anyone working in caregiver situations. There is also agreement that burnout has three central defining characteristics: emotional exhaustion, diminished caring, and a profound sense of demoralization.[44] Emotional exhaustion includes low energy, a sense of being drained and used up, depression, and low self-esteem. I refer to emotional exhaustion as that feeling of going nowhere useful while running in place. A second burnout component is diminished caring. This sense of not caring seems to permeate your very being. "I just don't care; it's hopeless!" is one such comment indicating diminished caring. Everyone seems to be a problem to you and for you. You are consumed by a sense of hopelessness and helpless apathy. The third component in burnout is a profound sense of feeling demoralized. A good example is the social worker who is called in to assist with a dying client and says, "I'm useless here, there's nothing I can do. Why are they asking for me?" when, in fact, this social worker is quite gifted in working with terminally ill patients. To be burned out is to feel overwhelmed in body, mind, and soul.

Burnout is nothing to be ashamed of. It means you once cared and gave it your all. In many ways burnout is a badge of courage and honor. Burnout is a warning sign. It is a reminder that it's time to take care of yourself. A time to seek and find your happy and safe balance in love, work, and life. Complete the exercise on the following page to find out what your burnout score is. As you complete your burnout exercise, think about what is going on in your life. What should you be doing to be good to yourself? Think about healthy strategies you might use to deal with stress and burnout.

⇒ **Directions**

Understanding burnout and learning to gauge your own burnout level is important. Complete the following questionnaire and compute your burnout score as directed at the end of the questionnaire. For each numbered component, respond using the following scale.[45]

1	2	3	4	5	6	7
	Once in a great while					
Never		Rarely	Sometimes	Often	Usually	Always

_____ 1. Being tired.
_____ 2. Feeling depressed.
_____ 3. Having a good day.
_____ 4. Being physically exhausted.
_____ 5. Being emotionally exhausted.
_____ 6. Being happy.
_____ 7. Being wiped out.
_____ 8. Thinking, "I can't take anymore."
_____ 9. Being unhappy.
_____ 10. Feeling run-down.
_____ 11. Feeling trapped.

_____ 12. Feeling worthless.
_____ 13. Being weary.
_____ 14. Being troubled.
_____ 15. Feeling disillusioned and resentful.
_____ 16. Being weak, susceptible to illness.
_____ 17. Feeling hopeless.
_____ 18. Feeling rejected.
_____ 19. Feeling optimistic.
_____ 20. Feeling energetic.
_____ 21. Feeling anxious.

Compute your score as follows. Total the values you wrote next to the following items: 1, 2, 4, 5, 7, 8, 9, 10, 11, 12, 13, 14, 15, 16, 17, 18, and 21.

Place this total on line A.	Line A _____
Total the values you wrote next to the following lines: 3, 6, 19, and 20	Line B _____
Subtract line B from the number 32.	Line C _____
Add lines A and C.	Line D _____
Divide line D by the number 21. This is your burnout score.	Line E _____

⇒ **Debriefing**

A score of 4.0 on this measure is the burnout cut-off score. If you are above 4.0, you are in burnout range. If your burnout score is high, don't panic. Many people function with high scores. What is important is to address this problem with helpful strategies. By systematically checking your burnout score from time to time, you can become more aware and stay in touch with stress and burnout. The first step to any meaningful change is knowledge.

Consider the following: (1) What's your burnout score? (2) Discuss your findings in group and class. (3) Discuss what health effects, both positive and negative, might derive from stress. (4) How might fear of death, and the stress associated with that fear, affect your living more fully day-to-day? (5) How might one deal with the stress of loss and grief? (6) Develop a "strategy list" for dealing with your stress. (7) Choose a self-help book on stress management and read it. (8) As concerns someone else who is dying, how might one lessen their stress. (9) List strategies for helping someone who is dying lessen their stress.

Caregiving Yourself

Life's short, eat desert first

Diane Apland

⇒ **Overview**

Any exploration of death and dying must also explore the needs of those who provide care for those experiencing dying and ultimately death. Caring for yourself is crucial if you are to continue caring for others effectively. Research in the area of burnout, caregiving, and stress has identified specific strategies used by professional caregivers. These strategies enable these professionals to effectively cope with stress and burnout associated with caring for terminally ill persons. These helpful strategies for dealing with burnout can be grouped into six categories and are discussed below. You may wish to read Larson, D. G. (1993). *The Helper's Journey*. Champaign, IL: Research Press, and Levine, S. (1987). *Healing Into Life and Death*. New York: Doubleday.

⇒ **Directions and Debriefing**

There are two parts to this exercise. For the <u>first part</u> of this exercise review the following checklist and check those you agree with. This exercise is most helpful if begun in small group and further addressed in full class. You may find keeping notes in your Active Journal section a useful tool as well. For each of the categories, add additional strategies which work for you and might work for other caregivers in their different or unique caregiving situations. The secret here is to make you aware of your positive skills in "taking care of yourself," and then sharing those "tips" with others. The second part is at the end of this checklist.

A. Education and Awareness

1. _____ I can identify my sources and symptoms of stress.
2. _____ I have training or other education in caregiving and death education.
3. _____ I understand my coping patterns.
4. _____ I am reading relevant reading materials or other self-help books in this area.
5. _____ I monitor myself for stress, burnout, and other negative effects of caregiving.

6. _____ _____
7. _____ _____
8. _____ _____
9. _____ _____

B. Attitude

1. _____ I know what I am seeking from caregiving.
2. _____ I have learned to prioritize.
3. _____ I know the rewards and failures in my caregiving.
4. _____ I know how to measure success and failure.
5. _____ I know my restrictions and limitations.
6. _____ I know when to "let go."
7. _____ I know when to slow down.

8. _____ I know when to delegate to others.

9. _____ _____

10. _____ _____

11. _____ _____

12. _____ _____

C. Supports

1. _____ I know what practical supports I need.
2. _____ I know what emotional supports I need.
3. _____ I know what spiritual supports I need.
4. _____ I am able to seek support from others.
5. _____ I am able to express and discuss my feelings.
6. _____ I am able to share and express my varied emotions.
7. _____ I have supportive people with whom I can and do talk.
8. _____ The kinds of other supports I use are:

9. _____ _____

10. _____ _____

11. _____ _____

12. _____ _____

D. Respite

1. _____ I take time away from my caregiving.
2. _____ I have support in place which allows me to take time away from caregiving.
3. _____ I know, understand, and use relaxation techniques.
4. _____ I have hobbies which are unrelated to my line of work.
5. _____ I have friends unrelated to work whom I associate with and enjoy.
6. _____ I have other activities unrelated to work which I do and enjoy.
7. _____ I understand the principles of meditation and use them.

8. _____ _____

9. _____ _____

10. _____ _____

11. _____ _____

12. _____ _____

E. Exercise and Diet

1. _____ I exercise regularly (aerobic and anaerobic). How? _____
2. _____ I eat good, balanced, and nutritious foods.
3. _____ I maintain a good diet.
4. _____ I am happy with my weight.
5. _____ I am happy with the aspects of my health over which I have control.

6. _____ I do not smoke.
7. _____ I do not over indulge in alcohol and drugs.
8. _____ I have regular visits to my doctor and have annual checkups.

9. _____ _____

10. _____ _____

11. _____ _____

12. _____ _____

F. Self-Nurturing

1. _____ I like myself.
2. _____ I acknowledge myself.
3. _____ I, for the most part, receive enough rest.
4. _____ I have and practice a good sense of humor.
5. _____ I do something enjoyable for myself each day.
6. _____ My home is comfortable and enjoyable.
7. _____ I have a pet(s) I enjoy.
8. _____ I read about personal growth.
9. _____ I keep a creative or other such journal.
10. _____ I do spiritual or philosophical reading and/or activities .

11. _____ _____

12. _____ _____

13. _____ _____

Use the second part of this exercise to explain and share what your responses, techniques, and strategies are for the statements you checked off. For the statements you have not checked, develop strategies to address and correct them. In class share some of the best strategies each group developed.

Notes: _____

_____

_____

_____

_____

_____

_____

_____

_____

_____

Poetry as a Caregiving Tool

Here lay Joe. Really good bro.
Stopped to fight. He shoulda go

Wall graffiti
Housing project

⇒ **Overview**

Poems as they pertain to the sick, the dying, and dead are everywhere! The poem above caught my eye on a bus ride past a rather nasty and violent ghetto that could be in any urban American city. Poems tend to reflect upon the truths and frailties of life. You see them in written wills, as epitaphs on grave tombstones, and as poetic musings of the mind found in sundry different places. Whether in free verse or poetic rhyme, people have pondered death since the ages first began. Many a suicide note has been a poem, as have the poems written by great soldiers before battle. Both those cared for and those who provide this care have found solace in poems. Poems have a way of capturing the universal human predicament.

Poems have a way of grasping the essence as we walk beside life, behind life, or ahead in life. Reading and writing poetry can indeed be a most cathartic tool.

⇒ **Directions and Debriefing**

Compose a poem about life and death from the perspective of either a caregiver or a person being cared for. As you compose your poem, think about your feelings, your thoughts, your fears, and your pleasures. Be generous in allowing yourself to feel. Be generous in your discussion with self, in group, and in class. (1) Did you find it difficult to write a poem about sickness, death, or dying? Why or why not? (2) How might creative writing be cathartic for both the cared for and the caregiver? Explain. (3) Why do you suppose most sympathy cards have poems in them? (4) How might you write a condolence letter utilizing poetry? (5) How might you use poetry with someone, such as a child, who is very ill?

_____
Poem Title

_____
_____
_____
_____
_____
_____
_____
_____
_____
_____
_____
_____
_____

Meditation

Man's main task in life
is to give birth to himself.

Erich Fromm

⇒ **Overview**

Whether the question is life or death, we must always wonder and we must always ponder. The emotional drain of caring for the ill, caring for ourselves, or simply returning back to life from the shrill ache of losing someone we love takes a heavy toll on our body, mind, and our very soul. Meditation is a wonderfully helpful and soothing tool for these times and for the other harsh realities of living life. Meditation can be done at any time to relax or "de-stress!" A meditation session usually lasts for about 20 minutes, but 5 minutes is long enough to provide you an example of the procedure and to realize how difficult it is to keep internal voices from jabbering at you. In a sense meditation is a form of mind discipline or mind control. It has many benefits other than just to relax or unwind. Prepare to meditate in class. An excellent resource is *Learning to Meditate* by Patricia Carrington, Ph.D. (Kendall Park, NJ: Pace Educational Systems, Inc., 1979). You can find other resources on meditation at your local bookstore or community library.

⇒ **Directions**

1. Sit on the floor, at your desk, or in a chair. Get comfortable and remove distractions. Prepare to meditate for 5 minutes. Focus on your breathing and counting. The object is to exclude other thoughts from consciousness. When distracting thoughts occur, try to refocus by thinking, "Now, this is my time to relax," and continue with your breathing and counting.

2. Sit with your legs uncrossed. Cup one hand loosely inside the other in your lap or a bit higher if that is more comfortable.

3. Close your eyes gently and relax. Begin with relaxing the muscles in your feet and progress to your face, letting all your muscles relax. (Tighten first, then release them.)

4. Breathe through your nose and count each time you inhale. As you breathe naturally, count from one to ten, then start with one again.

⇒ **Debriefing**

(1) Were you able to exclude other thoughts from your mind? (2) What kinds of thoughts interfered with your meditation? Thoughts about the past? Thoughts about the future? Were you in the "now" and in the "present?" (3) Did you have the feeling that there may be different levels of consciousness? (4) Do you think a person would benefit from meditating 20 minutes every day? twice a day? What are the benefits? Might you purchase a book on meditation? Discuss how meditation might be a good tool for stress management.

Wait for the wisest of all counselors, Time.

Pericles (495-429 B.C.)

⇒ **Overview**

Grief is a central ingredient in the human experience, not just an illness from which we recover. Grief is not a final outcome but rather a life transition. We as humans are capable of compassion, and thus can help each other in times of need and grief.[46] Whether through our personal involvement or through an understanding of resources available, we can make a difference in soothing the grief in each of us. Grief, bereavement, and mourning take an emotional toll on us all. Much of this loss, however, is the anticipation of loss--just pure and simple fear. Fear interferes with us living life more fully. Learning how to use the tools of life so as to enable us and others to go on with life after a loss is an important task for each of us to learn in life.

⇒ **Directions and Debriefing**

Role play can help desensitize us to our fear and harsh anticipation of death and dying. Such an outcome allows us to be more helpful to ourselves and to others. In this desensitization lies still another bonus. We are more able to "get on and live" our lives more fully! When death leaves a family member or close friend bereaved, there is much we can do to "help out." Role-play the following situations. You may feel discomfort at first, but you will be better prepared next time when the situation is not a role play. Consider the following during this exercise. (1) What are your thoughts and feelings? (2) Did you develop any helpful responses? (3) Do you feel better prepared for such situations? If so, why? If not, why? (4) How can we prepare for such eventualities in our life? (5) How have you handled past personal grief?

1. Your brother's two-month-old daughter dies in her sleep of Sudden Infant Death Syndrome (SIDS). How might you assist?

2. Your wife's father dies of a heart attack while playing golf. How do you respond to your wife's grief and your own?

3. Your neighbor of ten years, who is in her 70s, has just returned from the veterinarian. Her twelve year old cat has died. What can you do?

4. You are the CEO of a law firm where a colleague and partner has just committed suicide. Everyone is looking to you to bring the "firm together" in this terrible time of need. How do you begin? What do you do? Prioritize a helpful action plan.

5. An employee you supervise has been diagnosed with a terminal illness. What might be helpful?

6. You are a teacher, and one of your students has just died in an automobile accident. How might you work with other students in your class to "cope with this tragic loss"?

7. Your best friend's wife dies suddenly. How do you demonstrate you care? What do you do first?

Unfinished Business

*The great tragedy of life
is not that some men perish
but that they cease to love.*

W. Somerset Maugham

⇒ **Overview**

This exercise takes a look at the business of unfinished business and the need to finish this business so we can get on with our lives and enjoy life. Unfinished business is the psychological baggage we cart along with us throughout our lives. It is the love we didn't get or give, the smiles we withheld, the many thank-you's we failed to say. In short, it is the sum of our regrets about our conduct towards other people, primarily those we love, wanted to love, or from whom we wanted love. The process of completing unfinished business is often necessary for survivors during the grieving period. Sometimes caregivers even find themselves assisting the dying in this finishing work.

⇒ **Directions and Debriefing**

Working individually, think of one person in your life who means a lot to you and imagine if that person were to die tomorrow. What should you have said to them? Write your responses to the following questions. Write your thoughts in the journal section. (1) How did this exercise affect you? (2) How can we prevent having unfinished business?

1. What were some of your <u>happy</u> moments together?

_____

_____

_____

_____

2. What were some of your <u>unhappy</u> moments together?

_____

_____

_____

_____

3. What are the circumstances of your most <u>painful</u> memories with this person?

_____

_____

_____

4. When you think of this person, what <u>sadness</u> comes to mind?

_____

_____

5. What will you <u>miss</u> most about this person?

_____

_____

_____

6. What unfinished business do you wish that <u>you</u> had discussed with this person?

_____

_____

_____

7. What unfinished business do you wish <u>they</u> had discussed with you?

_____

_____

_____

8. If you had to do it all over again, what would you do <u>differently</u> in this relationship?

_____

_____

_____

9. What is it about your <u>communication</u> style or the other person's communication style that allowed these circumstances to occur and develop?

_____

_____

_____

10. Since this was an exercise with a person who has <u>not</u> actually died, what might you do <u>now</u> to correct any problems with this relationship? Will you do it? Explain.

_____

_____

_____

4

Preparing For Death

While Embracing Life

The dignity that we seek in dying must be found in the dignity with which we have lived our lives. "Ars moriendi is ars vivendi" - The art of dying is the art of living. The honesty and grace of the years of life that are ending is the real measure of how we die. It is not in the last weeks or days that we compose the message that will be remembered, but in all the decades that preceded them. Who has lived in dignity, dies in dignity.

Sherwin B. Nuland
National Book Award Winner
How We Die

"It's a nice sleep with no alarm clock in the morning," a patient of mine said as he lay hospitalized in the end stage of renal (kidney) failure. Sleep has long been associated with death. The Greeks personified sleep, *Hypnos,* as the twin brother of death, *Thanatos.* The cultural connection between sleep and death is most vivid. Orthodox Jews thank God each morning for returning them to life.[47] My own Italian Catholic family always referred to the body in a casket at a funeral home as so-and-so who was "sleeping." Was it any wonder my brother and I dreaded going to sleep at night? I in particular had nightmares for years.

"Preparing to meet death," "preparing for the good death," and "getting ready for my maker," are all expressions somberly associated with dying. What does death look like? What immediately comes to mind--An old man in black hood and scythe on shoulder, right? One researcher[48] in a clever study asked several hundred subjects to describe death using a multiple-choice guide as sort of a template for developing their composite of this historically dreaded individual. What would your composite drawing of death look like? In ancient Greek times, dreadful looking hybrid-human and winged female creatures called sirens and harpies were associated with death.[49] *Sirens* brought death and *harpies* destroyed memory.[50]

With all the eerie and frightening supernatural possibilities interfering with one's death, is it any wonder the Greeks noted that dying correctly was in fact an art form (*Ars moriendi,* or Art of Dying)? But what exactly does this mean? What is the appropriate death, how does one prepare for the good death? This chapter attempts to address this question by preparing you to help yourself and others. The nice thing about learning this "Art of Dying" is that you will better understand death, and by so doing, better live life--rhyme and reason and everything relate nicely.

The chapter starts off with an examination of your own thoughts on dying and a discussion of dying. No discussion of dying can go far without looking at fears and losses among those dying. Kübler-Ross's theory is looked at, and then the chapter moves into strategies for working with issues surrounding dying. How does one get their personal affairs in order? What is a Living Trust? What is wanted in a funeral? These questions are addressed. Living Wills and Advance Directives are explained. The chapter examines the rights of patients both sick and dying. Opportunities for examining one's life and for formulating final thoughts are examined as well. This chapter is a practical series of exercises, all designed to better understand death preparation.

During the final days of his dying, my late brother Gary quipped to me that I should have carved into his headstone the following: "I'd rather be bowling!" It was a witty and cute line drowned out by his anxiety and my sadness and real helplessness. Back in 1985, I was as much ill-equipped to deal with a 33-year-old brother dying as my brother was at actually dying. Some many hundreds of clients later, I am much better at this *Ars moriendi* stuff. My desire is to equip you and empower you so you don't find yourself at someone's deathbed scene speech-less, helpless, and wishing you were bowling. *Ars moriendi is ars vivendi*: The art of dying is the art of living! Indeed it is so.

Be ashamed to die
until you have won some victory for humanity.

Horace Mann

⇒ **Overview**

The discomfort of dealing with the loss of someone who is close to you pales when compared to the flow of emotions felt when actually making arrangements for someone's death. If you felt ill prepared and ill at ease at someone's deathbed, pause a moment, and consider how hard the task is working with someone who is dying and wishes for you to assist them in making their final arrangements. The simple fact is that most of us will have to consider death wishes for ourselves and others we love at some point in our lives. We may in fact find ourselves making such death plans with or without consent. When a parent or other immediate family member dies, someone has to make the plans. And that may well be you. Making such plans and such decisions from an educated and informed perspective can make all the difference in whether the task of planning someone's death is manageable or overwhelming. Making death plans can be disastrous on an emotional, financial, and personal level if we are unprepared. There are many considerations in preparing for someone's death. The following activity should be most helpful in addressing these considerations. Preparation and education are the crucial ingredients.

⇒ **Directions and Debriefing**

The perspective of this activity is that of a dying friend who has asked you to work with them in making their final plans and in preparing for death. The activity will serve as a useful learning and training opportunity. Review the following exercises listed below. These particular exercises are all located in this chapter. If you become familiar with them, you will be better able to assist yourself and others in making final death arrangements. Some of the suggested exercises and activities are most useful for the dying themselves to work on, if that is their wish and they are able. Some exercises are suggested simply because they provide ideas and thoughtfulness for the dying person or their primary caregiver to consider in this sensitive matter. (1) Once you have finished this formidable task, share what you have learned in group and class. (2) Keep track of your learning by using the "Active Journal-Keeping" section beginning on page 246. (3) When you have completed the exercises, write a reaction paper.

1. Getting One's Affairs in Order
2. Durable Power of Attorney for H. C.
3. Dying Person's Bill of Rights
4. Eulogy
5. Fears of Death
6. Fears in a Dying Person's Life
7. Final Letter
8. Funeral Wishes
9. Moment of Death or Thereabouts
10. Living with Death and Dying
11. Obituary
12. Poetic Will
13. Preparing a Living Will
14. The Good Death for You
15. Tombstone Epitaph
16. What Are Your Thoughts About Your Own Death?

What Are Your Thoughts About Your Own Dying?

*The greatest use of a life is to spend it
on something that will outlast it.*

William James

⇒ **Overview**

The purpose of this exercise is to help you better understand the natural process of death in our own lives so you might better live your life and be of assistance to others who might be nearing life's end. When you have completed this exercise read *"The Importance of Dying,"* which follows.

⇒ **Directions and Debriefing**

If you think you feel uncomfortable talking with a dying person or discussing a loss with a bereaved person, imagine what it might be like to discuss your own dying or terminal illness. What do you think your feelings would be if <u>you</u> were the one dying? Here are some points to consider and write about. Use these questions as debriefing questions for use in group or class when you are through.

1. What might be your greatest concern(s) and fear(s)? _____

_____

_____

_____

_____

2. How much do you want to know about your condition and prognosis? _____

_____

_____

_____

_____

3. Where would you want to be when you die (home, hospice, hospital, etc.)? _____

_____

_____

_____

_____

4. Who would you want to be with you as you die and at your deathbed?   _____

_____

_____

5. What does the "good or appropriate death" include in your mind? What might you need to achieve it? _____

_____

_____

_____

_____

6. What are your thoughts about afterlife? Religious? Spiritual? Philosophical?

_____

_____

_____

_____

7. What might caregivers, family, and support friends do to help you? _____

_____

_____

_____

_____

8. What might you learn and do now to lessen your concerns and fears of death? _____

_____

_____

_____

_____

9. In terms of understanding and appreciating life, what is the importance of dying? _____

_____

_____

_____

_____

_____

_____

THE ART OF CARE!

The Importance of Dying

In the spring of 1996, a Michigan jury found Jack Kervorkian not guilty for assisting in the suicide of two terminally ill people. He had already "helped out" in nearly two dozen prior suicides. Around the same time, the U. S. Court of Appeals in San Francisco ruled that hopelessly dying people have the right to decide how to end their lives and physicians have the right to help them do so. The "right-to-die" issues of euthanasia and assisted-suicide have raised a lively debate.

Euthanasia comes from the Latin "eu" meaning well and "thanatos," meaning death. Euthanasia has come to mean a "good death." No doubt the controversy will rage on about this good death. But why is it we're all so consumed about death? After all, it's a given and a certainty. As the late George Burns himself said: "What's this big deal about death all the time--it's been done!" Why is it we make something so natural so unnatural? Ours is a most ignorant society when it comes to death. Studies show that about 75% of Americans don't have wills. People seem to fear that to write a will is to somehow rattle the cage "Old Man Death" and thus have him take note. Most don't have a clue where to begin discussing the death of a pet with a child, let alone grandma's death. We don't know how to act at funerals or even how to write a decent condolence letter to the family of the deceased. Generally, the best case scenario is to send a casserole, usually tuna. And why is it, the casseroles are always tuna? No one likes them. If the good Lord were to come down and raise up the deceased so they might eat that casserole, they wouldn't eat it either. Promise yourselves you will never send tuna casseroles to funerals. Our culture is terrified of using the words death or dying--the "D" words as I call them. We prefer euphemisms such as passed away, left us, laid to rest, departed, or transcended. In fact, there are about 150 commonly used euphemisms and slang for death. My favorite is "crossed into cyberspace." Next time you're out shopping, take a look at some sympathy cards. They almost never use the "D" word. The marketing gurus on Madison Avenue know the American public is not comfortable with those words in its sympathy cards. I suspect they reckon: Isn't it bad enough we have to die? Do we have to talk about it too?

Hallmark Cards is the king of this type of denial. The cover on one of their cards reads: "They're not gone, they're away!" What denial. For gosh sakes, where did they go, bowling? What makes complex issues like euthanasia and assisted-suicide so difficult and controversial for most Americans is the simple fact that they haven't dealt with the more basic questions of death in general and their own death in particular. If we just can't bear to send a sympathy card which uses the "D" word, or discuss our own mortality and death, then how are we ever expected to resolve more complex issues like euthanasia and suicide? What is needed is a national program of death education which begins the process of desensitizing people's fear of an open and candid discussion of death. We've got to put a halt to impersonalizing issues of death and dying with euphemisms and buzzwords like "oncology ward," "left us," and "friendly fire." We need to look at death the way the health-conscious look at diet, exercise, and good health care. We as Americans should be just as knowledgeable about advance directives--such as living wills, powers of attorney, and probate matters--as we are becoming about IRA's and 401-K retirement matters. Our minds are cluttered with fear and anxiety over death. How will we ever be expected to live fully if we spend so much time running from our death phobias? I'm not saying death should be something we love and adore, after all, death does represent much uncertainty. From reincarnation to hell, there are lots of issues to consider when discussing death. A healthy appreciation of the role of death in our lives and some acceptance might go a long way in furthering our ability to enjoy and live life fully. It is said to appreciate the sun and day one must understand the moon and night. It's this comparison and contrast which makes each so beautiful and important.

Death education has similar value, as well as providing a powerful added incentive for both a life and for a society. When we each deal with issues of our own mortality and our own death we cannot help but happen upon questions of purpose, meaning, and spirituality in our lives as well. When we address questions about the end of life, we soon begin to appreciate the importance of the rest of life. The moral rewards to society would be noteworthy. The process of death education, by its very nature, also leads us to examine how to best live a full and meaningful life within a moral and spiritual context. If we have the courage to accept our mortality and own deaths, then our children and those who follow behind, will have the courage to live their own lives.

And that in essence is the importance of dying.

Fears in a Dying Person's Life

The grave itself is but a covered bridge
Leading from light to light,
through a brief darkness.

Henry Wadsworth Longfellow

⇒ **Overview**

Death is filled with many meanings. Mostly, at least at first, death is filled with many fears. *Fear* pertains to some apprehension with a focus, while *anxiety* refers to some worry or trouble of a more diffused and nonspecific focus and nature. The most common responses among persons dying are a sense of sorrow, a need to overcome, a need to participate, and a series of fears. Fear is one of the most important psychological responses. Fear of death and dying, also known as *thanatophobia*, is probably the ultimate fear, while another primary fear is the *anticipated pain of dying.*[51] Death fears may be broken down into four general and broad categories. They are (a) fears related to death and the dying process, (b) fears related to the meaning of death itself, (c) fears related to consequences of death for oneself and others one loves, and (d) fears related to the death or dying of others. [52]

⇒ **Directions and Debriefing**

Brainstorm some of these fears as well as other fears you might have regarding death and dying. (1) Discuss your findings in group and class. (2) What would your issues be if you were dying? (3) What do you do now when you are fearful about things and events in your life? (4) How might one best deal with their fears? Develop some strategies.

Notes: _____

_____

_____

_____

_____

_____

_____

_____

_____

_____

_____

_____

_____

_____

_____

_____

_____

93

Losses in a Dying Person's Life

It matters not how a man dies, but how he lives.

Samuel Johnson

⇒ **Overview**

The purpose of this exercise is to help you better understand losses associated with persons terminally ill and dying and to examine these losses from both the perspective of the dying and their loved ones.

⇒ **Directions and Debriefing**

Though there are many changes in the dying person's or terminally ill person's life, the word which most stands out is "loss." The most significant changes relate to a series of losses. In group, brainstorm some of these losses. (1) Confer with your instructor and textbook for some potential responses after completing this exercise. (2) Be sure to complete this exercise by listing as many losses as possible. (3) Were you surprised by the extent of the losses that develop during the dying process? (4) As a variation, describe losses other than through death, such a loss of love, etc. (5) Consider following this exercise with "Interactions After a Family Loss" on page 182.

_____

_____

_____

_____

_____

_____

_____

_____

_____

_____

_____

_____

_____

_____

_____

_____

_____

_____

_____

_____

Kübler-Ross's Five Psychological Stages of Dying

Watching a peaceful death is like watching a falling star.

Elizabeth Kübler-Ross

⇒ **Overview**

Our society prescribes restrictive norms for the display of emotions among men and women. The prescriptions for men are even more restrictive than are those for women. A person facing a terminal illness will face their own death with less difficulty if they show and express their emotions. Elizabeth Kübler-Ross introduced her five psychological stages of dying that the terminally ill go through in her book, *On Death and Dying,* in 1969.

I think it is important to note that the existence of Elizabeth Kubler-Ross's stages has never been demonstrated scientifically.[53] Furthermore, no evidence exists to show the dying in fact move from one stage to another stage, let alone stages one through five. Further, the popularity of Kubler-Ross's stages may be found in the caregiver's need to control. Caregivers often get confused with what is happening and what should happen, and thus they often tip their hand wrongfully. Stage theory is a nice way of making some sense out of a rather terrible situation. But is it accurate? I doubt it. Though there is major disagreement over whether dying patients progress through stages in a particular sequence or even at all, it seems clear all dying patients do experience many emotions in one fashion or another. We serve our patients best when we take our cues from the patient and let them set the framework for us to assist them. I suggest we leave stages for the actors. With my cautionary comments aside, I think it important to examine Kübler-Ross's stages of dying. Her contribution is significant and we are all in her debt.

⇒ **Directions and Debriefing**

Define and describe Elizabeth Kübler-Ross's five stages of dying. (1) Discuss the pros and cons of Kubler-Ross's theory. (2) Do you think there is a pattern in the dying process? (3) What do you suppose is meant by the expression "people die in death as they lived in life"? (4) What other emotions and factors might appear during the dying process?

1. Shock or Denial _____

   _____

2. Anger _____

   _____

3. Bargaining _____

   _____

4. Depression _____

   _____

5. Acceptance _____

95

Life Reflection Scrapbook

What is our life
but a succession of preludes to that unknown song
whose first solemn note is sounded by death.

Alphonse de Lamartine.

⇒ **Overview**

Death is something we dislike thinking about. Death is something we talk about even less. The worst aspect of death is not the dreadfulness or inevitability, but the way we squander death. Death is a lost opportunity for us all. We all share death. We all die. That is the human commonality. In many ways preparing for death is the final stage of growing up. If preparing for death is done well, we all are winners: in terms of peace, in terms of positive life values, and in terms of wisdom passed on to those young and old alike. This activity describes how to develop a life reflection scrapbook.

⇒ **Directions and Debriefing**

A life reflection scrapbook is a place to reflect upon the highlights, the learnings, the values, the beliefs, and the important moments of a life. It is a place where one is empowered to make what remains of their life meaningful. Life reflection provides an opportunity to say what you mean, pass on what is important in life to others, note what one has learned in life, and suggest what one wishes to be remembered for. A good life reflection scrapbook, like a good container of perfume, captures the essence of one's life. There is no limit to what one may put in one's scrapbook: pictures, poems, clippings, letters, essays, philosophy, recipes, guidance, locks of hair. Special moments from a special person. One particularly nice technique is to use the scrapbook to describe the story behind prized possessions which are to be given away either during the dying process or after death. Asking an elderly person to share what life was like during the war or growing up in a rural community is quite often enough to get them going on their reflections.

There are many kinds of questions that stimulate a life reflection. "Tell me something about your family." "What were some of the lucky breaks you received in life?" "What were some of the major events and milestones in your life?" "What are some of your favorite memories?" "Looking back now on your life, did it differ much from what you expected?" "What would you do differently in life, if you had it to do over?" and "Who among family members resembles you?" These are good stimulating questions. You've got to stimulate "that shiny web trail of words like a spider would leave, all silver," out of that person working on their reflections. A life reflection scrapbook is a family affair begun early in life or begun in earnest now that grandma is getting old and ill. It might be a project for friends taking care of a friend with cancer. The scrapbook might be a therapy tool for professional and volunteer caregivers working with death and dying patients.

However, when one chooses to use this activity, one result always seems to emerge. The life reflection scrapbook is a means of connecting the past with the present, leaving one person's loving legacy of what was and might be for future generations to learn and grow from. (1) (1) Discuss your thoughts and ideas regarding your scrapbook in group and class. Be creative! (2) How might you use video and tape recording in place of a scrapbook?

He who had bequeathed property
had mixed his labor with it during life
under the expectation he could
continue his power over it,
even beyond the grave.

John Stuart Mill

⇒ **Overview**

Two-thirds of all Americans don't have wills, not to mention advance directives, or other orderly information in the event of their deaths. There is this odd belief that to deal with the "business of dying" is to beckon death itself to come and get us. Nobody wants to do that. But the somber fact is one's personal affairs, if not in order, only drain the life out of the sick and dying and those left behind more quickly. Having an orderly will and advance directives can relieve the stress and pain of "those dying and those crying"--those over-whelmed by their illness and dying, and those overwhelmed by their loss and grief.

But even when we might agree a will is an important document to have, many still will not execute one. As many reasons exist to inhibit the writing of a will as exist to facilitate writing one. Some reasons include the belief one is too young, possesses too few possessions, is in good health, or has no children. How do you wish for your remains to be disposed of when you die? Do you want to be buried or cremated and your ashes skattered at sea? These are important questions which you need to decide upon now, while you are alive. Give some thought to how yo wish to leave this life.

⇒ **Directions and Debriefing**

The following exercise provides a checklist for the most commonly found "affairs to get in order." The checklist is suitable for both the caregiver who wishes to help the ill-prepared charge as well as for the rest of us. Getting one's affairs in order does not shake the "cage of death" but rather soothes the "beast of fear" in all of us. This activity works well with the following exercises: "Funeral Wishes" on page 101, "Death Certificate" on page 34, "Preparing A Living Will" on page 104, "DPAHC" on page 108, and "Final Letter" on page 123 of the workbook. (1) After you complete this checklist, develop a timetable for completing those areas not completed. (2) Discuss the entire process in group or class to see how many of your classmates have their affairs in order. (3) Were you surprised by the amount of items to be addressed if one is to truly get one's affairs in order? (4) Discuss the pros and cons of taking the time to get your affairs in order.

An excellent resource developed by Nolo Press Publishing Company is called *WillMaker*. This computer software program walks you through the process of writing a will on your computer. It's very simple and easy to use even for the computer novice. The final printed document meets all the legal requirements for a will and is easy to change in case some of your beneficiaries fall out of favor with you. You will find an exercise called "Using NOLO Press's WillMaker" on page 122 of the workbook.

97

Topic	Not Completed	Completed

1. Advance Directives

> Living Will
> Durable Power of Attorney for Health Care (DPAHC)
> Durable Power of Attorney for Legal Affairs

2. Funeral Wishes

> Final instructions
> Funeral payment arrangements
> Health insurance policy information

3. Executor or Trusted Friend(s) to Carry Out Wishes

> Appoint executor
> Reserve cash for immediate needs and costs

4. Legal Instruments

> Will
> Final letter explaining will
> Final letter to friend and relatives
> Organ donor card ready
> Charitable donations noted
> Possessions to be distributed prior to death, if applicable
> State and federal tax circumstances and prior returns
> Personal and business balance sheets ready
> Custody and care of children, if applicable
> Other legal requirements

5. Death Notification

> List of relatives and friends to be notified immediately
> List of relatives and friends to be notified as time permits
> Obituary and news media of choice
> Enough information available to complete death certificate

6. List of Assets and Debts

> Insurance policies with correct beneficiaries
> Employee benefits
> Banking (checking, savings, loan)
> Credit cards
> Credit union
> Real estate

Safe deposit box (key or combination)
Savings bonds
Stocks
Municipal and corporate bonds
Art and other collections

7. Name Adjustments, Deletions or Additions to Legal Records

Safe deposit box
Will
Real estate holdings
Banking accounts
Vehicles
Life insurance policies or other benefits
Other personal possessions

8. Distribution of Entry Keys

Safe deposit box
Home(s)
Vehicles
Real estate property

9. Personal Papers Assembled for Distribution

Personal correspondence
Journals
Private papers
Other key writings and papers assembled

10. Other Instructions and Concerns

Care of pets
a.
b.
c.
d.

_____

_____

_____

_____

_____

_____

99

THE ART OF CARE!

Living Trusts: A Will for Living!

Joseph and Suzanne were together for 13 years. Though never legally married, they thought in tandem, acted in tandem, and loved each other in tandem. With Joseph in the final stages of cancer, both discussed Joe's final wishes and final disposition of assets. Joe gave everything he owned to Suzanne. Not much of this was documented, however. When Joe died at age 41, Joe's family stepped in from back east and took everything. Two years later the matter is still in litigation. Suzanne now has very little. Unfair. All avoidable!

A *living trust* is a legal instrument which assures those you love are provided for when you die or are disabled. It serves the same purpose as a will except it eliminates much of the need for probate proceedings, executors, commissions, and attorney's fees. It allows those you select to have uninterrupted use of funds for monthly bills and other expenses. The living trust has significant benefits for alternative relationships such as those living together without benefit of marriage and for gay relationships.

Why the Popularity? The living trust takes effect during the maker's lifetime. It is flexible, simple, and inexpensive. The trust is revocable by the maker at any time. The maker can take an active role in the management of assets or appoint a professional investment manager, if assets are of such complexity and worth.

Protection and Security. The trust protects the creator and their loved ones in the event of illness, accident, disability, or absence. Assets are safeguarded while the creator is traveling, incapacitated, or involved in other matters. Provisions of a living trust can assure income is collected and expenses covered. The creator can choose to stay active or defer to the trustee to carry out his or her day-to-day fiscal wishes. This is particularly useful for people with chronic illnesses who may, from time to time, be disabled by their illnesses. The document is completely confidential and is not part of any public record. This added convenience allows for disbursement of assets to those you choose without revealing "your hand" until you die or implement the trust.

Estate Provisions. Upon death, the living trust acts the same as a will for the transfer of property held in trust. However, there is one wonderful addition: The trust nearly eliminates the need for court-related probate proceedings. The trustee continues with the management of the trust without loss, interruption, or inconvenience to loved ones and beneficiaries. There is no loss in continuity in business, property management, payment of bills, and collection of income. The living trust is a "very smooth" legal instrument. Generally speaking, trust assets are transferred to beneficiaries in much less time than it would take to settle a probate estate.

Tax Matters. When one creates a revocable living trust, the creator's tax liability generally remains unaffected. Gains from income and likewise losses are reported on the creator's state and federal income taxes. Although principal amounts and assets may be subject to estate taxes at the time of death, other estate planning techniques may counter this. The best advice is to consult a probate attorney to set up your trust. This one-time expense is well worth the cost.

A revocable living trust provides the peace of mind and protection for your hard-earned assets. Most importantly it provides a smooth transition of assets to those you love and want to reward for years of care, loyalty, and devotion.

Advance Directives. A living trust is part of the arsenal of "Advance Directives." These tools include "Power of Attorney for Health Care," "Power of Attorney for Financial Matters," and "Living Wills." These tools provide you with final say in which types of "heroic medical measures" you wish or don't wish when you are so ill or disabled you cannot make these decisions yourself. They allow you to appoint people to represent your wishes in medical decision-making when you are incapacitated. They also allow you to appoint a temporary trustee to manage your financial affairs until you recover and are able to resume these functions yourself. These tools allow you to present your case on how you wish to be treated as you approach death or are so injured or incapacitated that any quality of life, should you live, would be doubtful and in serious question.

It is important for each of us to plan ahead and make decisions in advance about not only our lives but about our deaths as well. As Elisabeth Kübler-Ross so eloquently noted: "Watching a peaceful death is like watching a falling star."

Funeral Wishes

Death puts life into perspective.

Ralph Waldo Emerson

⇒ **Overview**

An excellent method of exploring death and dying, and therefore life, is by indicating your funeral wishes. This exercise will show you the value of having your affairs in order and provide some reflection as to what your funeral wishes might be. Your will had better be able also to assist others in making such arrangements.

⇒ **Directions and Debriefing**

Complete the following sentences. You may check more than one where appropriate. You might also explain why you have chosen the responses that you have. This would be helpful to those entrusted in carrying out your wishes in the event of your death. After you have finished this exercise, date, sign, and give this information to an appropriate person who will ensure that your wishes are known and hopefully carried out. (1) In group or class, discuss your reactions, feelings, and emotions after completing this activity. (2) How might these guidelines be difficult for a person to carry out. What factors might affect whether they get done at all? (2) Has this exercise better prepared you? As a follow-up exercise, complete "Getting Your Personal Affairs in Order" on page 97.

1. Upon my death, I would like my body to be:

_____ embalmed _____ not embalmed _____ viewed at home _____ viewed at a funeral home _____ cremated _____ buried _____ entombed.

2. As for funeral clothing, I wish to be dressed in _____

_____

_____

_____

3. The mortuary, crematorium, memorial society, or other I wish to prepare my body is

_____

_____

_____

4. The type of casket or other carrier I wish to be placed in and transported in is _____

_____

_____

_____

_____

5. The price range for my funeral should be no more than _____

6. _____ I would like flowers sent. _____ I would not like flowers sent.

7. _____ In lieu of flowers, send donations to _____

_____

8. The final disposition of my body or cremains (ashes) should be as follows:_____

_____

_____

_____

9. My grave marker (tombstone) should read as follows _____

_____

_____

_____

10. I wish to

_____ have a viewing of my body in an open casket.
_____ have no viewing of my body, but casket present.
_____ have no casket present.
_____ have a wake (visitation hours).
_____ have a memorial service.

11. For my memorial service I wish the following:

_____ none
_____ religious service (type: _____)
_____ secular service
_____ music
_____ poetry
_____ speakers
_____ eulogy

12. I wish there to be _____ no obituary _____ an obituary placed in the following newspaper(s) and to read as follows: _____

_____

_____

_____

_____

13. The person(s) I wish to see to it that my funeral wishes are carried out is/are

_____

_____

_____

14. I request the following additional details be handled as follows: _____

_____

_____

_____

_____

_____

15. I prefer that all arrangements and aspects of my funeral be decided upon and carried out as follows: _____

_____

_____

_____

_____

_____

16. These are my last funeral requests. I have left this information with _____

_____

_____

_____

Name:

Signature:

Date:

*The hour which gives us life
begins to take it away.*

Lucius Seneca

⇒ **Overview:**

A living will is sometimes confused with a living trust. A living trust has to do with the disposition of a person's property while they are still alive. A living will has to do with life-sustaining medical treatment. Luis Kutner first proposed the concept in the 1930s and is credited with later coining the term "living will." A living will simply provides one with control over life-sustaining medical treatments during critical periods, such as when one is incompetent due to coma, advanced Alzheimer's, or other diseases and accidents. A living will is a legal document, executed while still competent, which describes kinds and types of medical treatment to either receive or refuse at some future date should you be unable to make decisions at the time by yourself <u>and</u> physicians believe there is little hope of improvement.

The problem with living wills is their lack of timeliness. Even the best intentions are often lost in the moment. For example, if you were in a frightful automobile accident, the last thing you, your family, your friends, or even your attorney would be considering is your living will. In most cases, everything would be done to save you. Your personal communications would tend to be lost in the "hospital-save-at-all-cost-machine mentality." Unless you wear your living will around your neck, your intentions may in fact go ignored. Your living will is a low priority on the paramedic's, nurse's, physician's or other emergency personnel's immediate list when critical decisions must be made with split-second timing. That is why it is so important to be aware of medical care options. If you want control over your life and over your death, stay informed and act accordingly. Do living wills, therefore, make sense? Are they worth the effort? For the big issues they do. If you don't want to be left in a "persistent vegetative coma," then a living will may prevent that. It is interesting to note that people are coming up with all kinds of creative ways of making their wishes immediately known: medic-alert bracelets, tattoos with DNR orders, and even posting a living will in cyberspace via the Internet.[54] If you don't want heroic effortsused to save your life after having been in a car wreck, then a living will may not be immediately helpful---other legal tools may be more useful.

Living wills are part of several legal instruments known collectively as advance directives. All states in some form or fashion--through common law, constitutions or statutes--uphold living wills and other advanced directives. Additionally, the Patient Self-Determination Act (PSDA) became law in 1991. This act encourages the use of advanced directives for patients in various medical care facilities throughout the United States. The most preferred advance directive is the Durable Power of Attorney for Health Care (DPAHC). A DPAHC provides a personal representative of your choice to make the decisions for you that you would make for yourself if you were able. A copy of a DPAHC used in California follows this exercise. You should check in the area where you live to see which documents are legal and available for such important decision-making. As the technological options for prolonging life increase, so too do the legal and moral options.

104

⇒ **Directions**

Linda Emanuel and Ezekiel Emanuel[55] (1989, 1990) developed a checklist for use with advanced directives which serves as a guide when developing a personal living will or other advanced directive. In this exercise, read and check, as you see fit, those types of life sustaining medical treatments you want or don't want should you become incapacitated due to coma, accident, or disease with little hope of improvement.

	Yes	No	Undecided	Use for a trial period. If no clear improvement, discontinue.

1. Cardiopulmonary Resuscitation
2. Mechanical Breathing
3. Artificial Nutrition and Hydration
4. Major Surgery
5. Kidney Dialysis
6. Chemotherapy
7. Minor Surgery
8. Invasive Diagnostic Tests
9. Blood or Blood Products
10. Antibiotics
11. Simple Diagnostic Tests
12. Pain Medications (even if they dull consciousness and indirectly shorten my life)

⇒ **Debriefing**

(1) Do you have any advance directives in place? (2) Do you feel they are important? Why or why not? (3) If you don't have any advance directives in place, explain some of the reasons why you do not. (4) How do you suspect you will actually die? (5) How did you feel having to consider these "life and death" options? (6) Do you want all options taken to prolong your life? Why or why not? (7) Which categories above did you have problems considering? Was it a positive or negative experience? Explain. (8) How might your wishes be affected by time and situations; for example, in accidents, while on vacation, when you are younger rather than older? What strategies might you use to assure your wishes are carried out? (9) How can you ensure your wishes regarding advance directives will be followed? (10) How did this exercise affect you?

The following is a sample of California's Declaration, or Living Will, developed by the national organization Choice in Dying.[56] It lets you state your wishes about your medical care in the event that you develop a terminal condition and are unable to make your own decisions. The living will becomes effective if your death would occur without the use of life-sustaining medical care. (One other doctor must agree with your attending physician's opinion of your medical condition.) Choice in Dying recommends that you complete both a DPAHC and Declaration (Living Will) to ensure your requests are met. You may contact this organization for the appropriate legal advance directives for your jurisdiction by writing Choice in Dying, 200 Varick Street, New York, NY 10014, or calling (212) 366-5540. The fax number is (212) 366-5337.

　　　　105

CALIFORNIA DECLARATION

If I should have an incurable and irreversible condition that has been diagnosed by two physicians and that will result in my death within a relatively short time without the administration of life-sustaining treatment or has produced an irreversible coma or persistent vegetative state, and I am no longer able to make decisions regarding my medical treatment, I direct my attending physician, pursuant to the Natural Death Act of California, to withhold or withdraw treatment, including artificially administered nutrition and hydration, that only prolongs the process of dying or the irreversible coma or persistent vegetative state and is not necessary for my comfort or to alleviate pain.

If I have been diagnosed as pregnant, and that diagnosis is known to my physician, this declaration shall have no force or effect during my pregnancy.

Other instructions:

DATE AND SIGN
THE DOCUMENT
AND PRINT
YOUR ADDRESS

NOTE: YOUR
WITNESSES
MUST SIGN ON
THE NEXT PAGE

Signed this _____ day of _____, 19____.

Signature _____

Address _____

_____

Reprinted by permission of Choice In Dying
200 Varick Street, New York, NY 10014
212/366-5540

WITNESSING PROCEDURE

WITNESSES MUST SIGN AND PRINT THEIR ADDRESSES

The declarant voluntarily signed this writing in my presence. I am not a health care provider, an employee of a health care provider, the operator of a community care facility, an employee of an operator of a community care facility, the operator of a residential care facility for the elderly, or an employee of an operator of a residential care facility for the elderly.

WITNESS #1

Witness _____

Address _____

_____

The declarant voluntarily signed this writing in my presence. I am not entitled to any portion of the estate of the declarant upon his or her death under any will or codicil thereto of the declarant now existing or by operation of law. I am not a health care provider, an employee of a health care provider, the operator of a community care facility, an employee of an operator of a community care facility, the operator of a residential care facility for the elderly, or an employee of an operator of a residential care facility for the elderly.

WITNESS #2

Witness _____

Address _____

_____

STATEMENT OF PATIENT ADVOCATE OR OMBUDSMAN

IF YOU ARE A PATIENT IN A NURSING HOME, A PATIENT ADVOCATE MUST READ AND SIGN THIS STATEMENT

I further declare under penalty of perjury under the laws of California that I am a patient advocate or ombudsman as designated by the State Department of Aging and that I am serving as a witness as required by Section 7178 of the Health and Safety Code.

Signature: _____

© 1995
CHOICE IN DYING, INC.

Courtesy of Choice In Dying
200 Varick Street, New York, NY 10014 (212) 366-5540   8/95

Death is one moment,
and life is so many of them.

Tennessee Williams

⇒ **Overview**

The Durable Power of Attorney for Health Care decisions (DPAHC)[57] is one of the more powerful advance directives used for preserving your decision-making ability regarding life-sustaining medical treatment during a time of incompetence. The DPAHC is used when, due to disease or accident, you have become incompetent to make your own decisions <u>and</u> there is little hope of improvement in your condition. A DPAHC legally permits you to appoint a personal representative of your choice to make the decisions for you that you would make for yourself if you were able to do so.

⇒ **Directions and Debriefing**

Before completing this exercise first complete the "Preparing a Living Will" exercise on page 104. You will find that exercise located elsewhere in your workbook. A copy of a DPAHC used in California follows. Read it carefully and then complete it. Prepare to discuss your reactions in group or class. If your state or jurisdiction has a DPAHC or similar instrument, secure copies of that legal document and complete it. Follow the same guidelines as stated above.

As a follow-up to this exercise, choose a personal representative; after discussions with your representative, actually complete a DPAHC. Have the document notarized or witnessed and leave an authenticated copy with your personal representative. Your witnesses should be "disinterested," that is, not in line to receive anything from your will. You may also want to have another personal representative in case your primary representative becomes disabled or is unwilling to carry out your DPAHC in time of need. Follow the DPAHC document completion requirements exactly for your state. Having completed your DPAHC, you will now be better prepared for the future. Now you know <u>you are in charge</u> in this important area of life. When finished, share your thoughts about this exercise. (1) Do you feel better having completed these legal documents? (2) If so, why? If not, why? (3) What do you think the advantage of having these documents on file would be to you and your family? to society as a whole? (4) How might such documents be abused? How might this situation be prevented?

The following is a list of commonly asked patient questions concerning a DPAHC. This pamphlet, entitled: *Your Health Care: Who Will Decide When You Can't,* was developed by the California Medical Association for residents of California and is used with their permission. You may also contact the organization Choice in Dying for their Durable Power of Attorney for Health Care (DPAHC) forms. The organization provides a full range of appropriate and legal advance directives for the jurisdiction you live in. You may contact them at: Choice In Dying, 200 Varick Street, New York, NY 10014. Telephone: (212) 366-5540 or fax: (212) 366-5337.

1. What is a Durable Power of Attorney for Health Care?

California law allows you to choose another person to make health care decisions for you if for any reason you are unable to speak for yourself. By completing a form called a "Durable Power of Attorney for Health Care" (DPAHC), you can appoint another person to be your health care "agent." This person will have legal authority to make decisions about your medical care if you are unconscious or otherwise cannot make these decisions for yourself. You can also write down your health care wishes in the DPAHC form (for example, a desire not to receive treatment that only prolongs the dying process if you are terminally ill). Your agent must follow these instructions and must honor any other wishes you have made known.

A properly completed DPAHC provides the best assurance that your wishes will be respected if you become seriously ill and cannot speak for yourself.

2. Is a DPAHC different from a "living will"?

Yes. "Living wills" typically are documents that state your desire not to receive life-sustaining treatment if you are terminally ill or permanently unconscious. The living will form specifically recognized under California law is called a Natural Death Act Declaration.

A Durable Power of Attorney for Health Care allows you to state your wishes about accepting or refusing life-sustaining treatment. Unlike a living will or Declaration, a DPAHC also can be used to state your desires about your health care in and situation in which you are unable to make your own decisions, not just when you are in a coma or terminally ill. In addition, only a DPAHC allows you to appoint someone you trust to speak for you when you are incapacitated.

You do not need a living will or Declaration if you have already stated your wishes about life-sustaining treatment in a DPAHC. The DPAHC form distributed by the California Medical Association includes an optional living will statement that you can initial if it reflects your desires.

3. Who can complete a DPAHC?

Any California resident who is at least eighteen (18) years old, of sound mind, and acting of his or her own free will can complete a valid Durable Power of Attorney for Health Care.

4. Do I need a lawyer to complete a DPAHC?

No. You do not need a lawyer for a standard printed DPAHC form (such as the form supplied by the California Medical Association) to be legally valid. The only exception is for individuals who have been involuntarily committed to a mental health facility who wish to appoint the conservator as the agent.

5. Who can I appoint as my health care agent?

You can appoint almost any adult to be your agent. You can choose a member of your family (such as your spouse or an adult child), a friend, or someone else you trust. (If you appoint your spouse and later get divorced, the DPAHC is automatically invalidated.) You can also appoint one or more "alternate agents" in case the person you select as your health care agent is unavailable or unwilling to make a decision. It is important that you talk to the people you want to appoint to make sure they understand your wishes and agree to accept this responsibility.

The law prohibits you from choosing certain people to act as your agent. you may not choose your doctor or a person who operates a community care facility (sometimes called a "board and care home") or a residential care facility for the elderly. The law also prohibits you from appointing a person who works for your doctor, for the health facility in which you are being treated, for a community care facility, or for a residential care facility for the elderly unless that person is related to you by blood, marriage, or adoption.

6. Can I appoint more than one person to share the responsibility of being my health care agent?

The California Medical Association recommends that you name only one person as your health care agent. If two or more people are given equal authority and they disagree about a health care decision, one of the important purposes of the DPAHC--to clearly identify who has authority to speak for you--will be defeated. If you are afraid of offending people close to you by choosing one over another to be your agent, ask them to decide among themselves who will be the agent and list the others as alternate agents.

7. How much authority will my health care agent have?

If you become incapacitated, your agent will have authority over any other person to speak for you in health care matters. Your agent will be able to accept or refuse medical treatment; to have access to your medical records; and to make decisions about donating your organs, authorizing an autopsy, and disposing of your remains when you die. However, if you do not want your agent to have certain of these powers or to make certain decisions, you can write a statement in the DPAHC form limiting your agent's authority. In addition, the law says that your agent may not authorize convulsive treatment, psychosurgery, sterilization, abortion, or placement in a mental health treatment facility.

It is important to remember that the person you appoint as your agent has no authority to make decisions for you until you are unable to make those decisions yourself. When you become incapacitated, your agent must make decisions that are consistent with any wishes you have written in the DPAHC form or made known in other ways, such as by telling family members, friends, or your doctor. If you have not made your wishes known, your agent must decide what is in your best interests.

8. Will my health care agent be responsible for my medical bills?

No, unless that person would otherwise be responsible for your debts. The DPAHC deals only with medical decision-making and has no effect on financial responsibility for your health care.

9. For how long is a DPAHC valid?

A DPAHC is valid for an indefinite period of time, unless you state in the form a specific date on which you want it to expire or the printed language in the form itself mentions a specific duration. Forms printed prior to January 1, 1992, generally expire at the end of seven years.

10. What if I change my mind after completing a DPAHC?

You can revoke or change a DPAHC at any time. Simply inform everyone who received a copy of the form that it is no longer valid and destroy the copies. You should complete a new form if you want to name a different person as your agent or make other changes. however, if you only need to update the address or telephone numbers of your agent or alternate agent(s), you may write in the new information, and initial and date the change. You may want to make a list of persons to whom you give a copy of the form so you will know who to contact if you revoke the DPAHC or make a new one.

11. What should I do with the DPAHC form after I fill it out?

Make sure that the form has been properly signed, dated, and either notarized or witnessed by two qualified individuals (the form includes instructions about who can and cannot be a witness). Keep the original in a safe place and give photocopies of the completed form to the persons you have appointed as your agent and alternate agents, to your doctor and health plan, and to family members or anyone else who is likely to be called if there is a medical emergency. Take a copy of the form with you if you are going to be admitted to a hospital, nursing home, or other health care facility. Photocopies of the completed form can be relied upon by your agent and doctors as though they were the original.

12. Is my DPAHC form valid in other states?

A DPAHC form that meets the requirements of California law may or may not be honored in other states. If you spend a lot of time in another state, you may want to consult a doctor, lawyer, or the medical society in that state to find out about the laws there.

13. Can anyone force me to sign a DPAHC?

No. The law specifically says that no one can require you to complete a DPAHC before admitting you to a hospital or other health care facility, and no one can deny you health insurance because you choose not to complete a form.

111

14. Can I get more information about the DPAHC?

Yes. Your doctor probably can provide you with more information. However, you should talk to a lawyer if you want legal advice.

Review the following attached Durable Power of Attorney for Health Care (DPAHC). Use the space below for notes for this exercise. <u>Warning</u>: Please keep in mind this DPAHC is only a <u>sample</u> and should not be used as it may be outdated by new legislation that may have been passed and enacted since this form was published. Accordingly, this form is only a sample and should not be used as a legal DPAHC. Contact the sources above for the most recent version for your jurisdiction.

Notes: _____

_____

_____

_____

_____

_____

_____

_____

_____

_____

_____

_____

_____

_____

_____

_____

_____

_____

_____

_____

Source: Copyright California Medical Association, 1995. Published with permission of and by arrangement with the California Medical Association. Copies of this form, as well as an accompanying brochure and wallet card, may be obtained from CMA publications at (415) 882-5175.

California Medical Association
DURABLE POWER OF ATTORNEY FOR HEALTH CARE DECISIONS
(California Probate Code Sections 4600-4753)

1. CREATION OF DURABLE POWER OF ATTORNEY FOR HEALTH CARE

By this document I intend to create a durable power of attorney by appointing the person designated below to make health care decisions for me as allowed by Sections 4600 to 4753, inclusive, of the California Probate Code. This power of attorney shall not be affected by my subsequent incapacity. I hereby revoke any prior durable power of attorney for health care. I am a California resident who is at least 18 years old, of sound mind, and acting of my own free will.

2. APPOINTMENT OF HEALTH CARE AGENT

(Fill in below the name, address and telephone number of the person you wish to make health care decisions for you if you become incapacitated. You should make sure that this person agrees to accept this responsibility. The following may __not__ serve as your agent: (1) your treating health care provider; (2) an operator of a community care facility or residential care facility for the elderly; or (3) an employee of your treating health care provider, a community care facility, or a residential care facility for the elderly, unless that employee is related to you by blood, marriage or adoption. If you are a conservatee under the Lanterman-Petris-Short Act (the law governing involuntary commitment to a mental health facility) and you wish to appoint your conservator as your agent, you must consult a lawyer, who must sign and attach a special declaration for this document to be valid.)

I, _____, hereby appoint:
(insert your name)

Name _____

Address _____

Work Telephone (_____) _____   Home Telephone (_____) _____

as my agent (attorney-in-fact) to make health care decisions for me as authorized in this document. I understand that this power of attorney will be effective for an indefinite period of time unless I revoke it or limit its duration below.

(Optional) This power of attorney shall expire on the following date: _____.

© California Medical Association 1995 (revised)

3. AUTHORITY OF AGENT

If I become incapable of giving informed consent to health care decisions, I grant my agent full power and authority to make those decisions for me, subject to any statements of desires or limitations set forth below. Unless I have limited my agent's authority in this document, that authority shall include the right to consent, refuse consent, or withdraw consent to any medical care, treatment, service, or procedure; to receive and to consent to the release of medical information; to authorize an autopsy to determine the cause of my death; to make a gift of all or part of my body; and to direct the disposition of my remains, subject to any instructions I have given in a written contract for funeral services, my will or by some other method. I understand that, by law, my agent may not consent to any of the following: commitment to a mental health treatment facility, convulsive treatment, psychosurgery, sterilization or abortion.

4. MEDICAL TREATMENT DESIRES AND LIMITATIONS (OPTIONAL)

(Your agent must make health care decisions that are consistent with your known desires. You may, but are not required to, state your desires about the kinds of medical care you do or do not want to receive, including your desires concerning life support if you are seriously ill. If you do not want your agent to have the authority to make certain decisions, you must write a statement to that effect in the space provided below; otherwise, your agent will have the broad powers to make health care decisions for you that are outlined in paragraph 3 above. In either case, it is important that you discuss your health care desires with the person you appoint as your agent and with your doctor(s).

(Following is a general statement about withholding and removal of life-sustaining treatment. If the statement accurately reflects your desires, you may initial it. If you wish to add to it or to write your own statement instead, you may do so in the space provided.)

> I do **not** want efforts made to prolong my life and I do **not** want life-sustaining treatment to be provided or continued: (1) if I am in an irreversible coma or persistent vegetative state; or (2) if I am terminally ill and the use of life-sustaining procedures would serve only to artificially delay the moment of my death; or (3) under any other circumstances where the burdens of the treatment outweigh the expected benefits. In making decisions about life-sustaining treatment under provision (3) above, I want my agent to consider the relief of suffering and the quality of my life, as well as the extent of the possible prolongation of my life.
>
> *If this statement reflects your desires, initial here:* _____

Other or additional statements of medical treatment desires and limitations: _____

_____

_____

_____

_____

(You may attach additional pages if you need more space to complete your statements. Each additional page must be dated and signed at the same time you date and sign this document.)

5. APPOINTMENT OF ALTERNATE AGENTS (OPTIONAL)

(You may appoint alternate agents to make health care decisions for you in case the person you appointed in Paragraph 2 is unable or unwilling to do so.)

If the person named as my agent in Paragraph 2 is not available or willing to make health care decisions for me as authorized in this document, I appoint the following persons to do so, listed in the order they should be asked:

First Alternate Agent: Name _____

Address _____ _____

Work Telephone (_____) _____   Home Telephone (_____) _____

Second Alternate Agent: Name _____

Address _____ _____

Work Telephone (_____) _____   Home Telephone (_____) _____

6. USE OF COPIES

I hereby authorize that photocopies of this document can be relied upon by my agent and others as though they were originals.

DATE AND SIGNATURE OF PRINCIPAL

(You must date and sign this power of attorney)

I sign my name to this Durable Power of Attorney for Health Care at _____, _____
                                                  (City)   *(State)*

on _____ . _____
         (Date)   *(Signature of Principal)*

STATEMENT OF WITNESSES

(This power of attorney will not be valid for making health care decisions unless it is either (1) signed by two qualified adult witnesses who are present when you sign or acknowledge your signature __or__ (2) acknowledged before a notary public in California. If you elect to use witnesses rather than a notary public, the law provides that none of the following may be used as witnesses: (1) the persons you have appointed as your agent and alternate agents; (2) your health care provider or an employee of your health care provider; or (3) an operator or employee of an operator of a community care facility or residential care facility for the elderly. Additionally, at least one of the witnesses cannot be related to you by blood, marriage or adoption, or be named in your will. IF YOU ARE A PATIENT IN A SKILLED NURSING FACILITY, YOU __MUST__ HAVE A PATIENT ADVOCATE OR OMBUDSMAN SIGN BOTH THE STATEMENT OF WITNESSES BELOW __AND__ THE DECLARATION ON THE FOLLOWING PAGE.)

I declare under penalty of perjury under the laws of California that the person who signed or acknowledged this document is personally known to me to be the principal, or that the identity of the principal was proved to me by convincing evidence;* that the principal signed or acknowledged this durable power of attorney in my presence, that the principal appears to be of sound mind and under no duress, fraud, or undue influence; that I am not the person appointed as attorney in fact by this document; and that I am not the principal's health care provider, an employee of the principal's health care provider, the operator of a community care facility or a residential care facility for the elderly, nor an employee of an operator of a community care facility or residential care facility for the elderly.

First Witness: Signature _____

Print name _____

Date _____

Residence Address _____

Second Witness: Signature _____

Print name _____

Date _____

Residence Address _____

(AT LEAST ONE OF THE ABOVE WITNESSES MUST ALSO SIGN THE FOLLOWING DECLARATION)

I further declare under penalty of perjury under the laws of California that I am not related to the principal by blood, marriage, or adoption, and, to the best of my knowledge I am not entitled to any part of the estate of the principal upon the death of the principal under a will now existing or by operation of law.

Signature: _____

---

*The law allows one or more of the following forms of identification as convincing evidence of identity: a California driver's license or identification card or U.S. passport that is current or has been issued within five years, or any of the following if the document is current or has been issued within five years, contains a photograph and description of the person named on it, is signed by the person, and bears a serial or other identifying number: a foreign passport that has been stamped by the U.S. Immigration and Naturalization Service; a driver's license issued by another state or by an authorized Canadian or Mexican agency; or an identification card issued by another state or by any branch of the U.S. armed forces. If the principal is a patient in a skilled nursing facility, a patient advocate or ombudsman may rely on the representations of family members or the administrator or staff of the facility as convincing evidence of identity if the patient advocate or ombudsman believes that the representations provide a reasonable basis for determining the identity of the principal.

SPECIAL REQUIREMENT: STATEMENT OF PATIENT ADVOCATE OR OMBUDSMAN

(If you are a patient in a skilled nursing facility, a patient advocate or ombudsman must sign the Statement of Witnesses above <u>and</u> must also sign the following declaration.)

I further declare under penalty of perjury under the laws of California that I am a patient advocate or ombudsman as designated by the State Department of Aging and am serving as a witness as required by subdivision (e) of Probate Code Section 4701.

Signature: _____   Address: _____

Print Name: _____   _____

Date: _____   _____

CERTIFICATE OF ACKNOWLEDGMENT OF NOTARY PUBLIC

(Acknowledgment before a notary public is <u>not</u> required if you have elected to have two qualified witnesses sign above. If you are a patient in a skilled nursing facility, you <u>must</u> have a patient advocate or ombudsman sign the Statement of Witnesses on page 3 <u>and</u> the Statement of Patient Advocate or Ombudsman above)

State of California   )

)ss.

County of _____)

On this _____ day of _____, in the year _____.

before me, _____,
                                  (here insert name and title of the officer)

personally appeared _____
                                  (here insert name of principal)

personally known to me (or proved to me on the basis of satisfactory evidence) to be the person(s) whose name(s) is/are subscribed to this instrument and acknowledged to me that he/she/they executed the same in his/her/their authorized capacity(ies), and that by his/her/their signature(s) on the instrument the person(s), or the entity upon behalf of which the person(s) acted, executed the instrument.

WITNESS my hand and official seal.

_____
(Signature of Notary Public)

NOTARY SEAL

COPIES

YOUR AGENT MAY NEED THIS DOCUMENT IMMEDIATELY IN CASE OF AN EMERGENCY. YOU SHOULD KEEP THE COMPLETED ORIGINAL AND GIVE PHOTOCOPIES OF THE COMPLETED ORIGINAL TO (1) YOUR AGENT AND ALTERNATE AGENTS, (2) YOUR PERSONAL PHYSICIAN, AND (3) MEMBERS OF YOUR FAMILY AND ANY OTHER PERSONS WHO MIGHT BE CALLED IN THE EVENT OF A MEDICAL EMERGENCY. THE LAW PERMITS THAT PHOTOCOPIES OF THE COMPLETED DOCUMENT CAN BE RELIED UPON AS THOUGH THEY WERE ORIGINALS.

Dying Person's Bill of Rights

*Every human being by virtue of being alive
is worth remembering,
and worth being cared for.*

⇒ **Overview**

One of the sad facts of dying is that often you become relegated to second-class status. The treatable patient receives vigorous treatment regimens and the dead patient is simply taken away. But the patients in between, the terminally ill patients, are sometimes simply ignored. They become a lower priority in the fast-care and carrying-out world of medicine. A recent 28-million-dollar four-year study[58] that followed more than 9,000 patients provided a searing indictment of the way Americans die in our nation's hospitals and has prompted calls for widespread changes in how doctors treat people in their final days. Highlights of the study found: (1) half of all communicative patients said they were suffering moderate to severe pain not relieved by medications, (2) nearly 40% spent at least 10 days in a coma, isolated from family in intensive care units, (3) nearly a third of the patients and their families spent all or most of their savings in a vain and unsought effort to postpone inevitable death, and (4) nearly half the patients with "do not resuscitate" orders had these orders ignored once they became unconscious, due to "woefully inadequate" communications by physicians. This is not the picture that most Americans want to face when their time comes. The irony of this situation is that the less we involve the patient, the more the patient withdraws and then medical staff provide even less care; a vicious cycle at best. From many years as a medical social worker, I would watch medical staff treat dying patients much like an oil change: a mechanical act that had to be done so they could get on with their real life, their real patients, those living patients who really wanted their medicine and treatments. The interest that terminally ill persons show towards their remaining life depends on what kind of quality care is provided, what kind of human concern and touch are shown, and what kinds of interactions occur. It is an uncomfortable fact that those who die in hospitals and other health-care institutions often end their days in emotional states of abandonment, alienation, discomfort, and anger. For these and other reasons, several different versions of Patient's Bills of Rights have emerged to provide notice to all who assist the dying that they have rights and are human beings worthy of love and quality care up to and including the moment of their death. These sad realities have contributed greatly to the emergence of the hospice movement in America. You will examine the hospice movement in your course and also find a hospice-related exercise later in the workbook.

⇒ **Directions and Debriefing**

Review "A Patient's Bill of Rights"[59] and "A Dying Person's Bill of Rights"[60] individually, in group, or in class. (1) Discuss your thoughts, feelings, fears, and emotions regarding their usefulness. (2) Would you add anything to these bills of rights? (3) Would you take anything out of these bills? (4) How might you, as an advocate, share and explain these bills with a patient and dying patient? (5) What do you think of the philosophy presented in both? (6) Which aspects of the bills are most important to you?

117

A Patient's Bill of Rights*1

Introduction

Effective health care requires collaboration between patients and physicians and other health care professionals. Open and honest communication, respect for personal and professional values, and sensitivity to differences are integral to optimal patient care. As the setting for the provision of health services, hospitals must provide a foundation for understanding and respecting the rights and responsibilities of patients, their families, physicians, and other caregivers. Hospitals must ensure a health care ethic that respects the role of patients in decision-making about treatment choices and other aspects of their care. Hospitals must be sensitive to cultural, racial, linguistic, religious, age, gender, and other differences as well as the needs of persons with disabilities.

The American Hospital Association presents *A Patient's Bill of Rights* with the expectation that it will contribute to more effective patient care and be supported by the hospital on behalf of the institution, its medical staff, employees, and patients. The American Hospital Association encourages health care institutions to tailor this bill of rights to their patient community by translating and/or simplifying the language of this bill of rights as may be necessary to ensure that patients and their families understand their rights and responsibilities.

Bill of Rights

1. The patient has the right to considerate and respectful care.

2. The patient has the right to and is encouraged to obtain from physicians and other direct caregivers relevant, current, and understandable information concerning diagnosis, treatment, and prognosis.

Except in emergencies when the patient lacks decision-making capacity and the need for treatment is urgent, the patient is entitled to the opportunity to discuss and request information related to the specific procedures and/or treatments, the risks involved, the possible length of recuperation, and medically reasonable alterna-

tives and accompanying risks and benefits.

Patients have the right to know the identity of physicians, nurses, and others involved in their care, and well as when those involved are students, residents, or other trainees. The patient also has the right to know the immediate and long-term financial implications of treatment choices, insofar as they are known.

3. The patient has the right to make decisions about the plan of care prior to and during the course of treatment and to refuse a recommended treatment or plan of care to the extent permitted by law and hospital policy and to be informed of the medical consequences of this action. In case of such refusal, the patient is entitled to other appropriate care and services that the hospital provides or transfer to another hospital. The hospital should notify patients of any policy that might affect patient choice with the institution.

4. The patient has the right to have an advance directive (such as a living will, health care proxy, or durable power of attorney for health care) concerning treatment or designating a surrogate decision-maker with the expectation that the hospital will honor the intent of that directive to the extent permitted by law and hospital policy.

Health care institutions must advise patients of their rights under state law and hospital policy to make informed medical choices, ask if the patient has an advance directive, and include that information in patient records. The patient has the right to timely information about hospital policy that may limit its ability to implement fully a legally valid advance directive.

5. The patient has the right to every consideration of privacy. Case discussion, consultation, examination, and treatment should be conducted so as to protect each patient's privacy.

6. The patient has the right to expect that all communications and records pertaining to his/her care will be treated as confidential by the hospital, except in cases such as suspected abuse and public health hazards when reporting is permitted or required by law. The patient has the right to expect that the hospital will emphasize the confidentiality of this information when it releases it to any other parties entitled to review information in these records.

7. The patient has the right to review the records pertaining to his/her medical care and to have the information explained or interpreted as necessary, except when restricted by law.

8. The patient has the right to expect that, within its capacity and policies, a hospital will make reasonable response to the request of a patient for appropriate and medically indicated care and services. The hospital must provide evaluation, service, and/or referral as indicated by the urgency of the case. When medically appropriate and legally permissible, or when a patient has so requested, a patient may be transferred to another facility. The institution to which the patient is to be transferred must first have accepted the patient for transfer. The patient must also have the benefit of complete information and explanation concerning the need for, risks, benefits, and alternatives to such a transfer.

9. The patient has the right to ask about and be informed of the existence of business relationships among the hospital, educational institutions, other health care providers, or payers that may influence the patient's treatment and care.

10. The patient has the right to consent to or decline to participate in proposed research studies or human experimentation affecting care and treatment or requiring direct patient involvement, and to have those studies fully explained prior to consent. A patient who declines to participate in research or experimentation is entitled to the most effective care that the hospital can otherwise provide.

11. The patient has the right to expect reasonable continuity of care when appropriate and to be informed by physicians and other caregivers of available and realistic patient care options when hospital care is no longer appropriate.

12. The patient has the right to be informed of hospital policies and practices that relate to patient care, treatment, and responsibilities. The patient has the right to be informed of available resources for resolving disputes, grievances, and conflicts, such as ethics committees, patient representatives, or other mechanisms available in the institution. The patient has the right to be informed of the hospital's charges for services and available payment methods.

The collaborative nature of health care requires that patients, or their families/surrogates, participate in their care. The effectiveness of care and patient satisfaction with the course of treatment depend, in part, on the patient fulfilling certain responsibilities. Patients are responsible for providing information about past illnesses, hospitalizations, medications, and other matters related to health status. To participate effectively in decision-making, patients must be encouraged to take responsibility for requesting additional information or clarification about their health status or treatment when they do not fully understand information and instructions. Patients are also responsible for ensuring that the health care institution has a copy of their written advance directive if they have one. Patients are responsible for informing their physicians and other caregivers if they anticipate problems in following prescribed treatment.

Patients should also be aware of the hospital's obligation to be reasonably efficient and equitable in providing care to other patients and the community. The hospital's rules and regulations are designed to help the hospital meet this obligation. Patients and their families are responsible for making reasonable accommodations to the needs of the hospital, other patients, medical staff, and hospital employees. Patients are responsible for providing necessary information for insurance claims and for working with the hospital to make payment arrangements when necessary.

A person's health depends on much more than health care services. Patients are responsible for recognizing the impact of their lifestyle on their personal health.

Conclusion

Hospitals have many functions to perform, including the enhancement of health status, health promotion, and the prevention and treatment of injury and disease; the immediate and ongoing care and rehabilitation of patients; the education of health professionals, patients, and the community; and research. All these activities must be conducted with an overriding concern for the values and dignity of patients.

* These rights can be exercised on the patient's behalf by a designated surrogate or proxy decision-maker if the patient lacks decision-making capacity, is legally incompetent, or is a minor.

A Dying Person's Bill of Rights

1. Right: To be treated as a living human being until death

2. Right: To maintain hopefulness, however changing its perspective

3. Right: To be cared for by those with a sense of hopefulness, however changing its perspective

4. Right: To express feelings and emotions about approaching death in an individualistic   way

5. Right: To participate in all decisions regarding my care

6. Right: To expect continuing medical and personal care even though cure goals may change to comfort goals

7. Right: To not die alone

8. Right: To be free of pain

9. Right: To have questions answered openly and truthfully

10. Right: To not be deceived

11. Right: To have assistance from and for family members in accepting death

12. Right: To die in peace and dignity

13. Right: To be an individual and not judged by others and their beliefs

14. Right: To explore religious and spiritual experiences regardless of their meaning to others

15. Right: To expect the sanctity of the human body to be respected after death

16. Right: To be cared for by genuine, sensitive, and knowledgeable people who try to understand needs and gain satisfaction in assisting one to face death

Notes: _____

_____

_____

_____

_____

_____

_____

_____

_____

_____

_____

Poetic Will

I leave.
You stay.
Two Autumns.

Buson

⇒ **Overview**

Poems as they pertain to death are everywhere! You see them in written wills, as epitaphs on tombstones, and in the poetic musings of the mind. Whether in free verse or poetic rhyme people have pondered death since the ages first began. Many a suicide note has been a poem, as have the poems written by great soldiers before great battles. Poems have a way of capturing the universal human predicament, that last important moment, and for grasping the essence of one's life just prior to death. As pertains to death such poems can be one's last emotional signature.

To my wife I leave a knife
so she may peel away
some other poor slob's helpless life.
And to her mother
I leave my blubber.

⇒ **Directions and Debriefing**

So began the opening paragraph of one deceased and rather frustrated husband's last will. For this exercise try writing your own "Last Will and Testament" in poetic format. Use either rhyme or free verse. Be lyrical or whimsical. Present a lecture or simply bow out gracefully. Before you begin make a list of what you want to leave and to whom you wish to leave your "material world," try your hand at some prose. Who knows, maybe it will end up as a "rap song." (1) What were some of your thoughts as you wrote your poetic will? (2) Use the space below for part of your poetic will. Treat the exercise like theater, and go gently into that "last curtain call." (3) What other types of writing might be helpful in managing loss?

_____

_____

_____

_____

_____

_____

_____

_____

_____

_____

_____

_____

_____

121

Using NOLO Press's WillMaker

It's as though to write a will
is to have death take note of you.
Thus most Americans choose not to write one.

⇒ **Overview**

Nearly two-thirds of American adults do not have a legal will. There is this ill-founded fear that to write a will is to rattle the cage of The Reaper, thus directing his attention our way. Granted, preparing for death is not a high priority for most of us, but it is nonetheless crucial. If you don't make decisions about property, health care, and your final arrangements, then the state, the doctors and your family will have to make them for you. This could be disastrous. More importantly, is this what you want?

WillMaker is a computer software package developed by NOLO Press (950 Parker Street, Berkeley, CA 94710, telephone: 510-549-1976). There are Macintosh and PC versions. NOLO Press is a leader in self-help law. With over 20 years experience and a team of in-house lawyers, I feel confident you will find WillMaker valuable, and from a consumer point of view, most sensible. According to NOLO Press, WillMaker has easily made more wills than any lawyer or law firm in history. The beauty of WillMaker is that it is simple, easy and flexible! WillMaker provides you with the tools to create three vital documents: a legal will, advanced directives for health care, and final arrangements.

With WillMaker you can create a legal will which provides for family, domestic partners, friends, and charities. It allows you to name a guardian for minor children, create a trust for property, name an executor and fulfill other components of a legal will. The ability to update the will is easy. The will when legally witnessed and signed is legally almost airtight. With WillMaker you can create a living will or other advanced directive for health care. Such a document allows you to specify which kinds of medical care you want provided or withheld in the event of terminal illness or permanent coma. With WillMaker you can (1) specify that you do not want your life prolonged artificially, (2) specify life-prolonging medical procedures you do want or do not want if you become unable to communicate your wishes, and (3) determine who to appoint to be sure your wishes are carried out. With WillMaker you can make final arrangements through creation of a document which explains to those you love your preferences surrounding death. You can plan body-organ donation, type of body disposition, ceremonies, and other funeral arrangements. You can arrange details for disposition of your remains and provide guidance for epitaphs, obituaries, and memorials.

⇒ **Directions and Debriefing**

This is a very popular software item. See if you can find a copy to use. NOLO Press also provides demo copies for educational and promotional use where the print capacity has been disabled. Using WillMaker, create your last will, advance directives, and final arrange-ment documents. If for yourself, place these documents with responsible people you trust. (1) How did it feel to take charge of your future and destiny? (2) Upon completion of this assignment, offer up your comments and feelings in class or group. (3) How difficult was it for you to deal with writing a will and deciding upon your advance directives? (4) Do you feel more in control having completed these important documents?

Final Letter

Men do not care how nobly they live,
but only how long, although
it is within the reach of every man to live nobly,
but within no man's power to live long.

Lucius Seneca

⇒ **Overview**

Nothing brings out such "sweet sorrow" as having to say a final "goodbye." Whether it be a child going off to college or a spouse leaving for war, nothing touches one's essence more than losing someone you love. Loss comes in degrees. The death of a spouse is certainly a more harsh loss than a son or daughter moving out or going off to college. To help facilitate a better understanding of loss and those important in your life, compose and write a final goodbye. Use the opportunity to show your strengths, weaknesses, victories, and sorrows to date.

⇒ **Directions and Debriefing**

Write a brief and open letter to all those important people--and yes, animals too--in your life. Address each of your loved ones by name. Limit yourself to three written pages.

Consider the following questions. (1) What were your feelings? (2) Were you surprised by those you included or excluded? (3) How do you suspect those who read your letter, if it had been real, might have reacted? (4) Did you reveal anything unique about yourself? (5) Did you use any humor? (6) Were you able to choose your words carefully enough so as to stay within the three-page limit? (7) What other techniques might you use to manage your grief when you find yourself experiencing loss? (8) Did you note other observations in doing this exercise? Use the following space for outlining your letter and for determining whom to include in your "final letter." Remember, use only three pages.

⇒ **Notes:** _____

_____

_____

_____

_____

_____

_____

_____

_____

_____

_____

_____

_____

_____

The Good Death for You

Death tugs at my ears and says: Live, for I am coming.

Oliver Wendell Holmes

⇒ **Overview**

"She dropped dead dancing. She never knew what hit her! Good for her." That's what they said of my grandmother when she died at age 96. She was literally dancing to band conductor Lawrence Welk on television. (The Welk show was popular on TV in the 70s, especially among older viewers.) None of us really knew what grandma really thought was an "appropriate death" for her. She never told anyone in her family, other than she was old and ready to go, as I recollect she said at one time or another to me. How would you want to die? We all have to. Do you want to go quickly, like when you're playing golf on a warm sunny summer day? Do you want to die in a hospital, in a hospice, or at home? We spend an awful lot of time talking about the "good life," but not much about the "good death." The process of a healthy death shouldn't be that much different from the process of a healthy life. The key is figuring out what is appropriate for you. That factor varies among individuals, and is influenced by many social and cultural factors.

⇒ **Directions and Debriefing**

In group discuss what factors help to determine what a good or appropriate death is. What do you believe would be a good or appropriate death for yourself? Prepare to come back together as a class and discuss the variety of "dying factors and states" that were discussed. Complete the following individually, in group, or in class. Use the space below to sketch in some of your thoughtful highlights.

The good death or appropriate death for me is: _____

_____

_____

_____

_____

_____

_____

_____

_____

_____

_____

_____

_____

_____

Moment of Death or Thereabouts

There is something beyond the grave,
death does not end all, and the pale ghost escapes
from the vanquished pyre.

Sextus Propertius

⇒ **Overview**

The purpose of this exercise[61] is to help you understand and reinforce learning about the connection between a belief and the purpose it serves. People possess beliefs about death that have meaning and are useful to them. In other words, they have beliefs which serve a purpose in understanding life and death.

⇒ **Directions and Debriefing**

On the next page answer the two questions. When you have finished this exercise, exchange your response papers. With your fellow classmate's exercise in hand, imagine that you have had a dramatic change of mind or spiritual conversion and that the new exercise response you now hold in hand represents <u>your new belief</u>. Consider these questions as you complete this exercise. (1) Consider how this new belief functions to serve you and the greater society. (2) What purpose do ritual, beliefs, and attitudes serve for each of us? For society? (3) What are some of your beliefs, values, and thoughts on afterlife? (4) Are you spiritual? philosophical? Explain. (5) Do you believe in reincarnation? (6) Do you believe we each have lessons to learn on earth? (7) Do you believe that life has a purpose for each of us? (8) What are your thoughts about this exercise?

Use the space on this page as "rough draft" space to formulate your thoughts. Place your final thoughts on the following page.

Side One: What do you believe happens at or shortly after the moment of death?

_____

_____

_____

_____

_____

Side Two: How does that belief serve your understanding of life and death?

_____

_____

_____

_____

125

⇒ **Question One**

What do you believe happens at or shortly after the moment of death?

_____

_____

_____

_____

_____

_____

_____

_____

_____

_____

_____

⇒ **Question Two**

How does that belief serve your understanding of life and death?

_____

_____

_____

_____

_____

_____

_____

_____

_____

_____

_____

_____

5

Particular Deaths and Particular Approaches

So live, that when thy summons comes to join
The innumerable caravan, which moves
To that mysterious realm, where each shall take
His chamber in the silent halls of death,
Thou go not, like the quarry-slave at night,
Scourged to his dungeon, but, sustained and soothed
By an unfaltering trust, approach thy grave,
Like one who wraps the drapery of his couch
About him, and lies down to pleasant dreams.

William Cullen Bryant
Thanatopsis

Chapter 5

Particular Deaths and Particular Approaches

There is an old Sufi tale about a loyal servant shopping in the marketplace for his master. While in the crowded bazaar, he happens upon the face of Death. Stunned by such misfortune, he runs home to his master's house. The shocked and shaken servant quickly explains his plight to his kind master. "Oh master, oh master, while in the marketplace I came upon the face of Death. Please, oh please, master, if I have been good and loyal, lend me your fastest horse so I might flee many miles from here to the city of Baghdad," said the servant on his knees, crying and begging. Out of kindness and fairness the master agreed. The servant thanked his master greatly and fled straightaway to the great city of Baghdad. That very afternoon, while finishing the shopping left undone by his servant, the master too falls upon the face of Death. Though somewhat shaken, the master does not flee but rather walks up to Death and speaks. "Why is it, Death, you came here today and gave my loyal servant such a look?" says this braver-than-most man. Death pauses a moment and with a haunting look smiles. "It is because I was so surprised to see your servant here, in this marketplace, in this city, on this day," says Death. "Why is that, Death?" asks the master. "Because," says Death with an eerie puzzled look, "I have an appointment with him tonight in Baghdad."

And so it is--Fate! It was just this poor servant's fate to flee not from Death but in fact into the waiting arms of Death. It is a classic Islamic tale. Life is in the hands of Allah. Nothing to do but accept our fate. Nothing more, nothing less. What are your beliefs about fate?

Chapter 4, "Particular Deaths and Particular Approaches," is about fate and chance, accident and happenstance, and there but for good fortune, perhaps, goes any of us. In this chapter you will find exercises and activities which examine euthanasia, AIDS, suicide, violence, capital punishment, and disenfranchised loss and grief. What makes these particular encounters with death significant is our response to them as human beings. Generally speaking, death is an uncomfortable picture for most of us to view. It's even worse when we're either in the picture or somehow involved with the picture. That is why it is so important to understand, develop, and utilize particular approaches which make the task of dealing with these "particular deaths" a somewhat more manageable task. After all, waiting until you are in pain to figure out how to address your pain is not the best approach for managing pain and suffering. Accordingly, you will find exercises--approaches, if you will--for the dying trajectory, euthanasia, biomedical ethics, Glaser and Strauss's four awareness contexts, and hospice programs. You will have an opportunity to examine Kübler-Ross's theory and your own dying. I've even thrown in "time-machine" travel for good measure.

I believe you will leave this chapter with a better "repertoire of skills" for understanding and managing the world of death and dying and those tragic deaths associated with AIDS, violence, accidents, suicide, capital punishment, and dementia. We may not, as some philosophers suggest, be able in fact to flee from our predetermined fate. But we can develop effective understandings, strategies, and approaches so we don't flee into the arms of Death, before our time, in some distant city like Baghdad. A richer life awaits you in this chapter.

Dying Trajectory

Sustained and soothed
By an unfaltering trust, approach thy grave,
like one who wraps the drapery of his couch
About him, and lies down to pleasant dreams

William Cullen Bryant, "Thanatopsis"

⇒ **Overview**

My father, in fine Italian fashion, once said that when it was his time to go he hoped he might go quickly and have a good stiff drink prior. Well, he didn't. A four-pack-a-day cigarette habit granted him no such wish. Instead, he had a rough year of dying of throat cancer. How quick we go from health to death is called the "dying trajectory."[62] Many factors affect this "living-dying" state. Among them are age, lifestyle, treatment, disease, and psychological factors. Grim as it may seem, the dying trajectory has important implications for those who must make plans and make sense out of the hand that has been dealt a loved one who has a life-threatening or terminal condition. Kübler-Ross[63] said: "When you are dying, if you're fortunate enough to have some prior warning, you get your final chance to grow, to become more fully human." Thus one can see some positive aspects of understanding the dying trajectory. Glaser and Strauss[64] describe three types of dying trajectories. (1) The *lingering trajectory* is where a life fades slowly and gradually. Focus is on care and comfort. (2) The *expected quick trajectory* has four aspects. They include a "pointed trajectory," where death occurs from a risky medical procedure; a "danger-period trajectory," where a person is in a critical period such as after emergency surgery; a "crisis trajectory," where a person has a condition which could change at any moment; and the "will probably-die" trajectory, where doctors feel nothing more can be done for the patient. (3) The third trajectory is the *unexpected quick trajectory*. It has two aspects. First is the patient who dies "suddenly and unexpectedly" and second is emergency-room death occurring during rescue operations.

⇒ **Directions and Debriefing**

See if you can match up the following patient situations[65] (see endnote 65 in the back of the workbook for answers) with the living-dying trajectories discussed above and in class and in your textbook. (1) Prepare to discuss what advantages and disadvantages there might be to having an understanding of dying trajectories for families, professionals, and other caregivers. (2) For those of you who have had losses, what trajectories did they follow? (3) How might you use the trajectory for those who might be determining or planning when they die (i. e., suicide)? (4) What might your own dying trajectory be? (4) Discuss your thoughts and comments about this exercise.

1. Patient hospitalized with liver cancer. There is nothing more that can be done.
2. Patient is in surgery for a heart-lung operation.
3. Patient in critical condition with post-operation infection.
4. Patient in recovery room after major heart surgery due to heart attack.
5. Patient in coma due to severe brain trauma as a result of automobile accident.
6. Patient dies suddenly in recovery room after surgery due to stroke.
7. Patient dies on operating table after being brought in with gun wound to head.

129

*Remember, friends, as you pass by
as you are now, so once was I.
As I am now, so you must be.
Prepare yourself to follow me.*

Headstone
Ashby, Massachusetts

⇒ **Overview**

Last I heard there were about six billion people living on planet Earth. About 100 million die every year. That's about 275,000 deaths a day. Will you be one of them? The day is still young! And tomorrow another 275,000 will meet their fate. In many ways, how we meet and accept our own death reflects how we get to live our lives.

The topic of death and dying is slowly coming out of the closet. One of the great pioneers of bringing an understanding of death and dying into the public consciousness and awareness is Dr. Elizabeth Kübler-Ross. According to Dr. Kübler-Ross, the news of one's terminal condition or dying sets into play a wide display of coping and defense mechanisms. The particular defense barrier thrown up identifies where the person is in the process of coming to terms with their own death.

According to Kübler-Ross, the dying go through five stages. Though more recent research shows that not all dying persons go through these stages in any set fashion or, in some cases, through them at all, these stages still have great relevancy. Understanding these stages has great value in understanding the process of death and dying. As outlined by Kübler-Ross, the stages of dying are (1) denial and isolation, (2) anger, (3) bargaining, (4) depression, and (5) acceptance. In the first stage the person believes a grave error has been made. This disbelief often turns to denial. Acceptance is often nowhere to be seen. The second stage is noted by anger and irritability. There is often a lashing out at others; a displacement of responsibility for one's plight onto others. The third stage is a time of striking up a bargain. It is a time of "I'll change," "I'll be good," "I'll go to church," "I'll give up smoking," or "I'll follow alternative medicine and diet paths." It is a time of hope and deal-making. The fourth stage is often most painful; it is filled with the knowledge and despair that, in many cases, all is lost, all is hopeless. The dying begin to see signs of the end in their health and in their "flesh and bones." The perception of one's impotence leads to varying degrees of depression. In the last stage comes acceptance; not a happy acceptance, but a quiet expectation of the inevitable. The person seems void of feelings and emotions and shows a sad mechanical resignation.

⇒ **Directions**

This exercise will allow you the opportunity to role-play and experience some of the emotions found in these stages and to observe how the stages progress over time as noted by Dr. Kübler-Ross's research. As with all such death and dying exercises, you may choose not to participate if you feel uncomfortable by this exercise. You will be assigned a number by counting off from 1 to whatever your total class size is. Your instructor or facilitator will have already chosen a number at random, written it down on a piece of paper, and secured it away in a safe place until needed later. <u>The setting and scenario are simply this</u>: Someone must die! At end of class today, the number will be revealed and that person will die. No more. No less! In small group process some of your thoughts about this monumental event from the following questions, statements, and directions.

1. What if it is your time to die? What if your number is called at the end of class?

2. What will your thoughts be if it is the person sitting across from you in your group whose number is called?

3. If you could be certain that it was your number that would be called, how might you utilize what little time you have left?

4. How much time is left on the classroom clock? How much time have you wasted already?

5. What are some of your thoughts about being in a class where one student is going to die? We do die, don't we? We all will die, won't we?

6. List some of your thoughts, feelings, and observations about your possibly being dead at class's end.

7. How do you feel about never knowing when you are going to die?

8. How does one find purpose and meaning in life knowing death may occur at any moment in our lives?

9. Why is it we go about our lives pretending we will not die?

10. When you have had enough time to process the aforementioned questions, your instructor will take your comments and relate them to Kübler-Ross and her death and dying stage theory. It will be most interesting to see which of your comments fits into the various stages. In addition to debriefing this exercise with your instructor or facilitator, you may also wish to make some journal entries in the back of this book.

11. Finally, announce whose number has been chosen to die. How does the person chosen to die feel? How does the rest of the class not chosen to die feel?

⇒ **Debriefing**

(1) What were your thoughts about this exercise? (2) Did you have fears and anxiety? (3) How might such an exercise teach us all the need to value today and live fully each day? (4) It is said people die in death as they lived in life. What do you think of that statement? (5) How do you think your stages of dying, as suggested by Kübler-Ross, might flow? (6) Discuss this topic in a short essay. (7) Demonstrate your understanding of stage theory. Many researchers feel Kübler-Ross's stage theory is not valid. What do you think? What are the pros and cons of stage theory?

_____

_____

_____

_____

_____

_____

AIDS: How Much Do You Know?

Why should I talk to you?
I've just been talking to your boss.

Wilson Mizner
On his deathbed to a priest

⇒ **Overview**

How much do you know about HIV and AIDS? The World Health Organization (WHO), part of the United Nations, reported on December 16, 1995, that 18.5 million people worldwide had been infected with the HIV virus. Of the 6 million people thought to have developed full-blown AIDS since the epidemic began in the late 1970s, 4.5 million have since died of AIDS-related complications worldwide. The infection rate is about 6,000 per day with over 1.5 million HIV victims being children.[66] Over 223,000 deaths have occurred in the United States. In 1992 alone, 33,566 deaths were reported due to HIV infection, a 13.6% increase over the previous year. In 1992, the most recent year for such data, HIV was the eighth leading cause of death among all people in the United States. AIDS is the number one cause of death among males ages 25-44.[67] Looking into the future, the worldwide HIV-related infection rate is predicted to spread to over 22 million people by early 1997. What are you doing to stay aware and protect yourself?

The virus that causes AIDS is called the human immunodeficiency virus or HIV. It is notorious for its ability to take over cells and command them at will, often leaving little trace of itself. For this reason HIV has been very difficult to detect and treat, let alone cure. The virus in its unique fashion disrupts and disables the immune system. That is why the cause of death is generally not the HIV virus but the opportunistic diseases which invade as a result of a depressed immune system. These AIDS-related deaths are a result of multiple illnesses and diseases that an otherwise strong normal immune system would not be infected by. Are there AIDS prevention programs in your community?

There are four basic routes of transmission. The first is *sexual transmission* and can occur in both heterosexual and homosexual sexual activity. What is important to remember is that the HIV virus is most readily transmitted through the exchange of bodily fluids that results in absorption into the bloodstream. Second is *infected needles.* This route provides entry into the bloodstream quickly. Drug addicts are a major source of HIV because they exchange needles and reuse them among themselves. Third is *blood transfusions.* Research has shown that the first known HIV infection in the blood supply began occurring in the late 1970s. Because the HIV virus may lay dormant for months if not years, many healthy-feeling but infected carriers continued to donate blood to the national blood supply. (Careful screenings, testing, and national standards now prevent this.) Many drug addicts, for example, sold blood to secure money for their habits. As a result of this HIV contamination, the national blood supply became infected and suspect. This placed at great risk and harm those needing blood at hospitals during surgeries and those whose use of blood is needed often, such as hemophiliacs. The fourth transmission is at birth, or *perinatal.* This occurs when a pregnant mother is positive for HIV and passes this infection onto her newborn. The good news is this form of transmission seems to occur in less than half of all such cases.

There are many more myths about AIDS than facts. There are even more unanswered questions. For those not HIV-infected it is often but for the purest of good fortune they have been spared. Still others have had the wisdom to take precautions and protect themselves from this tragic disease. For those infected it is a measure of a society's greatness to provide whatever it takes to fight this disease and to help meaningfully those infected and in need. The following exercises will heighten your awareness and test your knowledge about some basic AIDS facts.

Part I: Fact and Fiction About AIDS

⇒ **Directions**

For the following statements circle one of the following three choices: True (T), False (F), or Uncertain (U). When you are through, break into small groups and discuss your responses. Prepare to return to the full class discussion with your instructor to go over correct information.

You will find a brief discussion of the correct answers for all three of the following exercises in endnote 68 in the back of the workbook.[68]

1. T   F   U   AIDS is generally found among the poor, drug users, and homosexuals.

2. T   F   U   AIDS is spread through rats and insects like mosquitoes.

3. T   F   U   Everyone should be tested for the HIV virus at least once.

4. T   F   U   Heterosexuals should not worry about becoming infected with the HIV virus.

5. T   F   U   If you suspect you have been exposed to the HIV virus, you should be tested.

6. T   F   U   Men should be more concerned than women about acquiring AIDS .

7. T   F   U   Sharing drug needles is one of the more high-risk methods of becoming HIV-infected.

8. T   F   U   There is a high risk of HIV infection from being around or near someone with AIDS.

9. T   F   U   Those people who are caregivers to persons with AIDS are at a very high risk of acquiring the HIV virus.

10. T   F   U   Toilet seats and bathrooms are major carriers of the HIV virus.

11. T   F   U   Use of condoms is a foolproof method of preventing HIV infection.

12. T   F   U   Women using birth control pills cannot become infected with the HIV virus.

13. T   F   U   You can acquire the HIV virus from casual contact with someone who has the virus.

14. T   F   U   You can become HIV-positive from receiving blood or donating blood.

15. T F U You can become infected with the HIV virus by using the same glass or utensil that a person with AIDS uses.

16. T F U You can become infected with the HIV virus through hugging and kissing someone who is infected with the HIV virus or who has full-blown AIDS.

17. T F U You can tell by looking at a person if they have AIDS.

18. T F U AIDS is an urban big-city disease.

19. T F U AIDS is generally a fatal disease with no cure in sight.

Part II: Defining AIDS

⇒ **Directions**

Provide a definition of AIDS by matching the correct term with the correct definition by placing the letter from the right column next to the correct term in the left column.

		Term	Definition
1.	_____	Acquired	a. defense system of the body
2.	_____	Immune	b. a cluster of disease signs and symptoms
3.	_____	Deficiency	c. something not born with
4.	_____	Syndrome	d. lacking; functioning poorly
			e. HIV

Part III: Major Routes of HIV Transmission

⇒ **Directions**

Complete the following short-answer exercise by filling in the correct words in the blanks in the following discussion on modes of HIV transmission.

There are four major Human Immunodeficiency Virus (HIV) routes of transmission. The first route is at (1) _____. This transmission occurs when an HIV-positive pregnant woman delivers a baby. Though not always, the virus is oftentimes passed onto the newborn. The second transmission route is through (2) _____ sex. One method of protection during sexual intercourse, though not foolproof, is to use a condom. The third route of HIV transmission is through the (3) _____ of dirty or used needles. Intravenous (IV) drug users are at high risk of contracting the HIV virus. Some of the highest rates of HIV are found among IV drug users. The fourth route of transmission is through (4) _____ transfusions. Many blood donors, prior to HIV testing in 1985, were positive for the HIV virus but did not know it. As a result the national blood supply became contaminated. Those who received contaminated blood transfusions became HIV-positive for the virus. Today the nation's blood supply is subject to substantial quality assurance and testing, and HIV contamination is now considered minimal.

⇒ **Debriefing**

Consider and discuss the following questions which address the previous material on HIV and AIDS.

1. Were you able to define AIDS? Did you know the four major routes of transmission? Write about them again below to reinforce these concepts in your mind.

_____

_____

2. Were you knowledgeable about AIDS? Did you develop a heightened awareness about this disease?

_____

_____

3. Were you surprised by any information? If so, what? Did you have any misinformation? Discuss how misinformation is spread.

_____

_____

4. What myths do people have about AIDS that you have heard about or are aware of?

_____

_____

5. What are some of your fears about AIDS?

_____

_____

6. Do you know anyone with AIDS? Have you provided caregiving to anyone with AIDS? Explain.

_____

_____

7. Were there aspects in this exercise requiring more reflection than other parts?

_____

_____

8. Do you feel you need more information about AIDS? If so, in what areas? Discuss this

135

with your instructor or contact an agency which works with the AIDS epidemic in your community.

_____

_____

9. What are your thoughts and feelings about this exercise on AIDS?

_____

_____

_____

10.   As additional follow-up activities consider the following:

a.   Write a "reaction paper" to this exercise.

b.   Review the related exercise entitled: "NAMES Project AIDS Memorial Quilt," on pages 207-209.

Notes: _____

_____

_____

_____

_____

_____

_____

_____

_____

_____

_____

_____

_____

_____

_____

_____

_____

All in the Family

Golden lads and girls all must,
As   chimney-sweepers,
come to dust.

Shakespeare

⇒ **Overview**

I remember, a long time ago when I was a young therapist, working with a man in a counseling context. He was dying of cancer. It was as terminal a case as I had ever seen. He had no idea he was dying. No one told him. Not even I breached the issue. Yet everyone from family to staff kept urging this young man to eat, that if he did so, he would be out of the hospital in no time at all. One morning during a hospital visit, while feeding my client some jello at his urging, he died. It seemed so wrong to have led him on that way. The last forty years has seen great change in the willingness of doctors to "be up front" and inform their patients if they are dying.[69] In 1960 nearly 90% of physicians surveyed were inclined to not tell their patients they were dying. But by 1980 well over 90% of physicians were inclined to inform their patients of their terminal condition--a complete turnaround.[70]   Regardless of how candid medical professionals, caregivers, and family members are, their interactions fall into four categories of "awareness and interaction contexts" described in a classic study by Glaser and Strauss.[71] These four awareness contexts are (1) closed awareness, (2) suspicion awareness, (3) mutual pretense, and (4) open awareness. Closed awareness context is when caregivers and staff know of the patient's impending death, but the patient does not. All such talk of death is avoided. Suspicion context is where patients suspect they are dying but the truth is withheld. Mutual pretense context is when both the patient and caregiving staff know of the terminal condition but choose to mutually pretend otherwise. Open awareness context is when both staff and patient know of the terminal condition and openly acknowledge this prognosis. This preferred last context allows for more openness and mutual support.

⇒ **Directions and Debriefing**

In small group have members role-play a family situation where different family members and professional staff interact with the dying, utilizing these four interaction contexts. Select a dying 40-year-old-son with AIDS, a rigid mother, an emotional father, a confused younger brother, a strong-willed nurse, and a young female physician. The setting is a hospital room where the time of year is Christmas. The topic is about the dying son coming home for a short visit for Christmas. With each assigned role depict an interaction using one of these modes. (1) Be prepared to present before the class. (2) What might be some of the considerations in being candid and open? How should such matters be discussed inside and outside the family? (3) What are your feelings about honesty and truth in such situations? What are some of the implications for making a terminal illness public? (4) How might "unfinished business" be helped or hindered by these modes of interactions? (5) Are there differences for adults and children? Is denial good or harmful? (6) How might these modes affect stress? (6) What other factors might need to be considered? (7) What would you want from staff and caregivers if you were the one dying? (8) Any other questions? What was your reaction to this exercise?

137

Ideal Hospice Program

The surgeon who I was working for told me that to do any good
I would have to read medicine...about pain and it was indeed,
as he said, the doctors who desert the dying.

Dame Cicely Saunders,
Founder, International Hospice Movement

⇒ **Overview**

The first real heavy snows had settled upon California's high Sierra Mountains in earnest when I went to visit my brother Gary for the last time in late 1984. My brother was nearing death from a painful struggle with AIDS. During the visit, I remember summoning, at my brother's request, the resident physician to increase my brother's pain medication. The doctor balked at the idea, choosing instead to calmly lecture me on the addictive qualities of morphine and how he was fearful my brother might become addicted. I fell silent for a very long moment, mainly out of anger and outrage. When I composed myself, I inquired about how long he felt my brother had to live. The physician, with head bowed, said, "Not long, I'm afraid." At that point I put my finger under the chin of this physician and raised his chin up. I looked him straight in the eye and said shaking: "And you are worried about addiction?" He increased the pain medication. My brother had a heart attack two days later, from which they resuscitated him against his wishes. He lingered in mechanical horror for another day. When he died on January 13, 1985, at age 33, he had spent eleven continuous months in a hospital bed.

The AIDS pandemic has contributed overwhelmingly to the quality of how we die. Outrage and outcry by those with HIV have been instrumental in changing the options of how we die today. This change is most evident in the growth of the hospice movement. The term *hospice* derives from the Latin word *hospitium*, meaning hospitality. Other words deriving from it include host and hostess. In a nutshell the difference between hospice care and hospital care may be found in the word *palliative*. To perform *palliative care* means to address symptoms rather than their underlying causes--to provide comfort rather than cure. "It's what's to be done" when others say "There is nothing more we can do!" As one's condition worsens and sickness progresses towards death, palliative care can often take on all the urgency that curative care once did.

With all the media given to Dr. Kevorkian's "death machine" and to physician-assisted suicide, we hear very little about hospice care. This is most unfortunate, as hospice care is a viable alternative to the "live-forever-never-say-die high technology" dilemma many dying people find themselves hopelessly mired in. There are more than two thousand hospice programs throughout the United States that provide hope, care, and comfort. Many of these programs have a strong cadre of dedicated volunteers.

As a result of an international task force[72] on death and dying held in 1975,[73] a set of standards was developed for the terminally ill. These standards became some of the first for standardizing hospice care for the terminally ill. Two major philosophical principles emerged from this task force. They were that "Patients, family, and staff all have legitimate needs and interests" and "The terminally ill person's own preferences and lifestyle must be taken into account in all decision-making."

138

$\Rightarrow$ **Directions**

Based on the above introductory comments and guiding hospice principles, brainstorm developing an "ideal hospice program" for your community. This project might be a group, class, or out-of-class project. You might also visit a hospice program or invite a hospice care worker to address your class and comment on your "ideal hospice program." When you are done, compare it with the national standards that follow at the end of this exercise.[74]

1. Identify <u>hospice-setting</u> goals and objectives for patient care.

    a. _____

    b. _____

    c. _____

    d. _____

    e. _____

    f. _____

2. Identify goals and objectives for <u>patients.</u>

    a. _____

    b. _____

    c. _____

    d. _____

    e. _____

    f. _____

3. Identify goals and objectives for <u>family and significant others.</u>

    a. _____

    b. _____

    c. _____

    d. _____

    e. _____

    f. _____

    g. _____

4. Identify goals and objectives for <u>staff.</u>

a. _____

b. _____

c. _____

d. _____

e. _____

f. _____

⇒ **Hospice Program Standards**

A. <u>Philosophical Goals:</u>

1. Patients, family, and staff all have legitimate needs and interests.
2. The terminally ill person's own preferences and lifestyle must be taken into account in all decisions made.

B. <u>Patient-Oriented Standards:</u>

1. Treatment of symptoms is a major treatment goal.
2. Pain control is a major treatment goal.
3. Living wills, no codes, advance directives, Patient Self-Determination Act guidelines and other documents will be respected and used in developing a patient's total care program.
4. A patient should expect and receive a secure, comfortable, and warm caring environment.
5. Opportunities for visitation and other "leave-taking" should be provided and should be flexible and adaptable to patient needs.
6. Provide opportunities to make a patient's final moments and wishes meaningful and quality-oriented.

C. <u>Staff-Oriented Standards:</u>

1. Caregivers should have adequate time to form and maintain personal relationships with a patient.
2. Develop a mutual support network that will assist staff with their grief from a patient's death.

⇒ **Debriefing**

(1) Were there many differences between your "ideal" standards and the national standards? (2) How might you use your "ideal" standards and national standards to evaluate a hospice program you were considering using in your community? (3) What considerations would you want for hospice care of children? (4) Should there be "family-oriented standards as well? What might we expect <u>from families</u> in providing hospice-oriented" care? (i. e., some hospice programs require a primary caregiver be present in the home before hospice-related services will be provided.) (5) How might you learn more about hospice care? (6) Do you now feel you understand hospice care better? (7) Would you choose hospice care or traditional care if you had a terminal illness? (8) Would you volunteer to be a hospice worker? (9) How might you become an advocate for a hospice program in your community? (10) Contact a hospice program near you or the National Hospice Organization in Arlington, VA. Request briefing materials and bring this information to class.

140

Moral Dilemmas

A certain recluse, I know not who,
once said that no bonds attached him to this life,
and the only thing he would regret leaving was the sky.

Yoshida Kendo

⇒ **Overview**

It is very difficult to deal with questions of death if you don't also deal with questions of life. These questions include moral, spiritual, and philosophical issues. Personal morals, values, and beliefs are difficult to describe, let alone apply in our lives. The following exercise affords you an opportunity to examine some of your personal morals, values, and beliefs. Hopefully, it will spark some new or renewed thoughts on your own spirituality and philosophy for living life and for leaving life.

⇒ **Directions and Debriefing**

From your readings, discussions, and life experiences complete the following exercise. As you complete this assignment, consider the following questions. (1) What did you learn about "you and your morals?" (2) What was the difficulty and discomfort level? (3) Were you surprised by how little thought you had given to your personal morality over the past months and years? (4) What are your beliefs and values concerning living and dying? (5) what most do you like and respect in your values and morals?

1. Describe a moral dilemma you have had to manage and work through. Choose a real substantial dilemma which challenged your morals, values, and beliefs.

_____

_____

_____

_____

_____

_____

_____

_____

2. Describe how you managed and worked through your moral dilemma.

_____

_____

_____

_____

_____

_____

Morality -- Who Lives, Who Dies!

Happy people die whole,
they are all dissolved in a moment,
they have had what they wanted.

Robinson Jeffers

⇒ **Overview**

It is very difficult to deal with questions of life and death without also examining your moral, spiritual, and philosophical beliefs. The following exercise forces you to examine some of these issues. You will have an opportunity to observe firsthand how your stereotypes, prejudices and discriminatory thinking gets in the way of fairness and honesty.

⇒ **Directions and Debriefing**

For individual or small group activity, role-play that you are the authorized administrator in charge of a particular nuclear fallout shelter. Major nuclear meltdowns have occurred in five countries due to terrorism---all part of a worldwide plot! There are threats of worldwide devastation. The people listed below are in line at your door fighting to get into the shelter you administrate. Those waiting to get in cannot reach a decision among themselves as to who shall be left behind. You must decide. There is little time available, so only a brief computer search description is available on each. The shelter can handle seven people plus your committee. It is probable you will be the only people to survive and "left" to start over on earth. You must reach an agreement as to which seven people to save. (1) After your group has discussed and decided on the individuals you will save, note why you chose as you did. (2) Discuss any highlights of your discussion. (3) Be prepared to present to the class your decisions and why. (4) What did you learn about yourself? Were you prejudiced? Was it hard to ignore stereotyping? Were you inclined to discriminate? (5) How do prejudices and discrimination affect us all? How might we all become more fair in life with others?

1. 24-year-old African-American civil rights activist, graduate of Howard University
2. 47-year-old alcoholic police officer
3. 59-year-old female, former Congressperson, and now active community leader
4. adult male with dwarfism
5. drug felon from well-to-do family
6. female street prostitute, 6 months pregnant, no prenatal care, possible drug abuser
7. basketball star with HIV-positive status
8. gay male physician
9. male radical environmental ecologist and zealot
10. Mexican farm laborer, illegally in United States
11. middle-aged female fundamentalist religious zealot
12. middle-aged, obese, balding politician, recently forced out of office
13. mildly retarded youth, age 20, with a steady job
14. office secretary with physical disability
15. university cheerleader majoring in marketing

Euthanasia Debate

We are healed of a suffering only by experiencing it to the full.

Marcel Proust

⇒ **Overview**

In January of 1996, Stanford University Medical Center provided a woman with Down's Syndrome with a heart and lung transplant. For many, that decision raised ethical questions. Did she deserve this procedure? Would she understand what had happened and follow through on aftercare directions? Weren't there more suitable recipients who should have had a higher priority than she? A biomedical ethics committee decided to go ahead with this controversial operation. What are your thoughts about this?

Bioethics is the study of the moral and social implications of practices and developments in the medical and life sciences. An ethical dilemma arises when there is a conflict of loyalties, duties, obligations, rights, principles, or values. Whatever decision is made, some good and some bad will both result. In a dilemma, the reasons on each side of a problem have credibility and none is in any obvious way the "right" set of reasons. Some basic bioethics terms include (1) *beneficence*, doing good, (2) *non-maleficence*, doing no harm, (3) *individual autonomy*, referring to patient self-determination, and (4) *proportionality*, weighing benefits versus disadvantages to ethical considerations in a bio-medical decision.

Techniques for resolving bioethical dilemmas include: (1) gathering and assessing all the facts, (2) identifying the dilemma and the principles in conflict, (3) considering alternative courses of action, and (4) developing a plan of implementation and follow-up.

⇒ **Directions and Debriefing**

For this role-play activity, divide into two groups. One group must defend the right of euthanasia and the other group must defend the right-to-life. Be prepared to discuss the varied aspects of euthanasia, such as active and passive euthanasia. Present interesting scenarios such as those raised by the following questions. For the second part of this exercise, prepare your thoughts and comments regarding the following questions.

1. Should euthanating pets and other animals be banned?
2. Should deformed newborn infants be actively euthanatized?
3. Should death-row inmates have the right to euthanasia? Some say death-row is passive euthanasia.
4. Should the elderly be encouraged to choose euthanasia as a option to living life?
5. Should the homeless and chronically ill be euthanatized?
6. Should the institutionalized be euthanated?
7. Should euthanasia be allowed for those wishing to donate organs? What would the ground rules be?
8. What are some of your concerns about invoking life and death decisions?
9. How does a discussion about euthanasia challenge your thoughts about death and dying?
10. What are some of your "bottom-line" thoughts regarding when to and when not to allow euthanasia?
11. What are your thoughts about the death penalty, aggressive pain management, and organ donation?

Judge and Jury

My old body:
a drop of dew grown
heavy at the leaf tip.

Kiba

⇒ **Overview**

It is human nature, it seems, that automobile drivers like slowing down and staring at roadside accident scenes. We've all done it. Few drivers stop and help, often just assuming someone else will or has stopped. Life and death decisions are similar. We're interested in them but would probably rather not get involved. Yet such decisions are made daily by people in all walks of life. Many times the reasons are simple. They had no choice; they had to because it involved someone close to them. Here is an opportunity to try your hand at one such situation and thus test your skill, wisdom, and compassion!

⇒ **Directions and Debriefing**

In group discuss the following exercise[75] and make a decision about whether to prolong the boy's life. Consider the situation as a jury trial, electing a foreman and taking a series of secret ballots between discussions periods. Open the trial by having the foreman read the case. The group's task is to reach a group decision on whether to prolong the boy's life. Begin discussion and every so often take a ballot vote in secret. The foreman should announce the results of each balloting before proceeding with the next round of discussions. When members have agreed on a decision, or at least agreed not to actively oppose the decision, each member should explain to the class (1) their personal decision-making process, (2) what factors played a role in their decisions, (3) whether the case information was sufficient and they had enough information to make a decision, (4) how they felt about the discussions and the group decision, (5) if all group members were in accord with and satisfied with the decision, and (6) was the exercise interesting and educational or just disturbing and frustrating. Other questions to consider include: (1) How did the exercise affect your thoughts on death? (2) What do you think of the jury approach? (3) How might juries be abusive in capital punishment trials?

The parents of a 7-year-old boy with leukemia are meeting with a health-care team consisting of the child's physician, nurse, and social worker. The child has reentered the hospital in the terminal phase of his painful illness; he has previously experienced three spontaneous remissions and returned home, only to fall dangerously ill and return to the hospital each time. A fourth remission is not expected. The group must decide whether to begin the child on an expensive new experimental treatment. Although the treatment is not expected to be able to control the disease for the child, it might keep him alive for up to six months longer, and its use in this case would add to medical knowledge and possibly improve the survival rate of other sick children. However, the parents and the two younger brothers of the child have prepared themselves for his death at each return to the hospital. The emotional strain of the dramatic recoveries is reflected in the worsening relationship between the parents and in behavior problems in the children. The father is working a second job to help pay the medical bills. The mother alternates between wanting to keep her child alive at all costs and wanting to release him from pain. The doctor is committed to saving and prolonging life if at all possible, especially in the case of a child. The nurse has cared for the child during each hospitalization and considers herself having the primary responsibility for caring for the child. The social worker has given the parents financial counseling and has tried to give them psychological support during the long illness.

144

Every life is its own excuse for being.

Elbert Hubbard

⇒ **Overview**

This exercise[76] is a follow-up to the "Euthanasia" and "Euthanasia Debate" exercises. Ethical consideration in making decisions about who lives and who dies are generally made by bio-medical ethics committees. These committees are located in hospitals, universities, and sometimes in the community at large. They are generally composed of medical staff, clergy, social workers, and patient advocates from the community. Family input is encouraged. This decision-making process is often a "push-and-pull" painful one at best. It must be remembered that each committee member has an agenda they want represented. How decisions and a consensus are finally made is most illuminating about a society's values. As the following exercise will demonstrate, the "power of life and death," can be a painful process. For this exercise to have its intended meaning and impact, you should have some understanding of the following: (1) passive and active euthanasia, (2) the Patient Self-Determination Act (PSDA), (3) advance directives, (4) living wills and living trusts, and (5) an understanding of some of the landmark "right-to-die" cases and situations. These include Karen Ann Quinlan, Nancy Cruzan, and Jack Kevorkian and physician-assisted suicide. For a good discussion of these see Kastenbaum, R. (1995). *Death, Society, and Human Experience.* (Boston: Allyn & Bacon) and DeSpelder, L. A. and Strickland, A. L. (1996). *The Last Dance.* (Mountain View, CA: Mayfield).

⇒ **Directions and Debriefing**

You will be part of a bioethics committee in your community. Divide into four-person groups. Each group has an administrator, a doctor, a patient advocate from the community, and a member of the clergy. Together you must judge whether or not a patient should receive life-sustaining treatment. You will be given enough time, so choose your roles and begin identifying relevant concerns. Once your group has assigned roles, jointly arrive at decisions for the following situations. (1) How difficult was this role-play? (2) Was arriving at a consensus easy or hard? Explain. (3) Do you see any value in the use of such committees? (4) Should such committees be regulated or legislated? (5) How does one police such committees and their actions? (6) What are your personal views regarding the decisions you made in this role-play? In other words, did you have spiritual, moral, or philosophical problems with any of your decisions? (7) Could you serve on a actual bio-ethics committee?

The following are the bioethics cases to consider. A life depends upon your decision.

1. A 62-year-old patient who has suffered a heart attack is resuscitated and placed on a respirator. After 24 hours, an electroencephalogram (EEG) shows no brain activity. Should life support be withdrawn?

2. An emergency medical team is called to the scene of a "man down," where they find a 75-year-old resident of a posh district in a major metropolitan city with no vital signs. Is this patient D.O.A. or should resuscitation efforts be started?

3. An emergency medical team is called to the scene of a "man down," where they find a 75-year-old "skid row" derelict with no vital signs. Is this patient D.O.A. or should resuscitation efforts be started?

4. The patient is an anencephalic newborn with a congenital malformation such that there is no brain development. The parents request that physicians withdraw intravenous feeding. Should the ethics committee consent to the parents' request?

5. The patient is a newborn with Down's syndrome and intestinal blockage. The parents refuse to give their consent to surgery and request that physicians withdraw intravenous feeding. Should the ethics committee consent to the parents' request?

6. A patient dying of AIDS asks to be released from the hospital in order to return home and commit suicide. What is the hospital's responsibility?

7. A newborn is given no medical possibility of living longer than five to seven days because of a congenital, always fatal condition. The adjacent incubator in the neonatal intensive care unit holds a newborn who will die within 48 hours without a heart transplant. Is it ethical to shorten the first infant's life by a couple of days so that another child has a chance to live? Who should decide?

8. A husband and wife are diagnosed, respectively, with Alzheimer's and untreatable, terminal cancer. They mutually decide on a suicide pact, desiring to die as they have lived for the previous six decades--together. Do they have the right to end their lives like this?

9. A major medical center announces that it wishes to open a special wing to keep the bodies of neomorts (brain-dead corpses) functioning on life support until the organs can be harvested to aid patients with life-threatening conditions. Should the medical center be allowed to proceed ahead? Who should benefit financially from such harvesting of organs?

10. A woman who has received governmental assistance (welfare) for the last 45 years of her life is killed in an automobile accident. There is no known next-of-kin and she did not complete an organ donor card or leave other instructions about the disposition of her remains. Given that the woman was supported by the state for more than four decades of her life, does the state have any "vested interest" in deciding whether her organs can be used for transplantation? Should the hospital ethics committee make such a request of the state?

⇒ Notes _____

_____

_____

_____

_____

_____

_____

_____

_____

_____

_____

_____

_____

_____

Euthanasia: Who Dies?

He who lives only for himself is truly dead to others.

Publilius Syrus

⇒ **Overview**

"An act of painlessly ending the life of a person for reasons of mercy." That's how the *American Heritage Dictionary* defines it and that's what it was. It was also a profound act of love from a brother to his younger brother. I'm talking about euthanasia and the story is about a client of mine. Lee was a long-time cancer survivor. The cancer had come back with a vengeance. Lee, already very frail with colon cancer, was told he needed new cancer surgery and that it was doubtful he would even survive the operating table. Even if he did survive, Lee's quality of life would be worse than he had now, which was already very poor. As his therapist, I was summoned by Lee one day and he said, "Doc, it's time for me to move on down the line. Will you help me?" I knew exactly what he meant and wanted. I had watched many die in my life and watched many die from strong morphine doses all under the cover of pain management. Euthanasia comes in many forms. Lee's brother Albert, who was caring for him, arranged the deadly cocktail from existing medications. Albert ran the concoction by me to be sure it would "do the trick," as Albert put it. One fine clear San Francisco day, from a window overlooking Golden Gate Park, Albert presented the "cocktail" to Lee. I had been working with Lee closely and knew he was aware of all options. This was to be his final act of control and empowerment. "Are you sure, Lee?" I said. "Yes, yes, yes," he calmly replied. He hugged everyone and drank all. With an ever-so-slight breeze blowing in through the bedroom window, as white mesh curtains let filtered sun in, Lee passed on. It took less than forty minutes. It was as nice a death as I'd ever seen. I guess in the eyes of the law it was an assisted suicide by Lee's brother Albert. I provided the education. Lee's case is a classic example of the "Right to Die" controversy. That is, who has the right to die, under what circumstances may they die, and who may assist them to die?

A literal translation of *euthanasia* is happy (<u>eu</u>) death (<u>thanasia</u>). It has come to mean much more, as my opening comments suggest: a death absent of pain and suffering. And as a dance must have two, so does euthanasia. One must wish to die and another must help the one wishing to die do so. It must all occur within a framework of providing mercy in a situation of pain and suffering with little chance of recovery. Any discussion of euthanasia must include passive euthanasia and active euthanasia. *Passive euthanasia* is where medical staff choose *not* to do something. No longer keeping a brain trauma patient on life support is passive euthanasia as it is the intentional withholding of treatment in a case where there is little hope for recovery or any quality of life. *Active euthanasia* is where a treatment is given which will end life. A person who is suffering greatly with little chance of recovery is given a lethal injection to end their life. This is a form of active euthanasia. Who has the right to die? Who will make such decisions? Professionals who deal with such issues are known as *bioethicists*. They deal with issues of health-care technology and how this technology will be applied to people's lives. Complete the following exercise and see what it feels like to have the weight of life and death on your shoulders. Complete the debriefing questions at the end.

147

⇒ **Directions**[77]

You are <u>Chief of the Biomedical Ethics Committee of Central City Hospital</u>. Each day you must review clinical case presentations for euthanasia. Euthanasia has been sanctioned and formally legislated under the Euthanasia Act of America (EAOA). Its legality has been upheld by the United States Supreme Court. You are immune from any criminal and civil prosecution. Your actions are considered fully legal and not subject to review. No one else has any legal standing in these matters but you and your committee. You must rely on findings presented to you as prescribed by law.

Sign your name on the last page as indicated. Indicate your decision for each patient by signing your initials in the appropriate box signifying active euthanasia, passive euthanasia, or continuation of life. Prioritize patients to be euthanated first by your subordinate physicians. Law prohibits your involvement in the actual act of euthanating a patient. Decisions must be made and are final under the Euthanasia Act of America (EAOA).

In the matter of:

1. Medical Case Record #1994-A

Infant Asian male, born to 23-year-old Vietnamese refugee mother. Undesired pregnancy. Father unknown. Severe birth defects: cleft face extending up through frontal bone with no nasal bone, grossly deformed eyes, and microcranium webbing of hands and feet. Child cannot survive without stomach tube-feeding or intravenous fluids. Parents have not seen child.

Euthanasia Recommendation   (1) Active _____   (2) Passive_____   (3) Continue Life_____

2. Medical Case Record #1994-B

Hispanic male, age 38, with stomach cancer. Onset of symptoms came suddenly one day. Patient has been in surgery five times over last five months. Patient has a wife, age 36, has been married for over 15 years. There are four children. Family cannot afford radiation and chemotherapy treatment. The family needs welfare now. Without the treatment, disease will spread rapidly. Further surgery has been ruled out due to expense. Patient wishes no further treatments. Patient wishes to die at home with family and in dignity. Wife wants husband to live. With counseling, wife would probably change her mind. Best case scenario: Even with treatment, patient will live for only another nine to ten months in constant pain.

Euthanasia Recommendation   (1) Active _____   (2) Passive_____   (3) Continue Life_____

3. Medical Case Record #1994-C

African-American female, age 25, in a coma since March 1985, from drug overdose. Patient can periodically breathe without a respirator but usually needs it. Patient takes in nourishment through use of nasogastric tubes or intravenously. Patient has no cognitive functions left and is essentially in a "persistent vegetative state" (PVS). Patient's family pleads for respirator to be discontinued and given to another patient who needs it. Patient's family further requests that even if patient lives without a respirator that "she be put to sleep" mercifully for her sake and for their peace of mind. The patient's family prays each day in hopes this decision will be made.

Euthanasia Recommendation   (1) Active _____   (2) Passive_____   (3) Continue Life_____

4. Medical Case Record #1994-D

White male, age 51, gay, identified AIDS patient with 16-year history of HIV status. Full-blown AIDS for last six years. T-cell compromised count of less than 10 (normal is 1000-1200). Patient currently being treated for opportunistic diseases Kaposi's sarcoma (KS) and Pneumocystis carinii pneumonia (PCP). Current medications include AZT, DDI, DDC and 47 other medications. Patient is 6'2" with a current weight of 108 lbs., grave evidence of "wasting syndrome" common in AIDS patients. Patient has developed colon cancer and showing evidence of dementia as a result of toxoplasmosis (brain infection from HIV). Treating and consulting physicians advise patient will most likely not survive any operating procedures to remove cancerous tumors. Patient unlikely candidate for chemo or radiation treatment, as patient has no discernible intact immune system. Patient has good support system in community and lives in own home with brother who provides care for him. Full insurance coverage is available. Patient requests active euthanasia. Patient is in end stage of AIDS even without consideration of cancer complications. Patient "feels it is time to go."

Euthanasia Recommendation   (1) Active _____   (2) Passive_____   (3) Continue Life_____

5. Medical Case Record #1994-E

Female Hispanic child, 12 years old, only child, with acute leukemia. Child still ambulatory (can move about) in unit, but patient's stomach is swollen to twice normal size from treatments. Child is apparently in pain most of time. Patient's 29-year-old parents are unable to visit her except on weekends, since they live 100 miles away. Both work two jobs each to pay for treatments. Child is resigned to hospital life, having almost grown up on unit, with treatments since age 4. Child sadly asks nursing staff: "How much longer will I live?," and "Will I ever see Marie and Paul again?" (two children who have died recently on ward). She has seen many deaths since her arrival on ward. Staff and some parents of other children are asking why she can't be "released from her suffering." Child's prognosis is guarded at best.

Euthanasia Recommendation   (1) Active _____   (2) Passive_____   (3) Continue Life_____

6. Medical Case Record #1994-F

Australian male, age 64, legal and naturalized citizen, in intensive care unit with liver shutdown as a result of chronic cirrhosis of the liver. Long history of felony convictions, vagrancy, and alcoholism. This is patient's tenth admission for an alcohol-related bodily dysfunction. Patient wants to live but has nowhere to go should he live and be released. Patient is "panhandler" and begs money for alcohol. The hospital staff dislikes him. He has been disowned by his parents, deserted by his wife and children, and neither welfare nor the social service agencies wish to work with him any longer. He is a danger to himself and the community. Many in the community and on the hospital staff are asking for euthanasia.

Euthanasia Recommendation   (1) Active _____   (2) Passive_____   (3) Continue Life_____

7. Medical Case Record #1994-G

White infant female, born of 28-year-old prostitute. Mother HIV-positive. Not desired pregnancy. Patient born with inoperable spina bifida (congenital spinal deformation). Infant as child will never walk, may be able to live a few years in a wheelchair. Parents cannot afford expensive drugs or treatment for the infant. All insurance has run out. Three other children at home. Child's reflexes are normal as is intelligence. Infant HIV-negative at this time.

Euthanasia Recommendation   (1) Active _____   (2) Passive_____   (3) Continue Life_____

8. Medical Case Record #1994-H

White infant female, born of 36-year-old mother and 38-year-old father who is Jewish Rabbi. First child and most desired pregnancy. Child showed at birth signs of Down's syndrome (mongolism). Scholastic achievement during child's life will not be better than 4th grade level. May need institutional setting throughout most of adulthood. Child also has several deformities which are correctable by surgery. Parents want no surgery as they wish child to die and not face life of struggle. Parents can afford surgery. They have good income and adequate insurance.

Euthanasia Recommendation   (1) Active _____   (2) Passive_____   (3) Continue Life_____

9. Medical Case Record #1994-I

White infant female born to 23-year old mother. Desired pregnancy. Initial neonatal life had no complications. Infant found in crib at home not breathing and "blue" at 6 days of life. Infant was rushed to ER (emergency room). Immediate efforts to resuscitate infant in emergency room successful. Parents are now in the emergency waiting room, awaiting infant's formal admittance. Infant will be severely brain damaged. Intelligence level will remain that of an infant. Infant will have life of problems as past history shows children in this situation usually die of varied infections between ages 10 and 15. A decision is needed immediately. Parents not yet informed. Hospital staff can notify parents resuscitation successful or not successful. ER staff recommends active euthanasia.

Euthanasia Recommendation   (1) Active _____   (2) Passive_____   (3) Continue Life_____

10. Medical Case Record #1994-J

Undocumented Mexican migrant farmworker, female, age 31, suffering from acute leukemia. Hospitalization "off and on" for last 19 months. Patient is presently in the "sterile room" with severe immune compromise from combination of bone marrow procedure (identical twin donated) and chemotherapy. Patient subjectively experiencing acute nausea, vomiting, and mental distress. There is no cure for patient's particular disease strain at present, and patient's chances for a remission are high from review of previous and similar cases. She may live up to three or more years. The last few days patient has been asking to "dc" (discontinue) treatment and occasionally wishing for death, since her agony (manageable pain) and ordeal are so great. Her family (exhausted) agrees with any decision daughter makes. Hospital records note: "Personnel enjoy patient because she is friendly and morale-building with other leukemia and cancer patients."

Euthanasia Recommendation (1) Active _____ (2) Passive_____ (3) Continue Life_____

11. Medical Case Record #1994-K

White female, age 81, in the hospital for renal failure (kidney disease). Patient must spend five hours each day attached to hospital kidney dialysis machine. Patient is often frightened and in pain from daily ordeal. Patient is frail and knows her condition will be fatal sooner or later and has asked medical staff why she can't be taken off these "new-fangled" machines and be allowed to die in peace and comfort at home. She fights the treatments, refuses medications. Patient calls her children frequently asking to die in peace. Patient's children want her to be given the best of treatments until the very end and "at all costs." They have full insurance coverage and substantial financial resources to care for their mother. They are threatening legal action. The son is on the Hospital Board's Governing Committee and has donated in excess of one million to the Central City Hospital Building Fund.

Euthanasia Recommendation (1) Active _____ (2) Passive_____ (3) Continue Life_____

12. Medical Case Record #1994-L

White female, age 63, recently had amputation of both legs below knee due to gangrene from lifelong diabetes. Patient has no hope for a life with any quality. Patient feels she has nothing left to live for. Her children rarely visit and she doesn't feel close to anyone anymore. Patient's husband died 8 years ago, leaving her to live alone in their small home in the country. After she leaves the hospital, she will be placed in a local nursing home on the edge of the city, called a "zoo" by many. Patient says the country is better for her to be in than the nursing home close to her children. Patient says of her country home: "It is the only place which makes me happy!" Patient displays severe depression symptoms as a result of her deteriorating condition and situation. Medical chart records show patient has "begged doctors to let her die in peace." Patient has economic independence and can afford all medical care.

Euthanasia Recommendation (1) Active _____ (2) Passive_____ (3) Continue Life_____

13. Medical Case Record #1994-M

Hispanic male, age 55, long-time drug abuser, is conscious and communicative, though dependent upon a heart-lung machine for life, after below-the-arms paralysis from an alcohol-related DUI (drunk-driving) auto accident. Patient is famous rock singer of '70s ("The Deadly Grateful"). Patient has requested repeatedly that all "heroic efforts" be turned off. Patient states and social work staff confirm that family is well provided for. His relatives have all had time with him. Patient has discussed euthanasia with family members, and all agree it is the best action for him now. Social work staff reports: "Family have all grieved and are finished with grief, including him. Patient is confident of a happy afterlife with his perceived God. Patient is competent and "ready." Should patient live, he faces murder charges as a result of DUI automobile accident. A mother and 5-year-old child were killed. The father is currently in critical condition at same hospital.

Euthanasia Recommendation   (1) Active _____   (2) Passive_____   (3) Continue Life_____

Be it said in the matters so described above that:

I, _____ Chief, Biomedical Ethics Committee, Central City Hospital, do hereby make the following decisions in the following clinical case presentations under the Euthanasia Act of America (EAOA), by Drs. Mannino, Joseph, Francis, Hope, and others as so assigned by me; and do thereby and so sign my name attesting to the above.

_____, M. D.   Date: _____
   Chief, Biomedical Ethics Committee

⇒ **Debriefing**

1. What were some of your thoughts about this exercise? fears? concerns? hopes?

2. How many votes for active and passive euthanasia did you cast? How many votes to continue life?

3. Though for the most part you would not find such identifying information on medical charts, did you find you had prejudicial feelings when identifying information such as age, gender, race, sexual orientation, religious or ethnic background was used? Might such information be an issue in the fairness of such proceedings? A closing thought here: How might ability to pay affect the equation of who has care or not?

4. What options would you want if you were terminal with no hope of recovery? What options would you want if you were terminal, in and out of pain frequently, and suffering?

5. Do you think our society is evolving towards such harsh euthanasia guidelines as evidenced in the above make-believe scenarios?

6. In real-life situations involving euthanasia decisions, bioethics committees are usually convened to make these decisions (see exercise "Euthanasia Debate" on page 143). Keep in mind that the intensity of conflict in these committee discussions is greatly affected by the composition of these committees. Which

medical and/or nonmedical persons should be on them? Where should they be located? What kind of training is needed? Would you serve on such a committee?

7. Do you believe a person has the right to die? If so, under what circumstances?

8. Does a person have to be <u>actually</u> dying before having the right to die? What guidelines are needed?

9. How might living wills, advance directives, and the Patient Self-Determination Act (PSDA) make a difference in situations such as presented above?

10. What do you think of Dr. Jack Kevorkian's "death with dignity" crusade for physician-assisted suicide?

11. How does one determine if one is competent to make personal decisions involving the right to die?

Notes: _____

_____

_____

_____

_____

_____

_____

_____

_____

_____

_____

_____

_____

_____

_____

_____

_____

_____

_____

_____

_____

_____

_____

_____

_____

Violence in the News

The hour of departure has arrived,
and we go our ways.
I to die, and you to live.
Which is better God only knows.

Plato

⇒ **Overview**

In September 1994, a solemn event occurred. Thirty-eight thousand pairs of shoes were placed along the Capitol's reflecting pool to symbolize the 38,000 violent deaths due to guns in the United States in 1993. Shoes were used to symbolize these deaths because, as organizers noted, except for the best of good fortune, we ourselves could have walked in those shoes. It has been estimated by the U. S. Census Bureau that violence takes over 2 million lives each year in the U. S. As many as 100 million Americans have been affected by violent crime. According to a Gallup poll, the number of Americans who worry about being murdered in the 1990s is almost double the number who worried in 1981.[78]

The purpose of this exercise is to examine how the media touches our lives with depictions of death, leaving us all, in some way or another, instantaneous survivors. Through the vicarious mass media experience from books, newspapers, magazines, television, and movies, we all learn about death. This exercise will examine print media. For a good discussion of the effects of war and violence, see chapter six in *Embracing Their Memory: Loss and the Social Psychology of Storytelling* by John H. Harvey.

⇒ **Directions and Debriefing**

It is said violent death is as close as the nearest television, radio, or newspaper---if not even nearer in our personal lives. For this activity review newspapers and magazines. Cut out some articles which deal with incidents of violent death, terrorism, murder, or other conflict. Keep track of the kinds of violent deaths and the number of times they occur. One interesting method is to restrict yourself to one regular print media source. For example you might search a local regional daily newspaper such as *The San Francisco Chronicle* or use your hometown newspaper. National dailies, such as the *Los Angeles Times*, *The New York Times*, and *USA Today*, are also fine. Weeklies such as *Newsweek*, *U. S. News and World Report*, and *Time* will also do fine.

Prepare to discuss your findings. (1) Clip and attach to this page an article about death from a print media source. (2) Explain how the article affected you and informed you about death. (3) Below, jot down some of the more powerful sentences from the article. Why were they powerful? How did these sentences affect you? (4) What percentage of the news seems to be concerned with death and violence? (5) What trends did you note?

_____

_____

_____

_____

Art of Violence

Hearts learn by being wounded.

Oscar Wilde

⇒ **Overview**

Take a look at the picture on the following page.[79] A quick glance and you might have thought you were looking at a blueprint for a computer chip or some disciplined artist's geometric drawing. A closer look, however, will show 489 graphical depictions of human beings. This number is significant. It is the number of homicides in the United States in a typical week for 1992. There were 25,488 homicides that year.[80] Additionally, in 1993 there were 5,751 children and adolescents killed by guns. In other words, a child is shot to death every 92 minutes.[81] What are your thoughts about these statistics?

⇒ **Facts About Homicides**[82]

1. There were 25,488 homicides and 30,484 suicides in 1992.
2. Men are more often both the killer and the victim.
3. People between the ages of 15-24 are most at risk for murder.
4. At least three out of five murders are committed by people who are relatives, lovers, friends, neighbors or colleagues of the victim.
5. Homicides are more common in large cities.
6. Firearms are the weapon of choice in about 70% of all homicides.
7. The trend is toward higher and higher homicides rates in the United States.
8. Arguments are the most frequent provocation for homicides.
9. Homicide is the leading cause of death for women in the workplace.
10. Most homicides are done by killers who are of the same race as the victim.

⇒ **Directions**

Move beyond the impersonal to the personal by putting a name on one of the faces. Bring in a media clipping of a murder case in your community. Circle one of the faces in the picture on the following page to represent the murder in your clipping. Write in the person's name on the picture. Paste part of the clipping on the picture itself. For dramatic effect post these collages on your classroom wall as well. Take time to view each other's postings, then in small group prepare responses to the debriefing questions below.

⇒ **Debriefing**

1. What are your fears of becoming a homicide or murder victim?
2. Have you lost family or friends to homicide?
3. Is a killing that occurs during war-time considered a homicide?
4. When is a homicide justifiable?
5. Most homicides are by guns. What is your opinion regarding gun control?
6. How might one protect oneself from homicide?
7. How might one work to make the community safer?
8. Were you surprised by any of the ten "Facts About Homicides"? Which ones? Explain.
9. If you were surprised by any of these homicide facts, might it have been because your stereotypes were challenged? Comment. How do stereotypes and prejudices get in the way of "fair play" and reason?

155

Art of Violence

I make his bed everyday,
because I want him to have a nice bed to sleep in.
Yes, I know this is silly, because it's been seven years
since my son was shot dead in cold blood on these here streets.

grieving mother's comment in newspaper

Death Penalty Attitudes

There is no constitutional right to choose to die.

Chief Justice Joseph Weintraub

⇒ **Overview**

The death penalty, or capital punishment as it is also known, is very controversial. The public debate over capital punishment continues to rage in the media, in the courts, in the legislative bodies, and in the agony expressed by both the pros and cons of those for and against capital punishment. Though debate is lively, the United States is one of the last remaining Western nations not to abolish the death penalty. Public sentiment seems to be high in favor of the death penalty. Proponents of the death penalty argue that the death penalty provides (a) retribution for "high capital" crimes, (b) a deterrent to others, and (c) a method of removing the criminal's continued danger to society. Opponents argue that (a) there is no conclusive evidence in support of the need for retribution by our society, (b) there is no proof the death penalty provides general deterrence, and (c) there is no proof capital punishment provides prevention and protection. Opponents cite the low recidivism rate for murder parolees.

⇒ **Directions and Debriefing**

Well, with the above as background, what are your thoughts? Do you believe, as others do, that death penalty attitudes fall on a continuum, that is, there are certain crimes which deserve the death penalty or don't deserve the death penalty? Examine the following statements carefully and you decide where you fall on the death penalty continuum. In parentheses you will find some sensational national news-story triggers to help put the statement in better perspective. (1) Prepare for discussion in group and in class. (2) As you carefully ponder these statements, do you find yourself agonizing, making excuses, or withdrawing from having to make decisions? Is it appropriate to kill a human being under these circumstances? (3) Exactly where do you stand? Are you for or against? At the end of each statement there are some "scenario hints" from the news media to spark your thinking. (4) Try to identify other scenarios where your thoughts about the death penalty might differ.

1. Murder of a person requires the death penalty. What is more than one person? ("O. J. Simpson Arrested")

2. Rape is grounds for the death penalty. ("Catholic Nuns Killed and Raped!")

3. Major arson is grounds for the death penalty. ("Oakland Hills, California Burns!")

4. Armed robbery is grounds for the death penalty. ("Two Killed and Millions Stolen!"

5. An act of terrorism is grounds for the death penalty. ("World Trade Center Bombings")

6. A drunk driver who kills with his car is grounds for the death penalty. ("Mother and Son Auto Death")

7. Murder for hire and profit is grounds for the death penalty. ("Insurance Motive in Melendez Murders!")

8. Murderer with a radical ideology should get death penalty. ("San Francisco Zebra Killers")

9. Murder of a minor by a minor is grounds for the death penalty. (Kid Kills Kid!")

10. Murderer obeying the voice of God to kill is grounds for the death penalty.   ("Branch Davidians")

11. Domestic violence deaths are grounds for the death penalty. ("Husband Kills Wife and Kids")

12. Kidnapping is grounds for the death penalty. Kidnapping resulting in death. ("Polly Klass Found Dead!')

13. Major graft and corruption as a corporate officer or elected political official are grounds for the death penalty. ("Keating S&L Scandal Heats Up!")

14. Major environmental pollution is grounds for the death penalty. ("Valdez: Major Oil Spill!")

15. Murder in the "heat of passion" is grounds for the death penalty. ("Wife Kills Husband in Bed with Girlfriend!" or "Courthouse Mother Kills Defendant Accused of Sexually Molesting Son!")

Notes: _____

_____

_____

_____

_____

_____

_____

_____

_____

_____

_____

_____

_____

_____

_____

_____

_____

_____

_____

_____

_____

_____

_____

Death Penalty Pros and Cons

Take love away and our earth is a tomb.

Robert Browning

⇒ **Overview**

A long time ago, when I was a volunteer in the United States Peace Corps, I had a debate about the death penalty with another Peace Corps Volunteer. I was against and he was for. Later that month I invited him to view a public hanging in the Islamic Southeast Asian country where we both served. A drug smuggler was hung. The spectacle of the hanging had a profound effect on my friend. He no longer supported the death penalty after that. This is what often happens when you get involved in an issue. You really learn something, then you really change. And this is good. In 1996, one of the major films was *Dead Man Walking*, a film about a young man on death row. The film examines, in many ways, the pros and cons of the death penalty. We must make our own decisions and be honest to ourselves. It is important to be true to yourself and "follow you bliss," as the late storyteller Joseph Campbell said. Many of the issues of our time go unattended because some people simply will not discuss them, let alone take a stand on them. Abortion, welfare, crime, child abuse, foreign aid, and immigration are but a few of the perennial issues that many people have opinions on, but few real facts to justify their opinions. People are very quick sometimes to offer up an opinion on the death penalty until they actually get into a discussion. Then they are not so sure about their position any longer. Both life and death require taking a stand and having a position. After all, life and death are very big issues.

⇒ **Directions and Debriefing**

This exercise attempts to force the issue as regards the death penalty. As a class, divide into two groups. Group A should make a list of statements favoring capital punishment and Group B should make a list of statements opposing capital punishment. Work hard at drawing up responses which are as rational as possible. Prepare to defend your position when the class comes together. (1) What are the pros and cons? (2) Prepare a list of ideas that might prevent the need for capital punishment. (3) Did you see some truth in both sides of the argument? (4) What was your reaction to the exercise? (5) Has the debate changed your attitude at all? If so, why? If not, why? (6) Did examining the issue help you understand the issues better? If so, might examining questions surrounding death and dying also help you understand those issues better? (7) If you were a prison chaplain, how might you counsel someone on death row? (8) Could you be the executioner who pulls the switch or injects the lethal injection to someone on death row? (9) Close out your discussion with some dialogue about whether it is right or wrong to execute a human being. (10) Bring in articles from the print media which discuss capital punishment. (11) Do you think being informed about issues of death and dying will help you live a better life? Why or why not?

_____

_____

_____

_____

How Much Do You Know About Suicide?

Nothing can be meaner
than the anxiety to live one,
to live on, anyhow and in any shape.

George Santayana

⇒ **Overview**

I was only 22 when I experienced my first suicide. I was working at a resort in Lake Tahoe for the summer before joining the United States Peace Corps the following fall. There was a whole bunch of us who worked this brassy bright-lit casino. Mark was the joyous one of our group. But he changed. By mid-summer he seemed different. After several weeks of being severely depressed, Mark suddenly became bubbly and filled with a newfound zest for life. We, his friends, all thought he was finally coming out of it. Less than a week later, Mark died of a self-inflicted gunshot to his head. He was only 21. None of it made any sense to us, his friends. None of us knew the signs of suicide or how to help someone like this. Things might have been different had we known more about suicide. We were all sad the day Mark died. He was a good guy, a nice kid to know. It was a human tragedy. We all mourned his loss and were listless for some time.

At this point stop and complete the Suicide Knowledge Questionnaire at the end of this exercise. When finished, return and resume reviewing this exercise activity.

Some Facts. Depressed people commit suicide at a rate 25 times higher than non-depressed people.[83] The Centers for Disease Control reported 30,484 "official" suicides for 1992, the last year for which official statistics are available.[84] Most experts believe the figure is well in excess of 100,000 a year.[85] The official figures just don't capture those who crash themselves to death driving on the roads or who drink or drug themselves to death. There are thousands of suspicious deaths each year which are nothing more than disguised forms of suicide that aren't labeled as such. Some cultures have particularly high suicide rates. Native American youth have suicide rates five times greater than suicides rates among youth of the general population.[86] Gay and lesbian youth have higher rates as well. Social stigma hides many suicides. I remember reading in the newspaper some time ago of a retired policeman who shot himself. His wife lied and said an intruder had entered the premises and shot her husband. Investigators and fellow police officers who knew him all helped to cover up the real cause, so as to save embarrassment and allow her husband to have a Christian burial. It wasn't until many years later that the truth came out. Suicide is the ninth leading cause of death, only recently being replaced by AIDS, which is now the eighth leading cause of death. Suicide is the third leading cause of death among 15- to 24-year-olds.[87] Five million living Americans have attempted to kill themselves. For every completed suicide there are 8 to 20 suicide attempts. A suicide usually affects at least 6 other people, putting the number of people's lives touched by U.S. suicides, between 1970 and 1992, at about 3.5 million.[88] One of the more alarming social problems is the rise of youth suicide. Every nine minutes a teenager attempts suicide, and every 90 minutes a teenager succeeds. In any one week, 1000 teenagers will try suicide and 125 will succeed in killing themselves.

160

Since 1960, the suicide rate among American teenagers has jumped 200 to 300%.[89] Equally alarming is the increased suicide rate among the elderly. After declining for nearly four decades, the suicide rate among elderly Americans climbed nearly 9% between 1980 and 1992. The Centers for Disease Control reported that nearly 74,675 Americans age 65 or older killed themselves from 1980 through 1992--19% of all suicides for that period. In other words, Americans 65 and older make up about 13% of the nation's population but account for 20% of all suicides. Some preliminary figures for 1993 and 1994, show the rate rising even higher. Social isolation seems to be a major factor, with firearms the primary method.[90] In the general suicide population, the most common suicide method is firearms followed by poison, hanging, or strangulation.[91]

Some Reasons. Risk factors for suicide are as varied as those who commit suicide. Some themes appear again and again during psychological autopsies. A psychological autopsy is an investigative process performed by forensic mental health specialists. It is a tedious process by which the past is recreated and examined in an effort to determine what was going on in the mind of a person, so as to create the climate or milieu which led to their suicide. Some of these risk factors[92] include (1) family break-up and separation, (2) financial hardship, (3) dysfunctional family situations, (4) increasing social isolation and lack of peer relationships, (5) sex roles issues, (6) parental expectations for success and achieve-ment, (7) peer pressure, (8) media attention given to suicide and self-destructive themes in pop culture, (9) issues surrounding lack of personal control, self-esteem, and self-image, (10) emotional and other psychological issues, and (11) substance abuse.

Risk factors for the elderly include (1) loneliness and isolation, (2) chronic illnesses, (3) growing acceptance of suicide so as to not be a "burden" and die with "dignity," (4) depression and other mental illnesses, (5) lack of purpose, meaning, usefulness, and boredom, (6) multiple bereavements, (7) financial difficulties, and (8) substance abuse.[93]

Some Warning Signs. There appears to be a fairly reliable cluster of warning signs for those considering suicide.[94] This cluster includes the following signs:

1.	Getting Affairs in Order	- making amends, attempting to heal troubled relationships
2.	Giving Away Possessions	- especially treasured and loved possessions
3.	Verbal Cues	- saying good-bye, discussing suicide, wishing oneself dead
4.	Emotional Displays	- feelings of sadness, despondency, crying, "not caring anymore"
5.	Stamina Loss	- extreme fatigue, loss of energy, boredom, change of exercise routines
6.	Withdrawal	- pulling away from friends, less and less socializing, "stay-in" behavior
7.	Mood Swings	- quick to "snap" or yell, irritable, moody, apathetic, or energy bursts
8.	Concentration	- loss of concentration, easily distracted, memory problems, forgetting
9.	Work or School Problems	- absenteeism, poor grades, discipline, and daily declines in effort
10.	Personal Appearance	- unshaven, disheveled, poorly groomed, unclean, neglectful & uncaring
11.	Sleep Disturbance	- loss of sleep, excessive sleep, disruptive sleep, nightmares
12.	Appetite Change	- loss of appetite, eating more, "junk food" binges, substance abuse
13.	Physical Complaints	- stomachaches, backaches, headaches, and other ailments

Some Helpful Tips. Suicide is a scary subject. It is surrounded by mystery and myth. It can be a frightening ordeal to someone thinking about it, and a total devastation to the survivors. Remember the discussion of my friend Mark in the opening paragraph of this exercise? Why was it the week before he killed himself he seemed to have regained his old self? Now I know better. He had made the decision to commit suicide and was relieved by that decision. That upbeat energy burst in his remaining days was used to get his affairs in order and give prized possessions away. He also needed time to find a gun and plan his own death. In light of living a nightmarish life, death may seem preferable to one who is distraught and filled with despair. There is no simple and foolproof way to prevent someone from suicide. One expert[95] makes the point that "perhaps nobody really knows exactly what to do when dealing with an imminent suicide." However, there are some general rules and advice[96] that may prove helpful if you ever find yourself needed in such a dire situation. The following seven pointers may save a life someday. Take time to review them carefully. We, at times, are each other's keeper.

1.   Take suicidal talk seriously. It is not idle talk or a veiled threat. Ask them directly if they are considering suicide. A suicidal person is often glad to have someone to talk to. It may be the first time they have discussed suicide with anyone else. Such discussion may diffuse the desire to die.

2.   Provide empathy and social support. Be genuine and show concern. Try and link the suicidal person with professional help or other helpful networks. Know the resources in your community.

3.   Offer help. Suicide is a last-ditch cry for help. Don't walk away. Don't leave the person alone. Your help is better than no help at all. Simply being there and talking with them is very helpful.

4.   Identify and clarify the crucial problem. A suicidal person is often confused and in a sea of frustration and problems. Their thinking is cloudy. If problems can be identified and broken down they become more manageable and will seem less insurmountable.

5.   Suggest alternatives. The suicidal person often sees suicide as the only way out. Mediate options.

6.   Capitalize on any doubts. For most it is not easy to give up. The suicidal person is often racked by doubts in the wisdom of their decision to end their lives. Zero in on these doubts. They may be the best argument for life over death.

7.   Encourage professional help. Don't leave the person alone. Call for help or a suicide prevention
hot-   line. Make a difference. The time you spend may be enough to pull a suicidal person out of their peak desire to kill themselves, and get the help they need and deserve.

⇒ Debriefing

(1) Review your answers to the Suicide Knowledge Questionnaire. (See endnote 97 in the back of the workbook for correct answers.) Have you known anyone who committed suicide? (2) What were or might have been the reasons for the suicide? (3) What was your bereavement experience like? (4) What strategies might be used to help someone who is suicidal and has telephoned you? (5) With your instructor, design what components might be useful in a good community-based "suicide prevention program." (6) Locate and keep handy some suicide prevention materials from a community organization near you. Bring this material to class. (7) Role-play a situation involving someone considering suicide. How would you assist the person?

⇒ **Directions**

Read the following statements and choose true or false. Choose the answer for each statement which actually represents your belief. Do not leave any blanks. When you are finished, return to the section you were asked to return to at the beginning of this exercise.

T F 1. People who talk about suicide don't actually commit suicide or give a warning.

T F 2. All people who commit suicide have definitely decided they want to die.

T F 3. Improvement in a suicidal person means the danger has passed.

T F 4. Once a suicide risk, always a suicide risk.

T F 5. Suicide is an inherited trait in a person.

T F 6. Suicide occurs more often among people who are wealthy.

T F 7. Suicidal behavior occurs when the person becomes insane.

T F 8. Suicidal people are always depressed beforehand.

T F 9. The motive for a particular suicide is evident.

T F 10. Men attempt suicide more often than women.

T F 11. Women commit suicide more often than men.

T F 12. Poisoning, by either drugs or gas, is the most common form of suicide.

T F 13. Minorities have the highest suicide rates.

T F 14. The suicide rate for gay and lesbian youth is lower than for non-gay youth.

T F 15. After about 60 years of age, suicide rates begin to decline continuously.

T F 16. Suicide rates for college students reached an all-time peak in the 1960s and have declined somewhat since then.

T F 17. Suicide rates are higher for people who are terminally ill than for people who have chronic illnesses with no end in sight.

T F 18. There are 50,000 suicide attempts in the United States each year. Roughly one in eight of these attempts succeeds.

T F 19. Most people who commit suicide are under the age of 45.

T F 20. Though a serious problem, suicide is not among the top 10 leading causes of death in the United States.

Youth and Suicide

There are times in life when we
would like to die temporarily.

Mark Twain

⇒ **Overview**

Adolescence is a time of storm and stress. All of us remember, all too well I'm sure, the pain of adolescence. For some youth, that pain takes the form of suicidal ideation, a suicide attempt, or the act of suicide itself. For many young victims of suicide, the situation which brought on the desire to kill themselves was situational. As the situation eased so too would the desire to kill themselves. Their suicide became a permanent answer to a temporary set of problems. If only they had waited. If only they had sought help. If only they had asked us. "If" is an interesting word. What would you do if you now stood between a crying youth and death by his own hand--gun to his head? The clock is ticking. What to do?

⇒ **Directions and Debriefing**

For the following questions regarding youth and suicide, organize your thoughts so as to be able to participate in a meaningful and lively discussion of the issues which surround these questions. Jot down some of your ideas in the space following each question. Think of this exercise as an outline of your ideas for discussion later in class. Your instructor and readings will provide thorough background to assist you. Prepare thoughtful answers to the following. How might you better prepare for such a situation?

1. Youth have all sorts of emotional issues. The issues, I think, that are the most severe and important include:

_____

_____

_____

_____

2. Not all youth who commit suicide are depressed, but many are. What do you think are the main causes of depression among teenagers?

_____

_____

_____

_____

3. Many young people have suicidal ideation from time to time. It is a big step from thinking to doing, however. Have you known a young person who has committed suicide? What were your thoughts at hearing of their death? thoughts now on suicide?

_____

_____

4. What was the first death you personally experienced in your youth? Describe.

_____

_____

_____

_____

5. How might you counsel a class where a classmate has committed suicide? How might you counsel a family who has lost a young son to a self-inflicted gunshot and has died? How might you explain to a younger brother that an older sister committed suicide?

_____

_____

_____

_____

6. Describe the types of losses in a child's life from your perspective and experience.

_____

_____

_____

_____

7. If you had but one thing to say to a teenager considering suicide, what would it be? What would you say if you had five minutes with a young teenager who was holding a gun to his head and told you: "Tell me why I shouldn't pull this trigger and die now?"

_____

_____

_____

_____

8. Make note of tips and other resource information from this exercise. Develop a list of suicide hotlines and other related resources in your community.

_____

_____

_____

_____

_____

_____

_____

_____

Writing A Suicide Note

The thought of suicide is a great consolation:
with its help you can get through many a bad night.

Friedrich Nietzsche

⇒ **Overview**

If you wish to explore more about who you really are and who you really are close to, try this intense (therefore optional) training exercise on suicide. It's not for the weak of heart. Use caution and don't leave your note lying around, less someone think it is real. I suggest you restrict your writing to your workbook. It might best be an in-class exercise. <u>Be sure</u> to spend time debriefing with your instructor in class after completing this powerful exercise.

⇒ **Directions and Debriefing**

Write a suicide note. See which persons you would mention and what you would say in your note to them. Your instructor may wish to collect these notes and read some of them aloud. No identifying names should be mentioned. Those of you who have been involved in situations surrounding suicide may find it more appropriate to pass on this exercise unless you have worked through your issues. Restrict yourself to three pages.

(1) What emotions came to the surface while doing this exercise? (2) Did you come across some pathways of unhappiness? If so, how might you modify these paths in your life? (3) Which persons did you mention? (4) Did you find yourself appreciating life more or less as you wrote your note? (5) Did you experience any anxiety or fear? Were you scared to do this exercise? Why or why not? (6) Did losses in your life come to mind? Explain.

You, Alzheimer's, and the Dementia-Related Conditions

Alzheimer's Disease, a thief
who returned night after night to the same home,
slowly turned my grandfather into an abandoned house.

Ann Wiesner, age 17

⇒ **Overview**

I guess you could say Tony died some years before he actually died. In the town where I grew up in New York, Tony was everybody's favorite person. I felt particularly lucky because Tony was my neighbor who taught me how to play baseball as a kid. He actually gave me my first taste of wine and taught me how to play pool, but don't tell my mom! Old Tony grew the best tomatoes, never missed church, raised four children, and put most of them through college. He drove an 18-wheeler Peterbilt truck for 35 years. He said he was proud to be Italian, proud to be a Teamster union man, and proud to be an American. In our town, he was famous in the bowling league and volunteered for everything from the Lions Club to licking envelopes for the Democratic party. At first, it started out simply enough with just forgetfulness. We who knew Tony figured he was just getting somewhat senile; after all, he was close to age 70. But over the next couple of years things progressively worsened. Names escaped him and they never seemed to return. He would make a meal and sometimes forget to eat it. He soon, as more time slipped by, struggled to find the right word when talking. He'd forget where the car was parked and the police would have to bring him home. His dress habits became odd, sometimes he would wear two shirts instead of a shirt and coat for going outside in the winter. Tony began misplacing keys along with his memories, and soon, like a thief in the night, Tony was no longer Tony, but rather that person next door. His mood and behavior changed along with his personality; he seemed to lose all initiative. After awhile, no one knew who Tony was, least of all Tony. He became as vacant as a boarded up storefront. I remember his son, in tears, telling me one day that his dad was just a "dead man breathing." Though none of us knew it at the time, Tony had Alzheimer's Disease. Tony was robbed of life, and so were we who all loved him.

⇒ **Some Facts**

Dementia refers to a group of symptoms that characterize certain conditions and diseases. Dementia is defined as a decline in intellectual functioning that is severe enough to interfere with routine daily activities.[99] *Alzheimer's Disease* (AD) is the major dementia-related disease. AD is defined as a progressive, degenerative disease that attacks the brain and results in impaired memory, thinking, and behavior.[100] *Senile dementia* used to be the term for people over 65 with dementia. Today the medical profession no longer uses the term *senile dementia* as it does not recognize dementia as a normal part of aging, but rather a result of diseases such as Alzheimer's. In fact, dementia is *not* a disease in itself. There are several dementia related diseases and illnesses. These disorders include (1) Multi-infarct Dementia, or stroke and vascular-related disease, (2) Huntington's Disease, a hereditary disorder that begins in mid-life, (3) Parkinson's Disease, a chemical imbalance of dopamine in the brain, which leads to dementia later in its progression, (4) Pick's

167

Disease, a rare disease similar to AD, and (5) Creutzfeldt-Jakob disease, a rare and fatal viral disease. Other conditions can cause dementia-like symptoms. These include depression, drug reactions, thyroid disease, nutritional deficiencies, brain tumors, head injuries, alcoholism, infections (meningitis, syphilis, AIDS), and hydrocephalus. Today the most common forms of dementia are associated with Alzheimer's Disease (56%), strokes (14%), and a growing number of AIDS-related dementia cases. As pertains to AIDS, it is now clear that cognitive impairment affects between 55% and 65% of these cases.[101] Alzheimer's disease is not new, it was first diagnosed by German physician Alois Alzheimer in 1907. AD is more likely to occur as a person grows older. Approximately 10% of all people age 65 are affected. This percentage rises to 47.2% for those age 85 or older. AD can strike in the middle years as well--there are even documented cases as young as age 28. Over four million American adults are dealing with the progressive degenerative disease of AD, which is just one of several major dementia-related conditions.[102] The only 100% definitive diagnosis for AD, is to examine brain tissue during an autopsy. However, a thorough examination is 70-90% accurate in diagnosing AD. Dementia-related conditions strike equally men and women, all races, and all socioeconomic groups. From onset, the lifespan of a person with AD is from 3 to 20 years.

⇒ **Some Warning Signs**

The difficulty in diagnosing dementia lies in the fact that many of the signs and symptoms of dementia are found in all of us from time to time. Additionally, there are over 60 disorders which can produce dementia-like symptoms.[103] We all forget, we all get distracted, and we all get sidelined in our activities. We all forget a word or misplace things, and we all have swings in our moods on occasion. The key with dementia-related disease and illness is that these signs and symptoms are persistent and intensive and worsen over time. Some warning signs of dementia are listed below. Some or all of these signs and symptoms are found in all dementia cases. Which ones a person will get and at what intensity is not predictable at this time. Someone with several of these signs should be seen by a physician for a complete examination. The major dementia disease names are used below to help remind you of them. All dementia cases share the same signs and symptoms.

1. *Memory Loss.* We all forget things at times, and that's normal. Those in later-stage *Parkinson's Disease (PD)* related-dementia forget things more often and don't remember them later. A familiar name may not return to a person with this dementia condition.

2. *Task Difficulty.* We all get distracted in our everyday lives. But those with dementia related to *Huntington's Disease (HD)* don't seem to recover from their distractions. For example, such a person might prepare a sandwich and then forget to eat it.

3. *Language.* We're all at a loss for the right word at times. A person with *Multi-Infarct Dementia (MID)* forgets simple words and substitutes various words inappropriately. They "confabulate" by filling in sections of sentences with wording which appears to make sense, but in fact does not.

4. *Disorientation.* Everybody forgets the time or day of the week. We even forget where we are sometimes. Someone with dementia related to *Pick's Disease*, however, may not only forget where they are but get lost on their very own street.

168

5. *Judgment.* We don't always exercise good judgment in our lives, but someone with *AIDS-related Dementia* may forget where the car is, forget what's in the oven, or dress inappropriately. The key is they really never quite regain their judgment.

6. *Abstract Thinking.* For people with dementia, routine and familiar tasks become difficult tasks. Where they once were good at balancing a checkbook, the task now becomes a most disconcerting one. They fumble over math numbers and common everyday phone numbers.

7. *Misplacing.* Never a day goes by when we don't misplace something. Someone with *Alzheimer's Disease* (AD) is illogical in their misplacement. They might place milk in a closet or a watch in the refrigerator.

8. *Mood Changes.* Like the weather our moods can change at times. Events can bring about these changes in our life. That's normal. For someone with *Creutzfeldt-Jakob (CJD)* related dementia, their mood swings are rapid with no apparent reasoning. They can go from joy to tears to anger in just a few hours time.

9. *Personality Changes.* Over time subtle changes in a person's personality are often seen. But a person in *severe depression* may show dementia-related personality changes that are drastic and greatly exaggerated. This form of depression-related dementia can be reversed with treatment. It cannot with the other dementias.

10. *Initiative Loss.* We all get tired of the same old routines, whether they be housework, business activities, or obligations in general. But our initiative generally returns with time or after a respite. A person with dementia seems to constantly need cues and prompting to get involved and to embrace their world each day.

⇒ **Some Helpful Tips**

AD and dementia-related disorders are a growing concern in our society. As more of us age and live longer, it is doubtful any of us will escape contact with those suffering from the many disorders associated with dementia. The best way to understand and deal with someone with dementia is by educating yourself. The following are some broad-based tips concerning caregiving and communicating with someone who has dementia. The following are excellent resources for further reading. *Living with Dementia* by Fawn Moran. (San Francisco: Impact AIDS, Inc., 1992. Available from 3692-18th ST., San Francisco, CA 94110.) This material deals with AIDS-related Dementia. For AD and general dementia information, see *The 36-Hour Day: A Family Guide to Caring for Persons with Alzheimer's Disease and Related Dementing illnesses* by Nancy L. Mace and Peter V. Rabins, M.D. (Baltimore: Johns Hopkins University Press, 1991.) and *Understanding Alzheimer's Disease* by Miriam K. Aronson. (New York: Scribners, 1988.) Please note that how the following tips are used with a person with a dementia-related disorder will depend upon the intensity and progression of the disorder. Your initial contact should provide enough clues to gauge how to use these tips.

1. Respect. First and foremost, treat the person with dignity and respect. It is often easy to "talk down" to someone with dementia because of the use of simple words and sentences. They are adults, not children.

2. Communication. For those who will have only limited exposure to a person with dementia-related conditions, there are several tips which can make this experience less stressful or overwhelming. When communicating with the person, (a) be calm and supportive, (b) show interest in what is being said, (c) if you don't understand what is

being said, say so, and encourage them to use gestures, (d) offer the word or words if you think you understand what the person is saying but they are having difficulty finding the word or words themselves, (e) keep confusion, distraction, and noise to a minimum, (f) speak slowly and distinctly, (g) convey calm and smile, (h) approach the person from the front and allow them to determine the amount of space to be kept between you and them, (i) use short, simple, and familiar words and sentences, (j) repeat questions or information using the same phrasing and words used prior, (k) use non-verbal expressions such as a smile or hug.

3. <u>Special Needs.</u> Key areas of concern for those caring for someone with AD or an other dementia-related condition include (1) eating and swallowing, (2) nutrition and weight loss, (3) thirst and dehydration, (4) toileting and incontinence, (5) communication and (6) behavioral changes. These include suspicion, agitation, depression, and wandering. Each of these areas requires special knowledge and skills.

4. <u>Family Caregivers.</u> Often the "second victim" is the AD caregiver. It is important, therefore, for family members providing care to consider three components in providing for a person with AD or other dementia-related conditions. (a) First is "houseproofing," making the home safe for the person. What are the safety hazards from poisons, falls, fires, etc.? (b) The second component is providing a safe and healthy schedule of activities for the person. This would include personal care, meals, leisure-time, and exercise. (c) The third component involves exploring various forms of outside care. Such care might include respite, short-term, and long-term care. Other options include homecare, day care, short-term residential care, adult homes, nursing homes, and hospice programs. All of these option choices for a dementia patient will depend upon stage of disease and resources available to the person. Additionally, there are many legal remedies available for persons with dementia, such as advance directives, living trusts, guardianships, and conservatorships. These remedies are best used early during the onset of the condition.

5. <u>Information.</u> Contact the Alzheimer's Association for information, chapters, and resources near you. Don't try and "re-invent the wheel." Find and use support groups and resources available in your community. You can find out more about "tips" from the resources mentioned above or through brochures provided by the Alzheimer's Disease and Related Disorders Association, Inc. 919 North Michigan Avenue, Chicago, IL 60616.

⇒ **Debriefing**

(1) Complete the *Alzheimer's Disease and Dementia-Related Conditions Questionnaire* on the following page. (2) Review your answers individually, in group, or in class. (3) Have you known anyone with dementia? What were the circumstances of and experiences from being with this person? (4) How might you use the information you have learned from this exercise to help you when you are with someone who has dementia? (5) What kinds of resources are available in your community for these conditions? Contact the Alzheimer's Association and secure materials on dementia conditions and bring them to class. Role-play a situation involving someone with dementia. How could you help?

Alzheimer's Disease and Dementia-Related Conditions Questionnaire[104] [105]

⇒ **Directions**

The following statements are based on information you have read in the text of this exercise. Review the following statements and choose true or false. You will find a discussion of the correct responses in endnote 105 located in the back of the workbook.

_____ 1. There is a quick and easy diagnostic test for Alzheimer's Disease.

_____ 2. *Senile   Dementia* is part of the aging process.

_____ 3. Alzheimer's disease and other dementia-related disorders (AD) strike only the elderly.

_____ 4. *Dementia* is a class of diseases.

_____ 5. Infections such as the HIV virus can cause cognitive impairment and dementia.

_____ 6. Over half of all dementia cases are from strokes and vascular conditions.

_____ 7. The primary symptoms of dementia are impaired memory, thinking, and behavior.

_____ 8. Four million people are estimated to be infected with Alzheimer's Disease. Because the population is aging, it is estimated that by 2050, unless better treatments or a cure are found, over 14 million people will be infected with Alzheimer's Disease.

_____ 9. *Hardening of the Arteries* is another term for dementia.

_____ 10. Huntington's Disease (HD) is a hereditary disorder beginning in mid-life.

_____ 11. The cause of Alzheimer's Disease and other dementias is now known but there is no cure.

_____ 12. The Alzheimer's Association has more than 3,000 support groups and 220 chapters nationwide.

_____ 13. Common behavioral problems of dementia are suspicion, agitation, depression, and wandering.

_____ 14. Approximately 55-65% of all people with AIDS have some cognitive impairment.

_____ 15. Currently the only way to make a certain diagnosis of Alzheimer's Disease is by examining brain tissue during an autopsy.

_____ 16. Alzheimer's Disease is a recent discovery, having only been discovered in 1985.

_____ 17. Often the second victim in dementia cases is the caregiver--usually a spouse or other family member. One method of preventing a caregiver from becoming a victim is through the use of "support groups."

_____ 18. One of the great tragedies is the lack of legal options for AD and other dementia patients.

_____ 19. Dementia-related diseases and illnesses appear to strike some minorities more readily than other racial, ethnic, and socioeconomic groups.

_____ 20. The lifespan of someone with Alzheimer's Disease is approximately three years from onset to death.

Those who live in the future
have clearly passed by in haste,
the beauty of the present.

⇒ **Overview**

The purpose of this exercise is to take an objective "stand back" approach and examine death and dying customs and culture in our society. This exercise will also help to process several of the prior exercises found in this chapter.

⇒ **Directions and Debriefing**

Using role-play, complete the following exercise. This exercise may also be done individually. Imagine you are the captain of a time machine. Your research assignment is to travel to the middle of the next century. As a psychologist your assignment is to observe death and dying customs and practices observed by American society, a society which hopefully is still around in 2050. In group or individually, envision what your findings would be for the following questions. Be imaginative!

Once you have concluded your time-travel findings, discuss how this exercise reflects your beliefs and colors your values about life, the future, hope, and death and dying. In other words, provide a philosophical conclusion to your findings.

1. What is the situation regarding violence and war? What is the situation with capital punishment? Is suicide still a major concern with the young and some elderly?

_____

_____

2. What types of life-threatening diseases are prominent? What has become of AIDS and Alzheimer's Disease?

_____

_____

3. What are some of the new medical techniques, procedures, and equipment available?

_____

_____

4. What is the situation with genetic engineering?

_____

_____

5. What are some of the major ways people die? Where and how are the dying treated? How is pain managed?

_____

_____

6. How do people deal with grief, bereavement, and loss?

_____

_____

7. What has become of euthanasia? What is currently the situation with bioethics?

_____

_____

8. Has a new definition of death developed?

_____

_____

9. What is the situation with organ donations and organ harvesting?

_____

_____

10. What funeral practices prevail?

_____

_____

11. How are human remains disposed of?

_____

_____

12. What types of death rituals and customs are practiced?

_____

_____

13. What are the beliefs about afterlife and how do they vary from our here-and-now?

_____

_____

14. What whimsical observations did you note? What, for example, is in the newsmedia?

_____

_____

15. Did you want to return to the present or stay in the future?

_____

_____

_____

_____

6

Life and Loss:

Bereavement, Grief, Rituals, and Remembrance

I am standing on the seashore. A ship spreads her sails to the morning breeze and starts for the ocean. I stand watching until she fades on the horizon, and someone at my side says, "She is gone!"

Gone where? The loss of sight is in me, not in her. Just at the moment when someone says "She is gone," there are others who are watching her coming. Other voices take up the glad shout, "Here she comes!"

And that is dying.

Anonymous

Chapter 6

Life and Loss: Bereavement, Grief, Rituals, and Remembrance

I have a 19-pound black and white run-of-the-mill cat named Slyvester. He is big, so much so that he should have his own zip code. He looks like an oversized meatloaf. Late at night, when he struggles off my bed and down the stairs for his midnight snack, he could easily be mistaken for a drunken prowler. I'd be at a loss without Sly. He's an excellent conversationalist in that he tends to be so agreeable with most of what I say. He's quite topical, too, as long as the topic is TBF--tuna, beef, and fish. We Americans love our pets. Dogs, cats, birds, snakes, horses, hamsters, and even pigs abound in the American family no matter how defined. Big and furry to small and scaly, our society loves pets. In Paris it's even permissible to have your dog sit at your dinner table, if well-mannered. If Slyvester were to die tomorrow, I would not appreciate someone discounting him by advising me to simply go out and get another one. Would these same people suggest going out and getting another mother? I suspect not. But just how do you discuss the loss of a pet with a child or an elderly person? This chapter of exercises offers some insight into this question.

Do you know the difference between a eulogy and an obituary? How would you feel if tomorrow morning you picked up *The New York Times* and saw your own obituary listed among the death notices? How would you want your obituary to read? What would you want carved into your gravestone? How would you want to be immortalized?

"What a luxury," my grandmother said, when as a kid I'd complained of boredom. When she was a kid, she had no time to be bored; she was scraping a living seven days a week. How dead are you in life? What's the quality of your day-to-day life? This chapter explores life as well as death. You will find exercises for looking at pet loss, grief, defense mechanisms and simply getting in touch with yourself. You will have an opportunity to take a look at what the good death means to you as well. We will also examine how families interact after a family loss. Many exercises in this chapter are designed for recovery from loss. You will find exercises for rituals of remembrance, constructing your own sympathy card, and for learning how to write a condolence letter. There are numerous opportunities to learn about community resources for managing stress, loss, and grief as well. Finally, you will have the opportunity to examine mortality and immortality, and your very own moment of death. This is an action-packed chapter that goes from loss to remembrance.

Grief is just part of the story of bereavement, part of the process of returning to a full life for survivors of loss. For many who have struggled watching loved ones slowly waste away and die from AIDS, it is this *anticipatory grief* which is particularly painful. Anticipatory grief is grieving for a loss before it occurs.[106] The AIDS Memorial Quilt section will be a welcome tool to the arsenal of helpful strategies dealing with anticipatory grief and *complicated grief,* another term dealing with grief which doesn't seem to go away, even over time.[107]

Though this chapter is about saying good-bye and letting go of the sorrow of death and loss, it is much more. It is about not forgetting all that was good about those who have taken to "the high road," as my mother often said. It is about love, remembrance, and honoring and keeping tucked safely in our hearts all those we have liked and all those we have loved.

175

A Survival of Quality

*People are not afraid of death per se,
but of the incompleteness of their lives.*

Lisa Marburg Goodman

⇒ **Overview**

"Alive in years but dead in tears." My grandmother used to say that when, as a kid, I'd complain about being bored. Though alive, many of us are, in fact, dead in terms of the quality of lives we live. What about your quality of life? Are you more "dead than alive?" Fear of death can prevent us from maximizing each day. What might you be doing to better your life, improve your life, and simply enjoy each day of your life more? Think about this as you complete this exercise.

⇒ **Directions and Debriefing**

The following table[108] shows you how many more years you can expect to live according to government figures. These figures are based on your current age interval. (1) What are your thoughts and feelings regarding these data? Figures are just an expectation of years remaining in life. We have no data as to how healthy, happy, or how active and meaningful these remaining years will be. (2) Make a list of what you like and dislike about your life. (3) Develop a plan and timeline for change, if needed. Remember the clock is ticking, seize the moment! (4) What were your thoughts about your amount of time left?

Age Interval	Average Number Years Remaining at Beginning of Age Interval
5-10	71.6
10-15	66.6
15-20	61.7
20-25	56.9
25-30	52.2
30-35	47.5
35-40	42.9
40-45	38.3
45-50	33.8
50-55	29.3
55-60	25.1
60-65	21.1
65-70	17.5
70-75	14.2
75-80	11.2
80-85	8.5
85 and over	6.2

Comments: _____

_____

_____

_____

Price of Life

All the arts we practice are but apprenticeship.
The big art is our life.

M. C. Richards

⇒ **Overview**

What's a life worth? It is said, "At any price a life!" Do you agree? In our need to understand our world we sometimes impersonalize our world, and with it, our own very lives. We put a price on everything, sometimes pricing ourselves right out of the market, right out of our values, and right out of our lives. Read the following *New York Times* commentary by journalist William R. Greer[109] and discuss in group and class your thoughts. The purpose of this exercise is to help you assess how you value life--yours and others. What in fact is a life worth to you? At what price a life? That is your assignment. To prepare better for discussion, you may wish to first review the debriefing questions at the end of this exercise.

When a construction crane fell on Brigitte Gerney last month as she walked along Third Avenue, pinning her for six hours, the city leaped into action. Hundreds of police officers rerouted traffic throughout the Upper East Side. Two cranes were brought from other boroughs to lift the one that had fallen. Doctors from Bellevue Hospital set up a mobile hospital at the construction site. Emergency Services rescue workers risked their own lives to save hers. Once she was freed, the police halted traffic for 30 blocks along Franklin D. Roosevelt Drive to speed her trip to the emergency room.

No city official questioned how much the rescue effort cost the city, or whether saving Ms. Gerney's life was worth the price. To do so would have been unthinkable. "There's no point where you say that's too expensive," said Lieut. Thomas Fahey, speaking for the New York City Police Department.

And yet putting a price on human life is a common activity among life insurance companies, airlines, courts, industries, and agencies. The Federal Government routinely calculates the value of a life, having been required to do so by law: Executive Order 12291 issued by President Ronald Reagan in February of 1981. Ordinary citizens make much the same determination, albeit unconsciously, when they choose small cars over larger ones, take jobs hundreds of feet below the ground for higher pay, or buy inexpensive houses in a flood plain instead of more expensive ones in safer areas.

The fact that Americans put a price on human life, the processes for making such valuations, and the ways in which the results are used raise questions about our society: Is this necessary? What are the ethical and moral considerations? Given the answers, where does human life stand in this society's scheme of things?

People have been calculating worth of their lives and the lives of others for as long as archaeologists, anthropologists, and historians can document human existence. "It may be thought to be an aberration of our institutional values, but it's not at all unique in the course of humankind," said Kenneth Korey, an anthropologist at Dartmouth College.

"In tribal and band societies, for example, we find indemnification for the loss of a life that involves property transfers. How else can those groups set straight the fabric of the society when it is distressed by the disorder of a murder?" The Aztecs in the 15th century created an elaborate system of compensation for injuries and deaths; so did the Code of Hammurabi of ancient Babylonia. In both ancient and medieval law, a compensation, or sum of money, was paid by a guilty party to satisfy the family of the person he injured or killed. Indeed, in Old English the word "wergild," meaning "man's price," referred to the amount paid to the king, who had lost a subject; to the lord of the manor, who had lost a vassal; and to the family of the deceased.

But there is a fundamental difference, many social scientists say, between calculating the value of a life to compensate for its loss, a common practice throughout the centuries, and determining whether it is worth saving, a practice growing more common today.

"We cannot argue that in our society human life has gained in value or that we cherish life more than primitive people did," said Robert Zeitlin, an archaeologist at Brandeis University. "I think looking back at our society thousands of years from now, people will regard some of the things we do with absolute horror, the fact that we knowingly allow people to die from environmental hazards, for example."

Some philosophers say that the value of human life is infinite or incalculable. "Individual human beings are utterly irreplaceable," said Dr. Daniel Callahan, Director of the Hastings Center, a nonprofit research and educational organization devoted to ethical issues in medicine and biology. However, insurance agents, economists, legal experts, scientists and agency administrators are assigning life values ranging from a few dollars to many millions of dollars, depending on the formulas used.

One way of figuring value is to break down the body into chemical elements: 5 pounds of calcium, 1 and 1/2 pounds phosphorus, 9 ounces potassium, 6 ounces sulfur, 6 ounces sodium, a little more than 1 ounce of magnesium, and less than an ounce each of iron, copper, and iodine. Dr. Harry Monsen, an anatomy professor at the University of Illinois Medical School in Chicago, said that on that basis a human life today is worth $8.37, up $1.09 in six years because of inflation.

Another approach is to look at the going price of contract murder. Andreas Santiago Hernandez, 22, recently told the Los Angeles Police Department that he was paid $5,000 to kill Lorraine Keifer, the 67-year-old widow of a San Fernando Valley executive. Lt. Fahey says that in New York City a murder contract can cost nothing, if it is "for practice," or $10,000 and up.

The life-insurance industry also determines what people would have earned had they lived a full life. "What is the economic value of an individual?" said Robert Waldron, Director of the New York office of the American Council of Life Insurance. "It's their earning power over the course of their working life. It's unsentimental but it's fairly straightforward."

Lee S. Kreindler, a lawyer who, since 1952, has been representing the victims of airplane crashes and their families, says his formula is specified by law. But the law varies from state to state. In Georgia, for example, people are worth what they would have earned, while in New York they are worth what they would have contributed to their family. "A 35-year-old man killed in a crash, is unmarried but was making a great amount of money, " Mr. Kreindler said. "That's a small case in New York, but a huge case in Georgia.

The Federal Aviation Administration, when analyzing the costs and benefits of proposed regulations or revisions in old regulations, figures that a human life is worth $650,083, according to John Leden, a spokesman. The $83, he said, is for inflation. The Environmental Protection Agency chooses a number between $400,000 and $7 million-- the choice, agency officials say, is arbitrary-- with the average being "around $1 million or $2 million," according to John M. Campbell, the Deputy Assistance Administrator for Policy. The Occupational Safety and Health Administration uses a scale of $2 million to $5 million; again, the decision is arbitrary, agency administrators say.

The issue for Dr. Viscusi, an economist at Duke University who directed the Council on Wage and Price Stability in the Carter Administration, is not whether to perform such calculations, but how the answers are used. "The alternative," he said, "is to pull values out of the air and not make the public aware of what the trade-off is between money and risk on the job." He added: "We always have to get back to the fundamental trade-off between money and risk, because we don't have enough money to eliminate all risks."

⇒ **Debriefing**

Interesting article, isn't it? (1) So, in your eyes, what price is a life worth? (2) What are your thoughts about Greer's breakdown of what a human being is worth in terms of chemicals? (3) Do you agree with the rationale discussed by some of the government experts that value must be placed on all things or they lose value or have no value at all? (4) Can you envision situations where a person might be worth more dead than alive? Explain and discuss. (5) Should a society be responsible for the cost and care of all of its citizens? (6) If so, how are scarce resources to be distributed and rationed? (7) What are some biomedical and other ethical considerations which arise from reading Greer's article? (8) What were some of your thoughts about the cost of murder? (9) What are some of your feelings about the so-called out-of-control and spiraling costs of lawsuits and malpractice suits? (10) In a couple of sentences define what the value of a human life should mean.

The value of human life should mean _____

_____

_____

_____

Source: Greer, W. R. (1985, June 26). Value of one life? from $8.37 to $10 million. *New York Times*, p. 1.

Calendar of Death Events

They are never gone unless you forget them.

74-year-old Widow

⇒ **Overview**

Bereavement is a universal experience. There is no society, past or present, which is spared the agony of loss for the people they love and care for. Anniversaries, seasons, locations, and events can all rekindle grief to a point where it is reminiscent of the intensity the grief first had at the time of the actual loss. Grief can pay untimely and often unwanted visits again and again long after a loss has occurred. Like clockwork, a mother visits the grave of her young son years later and, like clockwork, she cries.

Culture flavors how one expresses grief and, over time, mourning styles can even change as well. I look back at how my New York Italian family expressed grief. When my father died, the elderly women wore black on black on black, their daughters wore less harsh dark clothing, and the grandchildren wore clothing with hopeful colors in them. I have watched many cultures grieve and mourn. I remember my Jewish neighborhood. I have watched the Chinese and Southeast Asian refugees of San Francisco mourn and express grief. The singing voices from the African-American funerals I attended are still vivid in my mind. Events in time and space and place and kind can all bring a return of grief.

A loss is lifelong. Sometimes the emotional charge is too. Most people pick up and move on with their lives, though they pause long enough and often enough to look over their shoulder to note an image, catch a scent, feel a pinch of heartache, a tear, a sudden whisper of emptiness, and then get on with their lives.

⇒ **Directions**

On the following page is a calendar of months. For each month write in the following: (1) List the various religious and national holidays which are associated with death (i. e., Christmas, Memorial Day). (2) List death-related historical events (i. e., Kennedy's assassination, the Oklahoma City federal building bombing). (3) List your special, private, and important days that remind you of death or of someone who has died who you were close to (i. e., anniversaries, birthdays). (4) Sketch in some of the various "symbols" that are used to denote death or dying (I. e., skull and crossbones). These may be commonly found symbols or your own personal symbols.

⇒ **Debriefing**

(1) Why do you think our society acknowledges death-related events and holidays? (2) Were you surprised by the number of death-related historical events and holidays? (3) Which historical events and holidays personally affect you? (4) Why is one season and not another harder on some people who are experiencing grief? (5) How might you counsel someone who is worried about their ability to manage their grief during the upcoming Christmas or Hanukkah holidays? How would you suggest they grieve, remember, and celebrate a memory during such a trying time of the year? (6) What are some of your other thoughts about this exercise?

January	February	March	April
May	**June**	**July**	**August**
September	**October**	**November**	**December**

Interactions After a Family Loss

All that live must die,
Passing through nature to eternity.

William Shakespeare

Overview

Sometimes, though not always, life has lessons. Death is one of them. How we go forward with our lives after a great loss can sometimes indicate what lessons we have learned. One of the great stressors in our lives is the loss of a loved family member. Such a profound loss provides us opportunity to examine our priorities, our values, and develop creative approaches to living our remaining lives fully. The word grief comes from the Latin and French word *gravare* which means "to burden." The word bereavement is Old English for *bereafian* or to "to rob away." How each deals with loss, with grief, and with bereavement is in many ways a personal art form. Those of us who have experienced loss also know many of the signs of loss. Loss leaves amidst the ruins of our heart and soul shock, denial, questions, anger, guilt, shame, depression, and hopefully, resolution as well.

Family members can help each other through the rough road of loss. Five pointers come to mind. (1) Openly communicate about the deceased and develop strategies and solutions for dealing with the loss. For example, if your mother has just lost her husband, develop strategies among family members for helping to fill and provide continued meaning in your mother's life. (2) Embrace each day through use of memories or rituals such as taking a walk, lighting a candle, or composing a poem about the deceased. (3) Develop a balance between solitude and sociability. Though solitude may rejuvenate us, so can social outings with friends provide us with support. (4) Maintain pleasant memories and actively recall them. Keeping a memories journal or diary is a helpful tool. When special holidays or anniversaries arrive, give yourself permission to be joyful (or be sad and shed a tear if need be) in your actions and your thoughts. (5) Listen to those who offer you assistance. Whether it be family, friends, or colleagues listen to them and accept their offers. The true test of an individual is their ability to not only help others in need but to accept from others when they themselves are in need.

⇒ Directions and Debriefing

In group develop strategies and solutions for dealing with loss for each of the following. First, develop some common and predictable consequences for each loss. For example, the loss of one's wife interrupts dinner outings and trips together. Secondly, strategize a workable solution for each of the consequences you develop. For the above example, children might develop a rotating schedule of spending dinner with their father or inviting him to their homes. A special outing might be planned for holidays or special anniversaries. How might this exercise help you cope in the future? (1) Review your findings from this exercise in group and class. (2) What was helpful? What was not? (3) What lessons for lessening a survivor's pain of loss have you learned from this exercise?

1. Husband, 67, dies of sudden heart attack

2. Gay brother, 33, dies of AIDS

3. Brother, 25, killed in auto accident

4. Sister's child, 8, dies of leukemia

Survivors Left Behind

To fear love is to fear life,
and those who fear life
are already three parts dead.

Bertrand Russell

⇒ **Overview**

Dealing with the death of someone you love makes you a survivor. To better understand the experience of loss and its dynamics, you are asked to discuss a personal loss in your own life. Review your textbook materials on grief and loss processes.

⇒ **Directions and Debriefing**

Choose a loss from your own life. This loss should be of someone you knew well and loved. In group share your responses to the following questions. If you have had no losses in your life, interview someone who has. Stay aware of the dynamics.

1. What circumstances led up to this death? Tell us about the actual event itself.

_____

_____

2. What other losses accompanied this bereavement experience?

_____

_____

3. How did you cope? Whom and what did you turn to for help? What strategies did you find helpful in dealing with your loss?

_____

_____

4. Describe the moment you knew your life had changed significantly?

_____

_____

5. What are your feelings about this loss today?

_____

_____

6. How long did it take for you to accommodate the pain and the loss? What did you do to get beyond merely surviving this loss? Explain.

_____

_____

_____

Loss of a Pet

He was the love I never had,
the wife I never married,
and the son I wished for, all in one.

An elderly man's comment on
the death of his dog of 22 years

⇒ **Overview**

Americans love pets! There are around 117 million dogs and cats chomping at the heels of mail carriers and quietly living out their nine lives in the United States.[110] Pets must be important to us, because nearly half of all families in America have one and many of us consider them family.[111] Science is beginning to check in with research that most pet owners could tell you: Having a pet softens life's rough edges and enhances life's richness.[112] Pets have been useful in reducing blood pressure,[113] with depression in medical patients,[114] with institutionalized mentally ill patients,[115] with the elderly who are isolated at home alone or in nursing homes, and after spousal bereavement.[116] Pet therapy with children is well-known.[117] Pets provide comfort, reduce loneliness, and lessen stress. They are a nurturing force during life and death, loss and grief, and in times of success and stress.[118] In short, pets are important in the lives of people. The death of a pet is often a child's first loss. How the matter is handled by parents and other family members shapes a child's attitude about death and dying later in life. In one study of college students, 28% reported their first experience with death as that of a pet.[119]

For adults, a pet is often the only source of companionship, particularly among the elderly. While sympathy is often provided when a loss is a person, sympathy for loss of a pet may vary from strong support and sympathy to outright laughter. The death of a pet may be particularly painful for adults because such losses may bring back memories of resolved and unresolved earlier losses in their lives.[120] Pets provide unconditional support and their loss should not be minimized. The fact that many take their pets seriously can be found in the fact that over 500 pet cemeteries exist in the United States.[121] One of the oldest pet cemeteries is at the United States Army Presidio in San Francisco, the resting place for many a cavalry horse and guard dog. One of the more difficult decisions facing pet owners is whether to euthanize, to "put to sleep," a pet who is aged or ill and beyond practical treatment. This painful decision often alienates owners and clouds some of the issues of euthanasia. There is no joy in invoking the power of life and death over another living being.

⇒ **Directions and Debriefing**

For this exercise develop counseling strategies for loss of a well-loved and "been-around-for-a-long-time" pet for both children and adults. Consider the following questions for discussion in class. (1) How would you feel if your pet died? (2) What might be effective in assisting you through your grief and loss in such a situation? (3) Prepare a list of issues to be addressed with children and adults concerning grief, loss, and bereavement of a recently deceased pet. (4) Were you surprised by how much or how little you had to offer in these situations? (5) Do you now feel better prepared? What else might you do to better prepare yourself for such counseling situations?

1. How might you help a 7-year-old boy whose cat Sylvester was killed by a car?

2. How might you help with an elderly man's loss of his dog Buster of 17 years?

3. How would you discuss euthanasia to a 12-year-old girl whose pet is terminally ill?

4. How might you deal with a 14-year-old boy's request for a proper burial for his pet dog Smoky who died of old age?

5. How might you show your support, sympathy, and compassion to a friend who just lost a long-loved pet?

Notes: _____

_____

_____

_____

_____

_____

_____

_____

_____

_____

_____

_____

_____

_____

_____

_____

_____

6. As a library project, research a listing of good book and article titles concerning pet loss. List this information below. Include at least one storybook format for children.

_____

_____

_____

_____

_____

_____

Unresolved Grief

They live ill who expect to live always.

Publilius Syrus

⇒ **Overview**

The funeral is over, the memorial has past, but your grief and mourning remain. Resolving grief and securing closure are important if we are to move on with our lives. Sometimes there is no funeral, or it was far away and you either missed it or were not able to attend. Maybe you just didn't receive the closure you needed, or were unable to express your sorrow and loss. Maybe an unresolved loss from years ago still haunts you.

⇒ **Directions and Debriefing**

The purpose of this exercise is (1) to assist you in dealing with loss, (2) to help you continue your process of grief work, (3) to develop a ritual you can personalize for yourself when loss occurs in your life, and (4) to empower you to live life more fully even while grief is a part of your life. In this exercise you focus and meditate on a small votive burning candle. In a secure and private setting, such as your home, sit and relax while watching the candle burn. (You may need to use some relaxation techniques.) During this time focus on your particular loss which is unresolved. Stare into the candle, breathing slowly, and peacefully address the following statements. Feel free to add your own as well. If you have experienced a recent loss, you may not be ready yet to release this person or persons. (1) Describe this exercise for you and discuss its merits in group or class. (2) How helpful was it for you? How might you improve it? (3) What types of rituals do grieving people use? (4) What other rituals might be helpful? List some.

1. Think about your personal loss, reviewing the history that you shared.

2. What are your immediate feelings regarding this person?

3. Think about what you liked and disliked about the deceased.

4. What will you miss in the person, now that they are gone?

5. If you harmed the person in any way, ask for forgiveness, forgive yourself and release the feelings. Vow to correct the wrong if possible, or "make good" in other ways.

6. What would you like to say to this person? Formulate your words and say them either privately or aloud to this person, now gone.

7. What feelings or thoughts of loneliness, guilt, anger, or other emotions do you have about the dead?

8. How might you carry on any good the person did in their lives?

9. How might you become a happier person from your experiences with the deceased?

10. <u>Process</u>: As the candle begins to flicker and burn out, release the one you loved to "the ages," or to your god as you define god. Keep with you the love and positive memories and return to your moment, to your present world, poised to live a fuller, healthier, kinder, gentler, and wiser life.

Grief and Defense Mechanisms

"Life was meant to be lived,
and curiosity must be kept alive.
One must never, for whatever reason,
turn their back on life."

Eleanor Roosevelt

⇒ **Overview**

Like a cold chilly winter wind, grief is something most of us would prefer to flee from. But if we're ever to see the spring, we must mourn and do our grief work. William Worden, in his book *Grief Counseling and Grief Therapy*, [122] nicely concluded the findings of a federally funded bereavement study called the Omega Project. Mourning is necessary for anyone experiencing a loss and grief, said Worden. The successful resolution of grief is not something which occurs automatically. Moving through grief and back into the functioning real world is important. *Grief work* takes time, energy, and hard work. If grief is not resolved, future growth and development may be impaired. A person may move through their remaining life an emotional cripple. Worden described four tasks of mourning that each grieving person must accomplish. They are (1) accepting the reality of the loss, (2) experiencing the pain of grief, (3) adjusting to an environment in which the deceased is missing, and (4) withdrawing emotional energy and reinvesting in another relationship. These tasks can be hindered and manipulated by our psyche.

Grief is very much a psychological process. It often incorporates a great many defense mechanisms. These defenses, though often appropriate, may stand in the way of moving through the *grief work*. Review the following examples of grief defense mechanisms and see if you can come up with other examples used by survivors in minimizing and blocking their grief. If you have an understanding of how grief is interfered with by our defense mechanisms, you will better be able to help yourself and others deal with grief in your every day life. Review the following defense mechanisms, examining how each relates to grief. How many have you seen in others who have experienced losses?

⇒ **Directions and Debriefing**

For each defense mechanism, you will be given a clinical definition[123] followed by a grief-related example.[124] In the fill-in space provided beneath each example, brainstorm another example. Prepare to discuss your examples and thoughts in group, class, or in your Active Journal. (1) Consider which defenses you have used or might be prone to use in situations of personal loss, mourning, and grief. (2) Which defenses have you seen used by those you know and love? (3) Can you think of any classical defense mechanisms used in such situations on television or in the movies? (4) How does one pull oneself away from being manipulated by defense mechanisms? (5) How might some of the tasks of grieving be hindered by those around us? (6) Are there times when defense mechanisms are healthy and useful? If so, when? Explain. Take time in completing this exercise, taking close note of how you might respond.

Brutalization. Physically or verbally forcing yourself on others with complete disregard for their feelings or needs. An example might be your becoming overly critical of your

187

son's friends or becoming overprotective of your granddaughter. Another example?

_____

_____

Conversion. Physical symbolization of certain behaviors and illnesses. The widower who believes that he has the same form of cancer disease that killed his wife. Your example?

_____

_____

Denial. Upsetting or threatening thoughts and emotions related to stressful events are not allowed into conscious awareness. An example might be denying the death by going out soon after your partner's death and buying a major new appliance even though your financial situation has greatly changed negatively since this death. Your example?

_____

_____

Displacement. When it's unsafe or inappropriate to express aggressive or sexual feelings toward the person who is creating stress for you, that feeling can be directed toward someone safe. Expecting another person or object to behave like the deceased. An example might be a widow who expects her son to change careers and take over his deceased father's business. Another example?

_____

_____

Identification. Adopting values and behaviors of other people. A sad example is the widow who chooses not to remarry, even though she has suitors, because her widowed parent chose not to remarry. Another example?

_____

_____

Insulation. Withdrawing physically or refusing to talk about certain things. For example you avoid any of your married friends because they remind you of your lost husband. You can't accept the pain, so you avoid such painful situations. Your example?

_____

_____

Introjection. Following the advice or expectations of another person, even though it is not what is really wanted. A common example is the widow who moves from her beloved home, where she lived with her deceased husband, into her son's or daughter's home. The widow allows herself to be manipulated and become a victim. Example?

Isolation. Blocking out possible new associations and experiences. An example might be the widower who refuses to go out and play his regular game of golf or interact with anyone anymore since his wife died. Your example?

Projection. One's own dangerous or unacceptable desires or emotions are seen not as one's own, but as the desires or feelings of others. "Projecting" feelings on to others that you really hold. An example might be a widow who is envious of her friends who still have their husbands. She believes and accuses these women of being glad for her widowhood. Your example?

Rationalization. Stress is reduced by "explaining it away" in ways that sound logical and socially acceptable. Justifying certain behaviors for which there is no real justification. An example might be buying a new car and calling it an economically sound purchase even when it is not, in light of the recentness of the death and one's limited finances.

Reaction-Formation. Conflicts over dangerous motives or feelings are avoided by unconsciously transforming them into the opposite desire. Replacing an original behavior with an opposite one. An example might be the person who was religious before a spouse's death, but ceases going to church altogether after their death. Example?

Regression. Stress may be reduced by returning to an infantile pattern of behavior. Behaving in ways that were more appropriate earlier in life. An example is someone who, after a death of a loved one, becomes dependent upon their parents or children for making important decisions in their life. They become immobilized. Your example?

Repression. Potentially stressful, unacceptable desires are kept out of consciousness without the person being consciously aware that the repression is occurring. An example would be the inability to express any negative feelings about the deceased even though the relationship had been a stormy one at times. Your example?

_____

_____

Self-Brutalization. Engaging in self-destructive behavior. For example you begin gaining a lot of weight, drinking too much alcohol, and spending too freely--all contrary to the real you. Another example?

_____

_____

Somatization. Developing physical symptoms that are really psychosomatic in origin and are related to the loss. Examples include headaches, stomach problems, high-blood pressure, etc. Another example?

_____

_____

Sublimation. Stressful conflicts over dangerous feelings or motives are reduced by converting the impulses into socially approved activities. An example might be ending involvement in unhealthy and addictive relationships that reduce the anxiety of being alone and choosing instead to return to school or seek employment. Your example?

_____

_____

Undoing. Overperforming in one area to extinguish other expectations. An example might be you having your house redone even though you had just announced plans to move after the death of your husband. Another example?

_____

_____

Victimization. Submitting to what another person wants, regardless of its personal effect on you. An example might be selling your house to relatives even though the sale benefits only relatives and you don't really want to move from the home you love and lived in with your deceased partner. Your example?

_____

_____

_____

_____

Sympathy Cards

Ice in a hot world:
my life
melts.

Nakamichi

⇒ **Overview**

Society has a way of mirroring how we perceive events and circumstances through the products it sells. For example, if we want to understand society's views, beliefs, attitudes, and values on death, look to the sympathy card market. Though they come in thousands of different formats, most sympathy cards present similar themes of how we view death in our society. An interesting technique for discovering our own "hidden" view of death is through examination of the types of sympathy cards we would buy ourselves. We can learn much about our own beliefs and our own cultures by what we find acceptable in the purchase of a sympathy card.

⇒ **Directions and Debriefing**

Bring in two sympathy cards. (You'll have to spend a little money, but you'll have them for later use.) One card should be a sympathy card you like, would choose, and would buy. The other card should be very different from any card you would choose and buy. Also, while shopping, search carefully and see if you can find <u>any</u> sympathy cards which use the words dead or death in them. Why do you suppose there are so few, if any? Be prepared to discuss your cards in group and as a class. Carefully consider the following questions. As a follow-up, complete the exercise entitled "Developing a Sympathy Card" which follows this exercise.

1. What most impressed you about your cards?

2. What was different about your cards?

3. What thoughts came to mind when you were reading them?

4. Did you react negatively to some of the cards? If so, to what and why?

5. What do sympathy cards tell you about death and dying in American culture?

6. What euphemisms for death were used?

7. Did you notice sympathy cards for particular age groups or other groups?

8. What concept of death is presented? Is the designer most concerned with emotional, biological, social, spiritual, or philosophical understandings of death?

9. Were you able to find a card which used the word dead in it?

10. Do you send sympathy cards? What might one do in place of sending such a card?

11. What are some negative aspects of sending sympathy cards?

12. What appear to be some of the "universal ingredients" in a sympathy card? List and describe them.

Developing a Sympathy Card

*Death is a liberation
into a freer life. Peace Pilgrim!*

1995 sympathy card

⇒ **Overview**

If one wishes to discover the fear American society holds for death, one need but only look at a selection of sympathy cards. Rarely will you find a sympathy card which uses the "D" word--dead or death. For nearly five years, I offered my students an automatic A on their first exams if they could find and bring in a mainstream American sympathy card which used the word "dead" or "death" in it. For five years no takers. It was not until 1994, that one student found a card which used the word dead but even then it did so in a dismissive fashion. The inside of the card began: "...they are not dead they have only moved on..." As you can see, the word "dead" is used but then discounted in favor of the euphemism "moved on."   From a sociological perspective, if one wants to understand the prevailing values and fears in American society, look to Madison Avenue, to the advertising and marketing world. Advertisers and marketing experts will rarely violate the sensibilities of our needs and fears. The Hallmark Card Company is no fool. Its advertising and marketing staff know Americans are uncomfortable with death and dying and they just will not buy cards which use the "D" word. So they don't make any, at least not until recently.

⇒ **Directions and Debriefing**

In this individual or group exercise create your own sympathy card. The card should: (1) address death and dying candidly, (2) examine some aspect of death from a biological, societal, philosophical or spiritual perspective, and (3) address a particular kind of death, age, and group. For example, you might create a sympathy card which is specifically for parents who have just had a son die of AIDS, or for a child who has recently had a father or mother die of cancer.

Use the space on the next page to construct your "new age" sympathy card. (1) Prepare to show and discuss your creation in class as directed. (2) How tough was coming up with an appropriate quote, saying, or poem? (3) Do you feel there is a need for sympathy cards which use the words "death" and "dying" in them? (4) Would you actually use such cards if they were available? (5) What kinds of sympathy cards do you personally like? (6) How might the advertisers on Madison Avenue work with the public to develop more appropriate sympathy cards? (7) Assuming you had the card you designed professionally printed, would you send it? Who would you feel comfortable sending it to? Who would you not send it to?

Develop Your Sympathy Card Here

Text

Cover

Book of Remembrance for Multiple Losses

Time is the great physician.

Benjamin Disraeli

⇒ **Overview**

The loss of human life is always a tragedy whose timing is always poor. But multiple losses can heighten the devastation in grief and bereavement issues even further. Multiple loss, generally speaking, is the loss of one or more persons close to the bereft while they are still working through the grieving process from a previous loss. Such losses are often within two years or less. Multiple losses occur as the result of disaster, war, and accidents. Other such situations include murder, the AIDS epidemic, and loss associated with being a professional or volunteer caregiver. Multiple losses may lead to psychological conditions, such as Post Traumatic Stress Disorder (PTSD) and deepened forms of depression. Learning to manage multiple loss issues requires proven additional strategies.

⇒ **Directions and Debriefing**

This activity,[125] though useful for any loss, is particularly designed for those persons with multiple loss and bereavement issues. They include (1) multiple losses within a short time frame, (2) professional and volunteer caregivers who work with death and dying, and (3) AIDS epidemic survivors, especially those in the gay community who have lost partners and many friends.

The purpose of a "Book of Remembrance" is surprisingly simple, psychologically soothing, and therapeutic. The remembrance book provides a centralized place to channel one's love, remembrance, respect, memories, and ritual for those loved but now deceased. This sense of closure is very useful and valuable. The book also allows for renewing your remembrance for those loved and now gone. The book will provide an act of love all of your life. Discuss the following: (1) Share your ideas and approaches to using this strategy in group and class. (2) What other variations might work? (3) What types of remembrance ideas did you develop?

1. Choose and develop a suitable workbook, journal, or scrapbook for placement of pictures, written memories, poems, sketches, and other memorabilia concerning the deceased.

2. Develop an appropriate but "tailored for you" ritual for remembering and honoring those special people now gone in your life. Whether you use a votive candle or a special prayer, develop your own special sense of closure ritual.

3. Use the memory book to record happy and joyful memories, special incidents, and other special reflections.

4. Each time a new loss occurs, add to your remembrance book and recite your prayer or allow for some time of reflection. Light a candle or burn incense. Do this for all those in your remembrance book. Date and sign your name after each occasion of remembrance. The key is to encapsulate the deceased person's relationship to you.

5. How you use and develop your memory book is entirely up to you. For example, there is a hospital ward in San Francisco which deals exclusively with AIDS patients. Each time a patient dies, staff members enter personalized entries in their special ward remembrance books.

Obituary

I never wanted to see anybody die,
but there are a few obituary notices
I have read with pleasure.

Clarence Darrow

⇒ **Overview**

How would you feel if tomorrow morning you picked up *The New York Times* and saw your own obituary listed among the death notices? How would you want your obituary to read? Whereas a eulogy is a statement of praise, a laudable series of comments, or a message of praise by someone honoring someone at a memorial or funeral, obituaries are quick, concise bullets which notify and highlight a person's death. Obituaries generally appear in newspapers or other media as a means of notification of someone's death to the community.

This exercise will allow you to examine your mortality as well as provide perspective for looking upon your life at present. The chance to look back on your life is invaluable for new growth and appreciation of what you have achieved and overcome so far. When you construct the story of your life you cannot fail to examine the self--from the past, present, and future perspectives. If you find incongruities in your life as a result of this exercise, you might benefit from examining them more closely. Use the Active Journal section in the back of your workbook for this purpose.

⇒ **Directions and Debriefing**

In this exercise you are asked to write your own obituary. But it's too easy to write your obituary as though you might die tomorrow. So write your obituary from the vantage point of your wishes, hopes, dreams, and accomplishments. In other words, write your obituary as the *fully actualized self* you want to be and are becoming. This task requires patience, honesty, fantasy, hope, and promise.

What's particularly tough about writing obituaries is that they must be brief; generally, no more than a couple of paragraphs. But let's pretend you're well-known. People want to know about your death. You can have a full typed page which is about two columns in a average newspaper. The obit editor is being generous with you so make the most of it. Now the task is to get a lifetime into two columns. Good luck. Think reflectively!

In group or during class discussion read some obituaries aloud. Questions to discuss include (1) How did it feel to do this exercise? (2) Did you make any discoveries about yourself? (3) Did you find any incongruities in your life which need further examination? (4) How does it feel to write and read your own obituary or have it read to the class? (5) Are you happy with your life to date? If not, why not? (6) What might you do differently? Discuss strategies for making changes in your life if they are needed.

_____

_____

_____

195

Eulogy

We cannot, after all, judge a biography
by the number of pages in it;
we must judge by the richness of the contents.
Sometimes the 'unfinished' are among the most beautiful symphonies.

Victor Frankel

⇒ **Overview**

What would you want said at your own death, at your own funeral? How would you want to be eulogized? A *eulogy* is a statement of praise, a laudable series of comments, a message of praise honoring, generally speaking, some greatness--no matter how humble--in another person. Eulogies are most common at funerals. A eulogy is different from an obituary. An *obituary* is a death notification which appears in a newspaper or other media as a notification of someone's death to the community. This exercise will give you an opportunity to begin assessing what it is you want to do with the rest of your life. It will also allow you to reflect upon what you have done in your life that pleases you. This exercise is a powerful opportunity to review your life today and make changes accordingly.

⇒ **Directions and Debriefing**

Write your own eulogy. It's too easy to write your eulogy as though you might die tomorrow. Write your eulogy from the vantage point of your wishes, hopes, dreams, and accomplishments. In other words, write your eulogy as the *fully actualized self* you want to be and are becoming. This task requires patience, honesty, fantasy, hope, and promise.

This exercise will allow you to examine your mortality as well as to look upon your life to date. The chance to look back on your life is invaluable for new growth and appreciation of what you have achieved and overcome so far. When you construct the story of your life you cannot fail to examine the self--from past, present, and future. If you find incongruities in your life as a result of this exercise, you might benefit from examining them more closely. Use of a creative journal might prove most helpful.

During class discussion, without mentioning names, read some eulogies aloud. Consider the following questions: (1) How did it feel to do this exercise? (2) Did you make any discoveries about yourself? (3) Did you find any incongruities in your life which need further examination? (4) How does it feel to read your own eulogy or have it read to the class? (5) What have you done in your life that you are proud of? not so proud of? (6) How might you enrich your life and live more fully? Attach more pages as needed in the workbook. (7) As a possible follow-up exercise, write another obituary at the end of your course. Compare and contrast how your values and other contents might have changed.

⇒ Notes: _____

_____

_____

_____

Gravestone Pictures

There's an old saying which says: "May he rest in peace!"
My question is, what did he do in life to deserve such rest and peace?

⇒ **Overview**

This cemetery activity will help you understand the importance of ritual and remembrance in death. The wide range of variation in recognizing those no longer alive is in itself tribute and evidence that diversity makes the human species significant and interesting. Cemeteries are of great social interest from which we can better understand ourselves and our fears. Many of these fears are simply that--fears--and thus groundless.

⇒ **Directions and Debriefing**

For this activity you will need to visit a cemetery. Bring a camera and some writing material. Take photographs and write down the prose from headstones you find especially interesting. I'm sure there are some very interesting tombstones in the cemeteries in and around your community. (1) Bring your photographs and prose back to the next class for display on the blackboard and walls. Discuss the pictures as a group. (2) While doing this exercise, keep in mind what the deceased was remembered for. How do you know? What image or belief of death is presented?

A note about gravestone rubbings. I used have my classes do gravestone rubbings, but many old headstones are not sturdy and stable enough to tolerate a rubbing. History is being destroyed by untrained, careless gravestone rubbers. It is also very difficult to remove crayon and pencil markings off headstones that are not properly covered. Even among those who are skilled, often the rubbings don't come out well. So I've modified this exercise to photographs rather than rubbings. Please keep this precaution in mind.[126]

⇒ **Debriefing**

1. What kind of tombstone do you want for yourself?

2. How would you like your inscription to read? Write one!

3. Write an obituary about your death.

4. What about the surroundings in the cemetery? Did you like them? Did you find them peaceful?

5. Was there anything about the surroundings that were disconcerting, fearful, or anxiety-producing?

6. What were your thoughts as you walked throughout the cemetery?

7. Many cemeteries have crypts, mausoleums, rose gardens for cremains (cremated remains), or other large settings for the repose of remains. Which do you want for your remains?

8. Do you want to be buried, cremated, and/or placed in an above-ground mausoleum? What are your thoughts about cryonics?

_____

_____

_____

Tombstone Epitaph

And when he goes to heaven
To Saint Peter he will tell:
Another Marine reporting, sir;
I've served my time in hell!

Epitaph on grave of Pfc. Cameron
Marines Corps, Guadalcanal (1942)

⇒ **Overview**

The purpose of this exercise is to get you thinking about what your life is worth to you now, today. There is no better way of evaluating your life to this point in time than by having to summarize your life in just a few words, such as on a tombstone. This exercise is meant to have you evaluate not what you hope to be but where you are as a person <u>right</u> now. The hope is that from such reflection, such candor, you will truly get on with your life and live more fully and happily. Enjoy this learning tool.

⇒ **Directions and Debriefing**

Imagine you were to die today. What is it you would want said on your tombstone? The key to this exercise is not to come up with some saying, statement, or quote which might represent your "ideal" self, but rather to come up with some statement which represents the "true" you as you see yourself today. If after you process your tombstone statement you find yourself unhappy about it, perhaps some soul searching might be in order to better correct the path you currently find your life on. A good place to continue or to begin this work, is in the Active Journal section in the back of your workbook. What is the condition of <u>you</u> today? Think about that.

1. What does this exercise say about death? _____
   _____
   _____

2. What would your statement be? _____
   _____
   _____

3. What are your thoughts? _____
   _____
   _____

4. Are there any life changes you feel you need to make?_____
   _____
   _____
   _____

Each day is a little life;
every waking and rising a little birth;
every fresh morning a little youth;
every going to rest and sleep a little death.

Arthur Schopenhauer

Overview

Poetry is an excellent way of getting in touch with oneself. Through the use of poetry we are often able to get to the heart of our soul. A topic like death and dying cannot help but force us to examine who we are, what we want, where we are going, and who we want to be when death finally takes us. The following poems have been selected because they make us examine our inner selves. And that is good.

⇒ Directions and Debriefing

For the following two poems, "Warning" and "Philosophical Poem," provide a written response as to what your reactions were. Use the space provided below. (1) In group or class discuss what you have noted and learned. (2) What was the message in each of the poems? (3) How do they relate to you and your life? to life in general? (4) What are their messages for society? (5) What points did you like best? Points you liked least?

Warning[127]

When I grow old I'll wear purple with a red hat that doesn't go and doesn't suit   me. And I shall spend my pension on brandy and summer gloves and satin sandals and say we have no money for butter.

And I shall sit down on the pavement when I'm tired, and gobble up samples in shops and press alarm bells and run my stick along the public railings and make up for the sobriety of my youth. I shall go out in my slippers in the rain and pick the flowers in other people's gardens and learn to spit.

You can wear terrible shirts and grow fat and eat three pounds of sausages at a go or only bread and pickles for a week and hoard pens and pencils and beermats and things in boxes.

But meanwhile we must stay respectable and must not shame the children; they mind more than we do, being noticeable. We will keep dry and wear sensible clothes and spend according to good value, and do what's best for us and for our children.

But maybe I ought to practice a little now, so people who know me are not too shocked and surprised when suddenly I am old and start to wear purple.

Jenny Joseph

Philosophical Poem

You have an existential obligation to achieve four modest goals within your own life.

First, you must strive to become the very best you are capable of. You are responsible for your actions and master of your development. Secondly, you must contribute something to life, no matter how little, but nonetheless something, so that life is better than when you entered life--even if only slightly. Thirdly, you must convey to others, even if only to one other human being, a conviction from within your heart, a truth if you will, that tomorrow will be better. Fourthly, you must strive to develop a personal philosophy and sense of spirituality--which in part recognizes that every encounter with another is a holy encounter.

Life is a piece of art, not a piece of cake. Each and every life is a work of art. Each and every day a brush stroke upon your canvas. You have the obligation to contribute brush strokes daily to your life, to your work of art, to your canvas. It is my love, my hope you will step lively, and step lightly. Most of all brush stroke boldly.

What the mind understands today, the heart accepts tomorrow. And slowly, like small change, we count our victories in life.

From *Selected Poems* published by Teddy Bear Publishers. © 1992 J. Davis Mannino. Reprinted with permission

Mandala

Death is the veil which those who live call life:
They sleep, and it is lifted.

Percy Bysshe Shelley

⇒ **Overview**

According to Carl Jung, in his book *Man and his Symbols*[128], one finds among the mythological representations of the self much emphasis on the four corners of the world. In many pictures god or the "Great Man" is represented in the center of a circle divided into four. Jung used the Hindu word *mandala* (magic circle) to designate a structure for this order, an order which is a symbolic representation of the nuclear atom of the human psyche; an essence we do not know or are not in tune with. Myths about god and death have strong meanings in most cultures.

In this connection it is interesting to note some examples. For example, a Naskapi hunter pictorially represented his Great Man not as a human being but as a mandala. Whereas the Naskapi experience the inner center directly and naively, without the help of religious rites or doctrines, other communities use the mandala motif in order to restore a lost inner balance. For instance, the Navaho Indians try, by means of mandala-structured sand paintings, to bring a sick person back into harmony with himself and with the cosmos--and thereby restore his health.

In Eastern civilizations similar pictures are used to consolidate the inner being or to enable one to plunge into deep meditations. The contemplation of a mandala is meant to bring an inner peace, a feeling that life has again found its meaning and order. The mandala also conveys this feeling when it appears spontaneously in the dreams of people who are neither influenced by any religious tradition nor know anything about such occurrences. Perhaps the positive effect is even greater in such cases because knowledge and tradition sometimes blur or even block the spontaneous experience.

According to Jung whenever a human being genuinely turns to the inner world and tries to know himself--not by ruminating about his subjective thoughts and feelings, but by following the expressions of his own objective nature such as dreams and genuine fantasies--then sooner or later the true and real self emerges. The ego will then find an inner power that contains all the possibilities of renewal.

⇒ **Directions and Debriefing**

For this exercise follow your instructor in a relaxation technique, and with coloring materials provided, color your mandala allowing only your inner natural force and self to guide you and your use of colors. Allow your life force to flow and guide you. Take about 30 minutes, more or less, and be prepared to discuss your mandala. This may also be assigned as a homework assignment. The mandala is on the following page. (1) What were your thoughts about this exercise? (2) Explain how they related to life and death. (3) Examine various cultures you know and have studied and relate some of the folklore, values, myths, and storytelling to issues of life and death.

Support Groups for Loss and Grief

A civilization that denies death ends by denying life.

Octavio Paz

⇒ **Overview**

We are a country of volunteers, support groups, and community organizations, from Lions clubs to Save the Whales clubs. We have historical clubs and hysterical comedy clubs. And this is good. In your own community you will most likely find, in addition to such familiar names as the Rotary, AA, VFW, and 4H clubs, various other support groups for dealing with loss and grief. Whether it be an activist group like MADD (Mothers Against Drunk Drivers) or a home hospice program for AIDS patients, your community--like thousands of others across the land--probably offers more than you know in self-help, support, and care for many kinds and types of needs and losses communities experience each year. See the extensive telephone list on the next page.

⇒ **Directions**

In this activity research the resources your community provides in general and in particular to persons experiencing loss and grief. Having knowledge of this information may prove most helpful to you, your friends, and your loved ones sometime soon. Tip: "Let your fingers do the walking!" List names, kinds of support offered, and phone numbers below for the relevant organizations. Bring brochures, pamphlets, and other information to class and share it with your fellow students. Look for suicide prevention hotlines and other such specialized programs as well during your research.

Organization Name	Kinds of Support Offered	Phone Number
1.		
2.		
3.		
4.		
5.		
6.		
7.		
8.		
9.		
10.		

Overview

The following national organizations deal with issues surrounding death, dying, life-threatening illness, loss, and bereavement. Telephone numbers were current at the time of printing. Organizations are listed in alpha order. Check your local directory for listings of helpful organizations in your community. Keep them handy for future reference and when the need is at hand. Better yet, volunteer to "help out" in an organization near you. Use this resource list in conjunction with the exercise "Support Groups for Loss and Grief" on the previous page. Contact some of the following organizations and ask that information be sent to you. As a class project collect this information and share it in class.

AIDS Hotline	800-342-AIDS
AIDS Resource Center	212-633-2500
Alliance for Cannabis Therapeutics	202-483-8595
Alzheimer's Disease and Related Disorders Association	800-272-3900
American Association for Retired Persons-Legal Council for the Elderly	202-434-2170
American Association of Suicidology	202-237-2282
American Cancer Society	800-ACS-2345
American Cemetery Association	800-645-7700
American Cryonics Society	800-423-2001
American Foundation for AIDS Research (AMFAR)	213-857-5900
American Heart Association	214-373-6300
American Hospital Association	800-424-4301
American Medical Association	312-464-5000
American Pain Society	708-966-5595
American Sudden Infant Death Syndrome Institute	800-847-7437
Association for Death Education and Counseling	203-586-7503
Cancer Care	212-221-3300
Center for Attitudinal Healing	415-331-6161
Cancer Information Center	800-4CANCER
Centers for Disease Control and Prevention	800-232-1311
Centers for Disease Control, National AIDS Clearinghouse	800-458-5231
Children's Hospice International	800-242-4453
Choice in Dying	212-366-5540
Continental Association of Funeral and Memorial Societies	800-458-5563
Foundation of Thanatology	212-928-2066
Friends and Relatives of the Institutionalized Aged	212-732-4455
Gerontological Society of America	202-842-1275
Hemlock Society	800-247-7421
Hospice Association of America	202-546-4759
Hospice Education Institute	800-331-1620
Hospice Foundation of American	202-638-5312
HospiceLink	800-331-1620
International Association for Near-Death Studies	203-528-5144
Leukemia Society of America	212-573-8484
Make-A-Wish-Foundation	800-722-9474
Mothers Against Drunk Driving (MADD)	800-438-MADD
Names Project Foundation (The AIDS Quilt)	800-USA-NAMES
National Abortion Federation	800-772-9100
National Academy of Elderlaw Attorneys	602-881-4005
National Council on the Aging	202-479-1200
National Funeral Directors Association (NFDA)	414-541-2500
National Hospice Organization	800-658-8898
National Kidney Foundation	212-889-2210
National Selected Morticians (NSM)	800-323-4219
National Self-Help Clearinghouse	212-354-8525
Neptune Society	909-359-2021
Project Inform (HIV information)	415-558-0684
Shanti Project (AIDS support program)	415-864-2273
Starlight Foundation International (terminally ill children)	310-207-5558
United Network for Organ Sharing (UNOS)	800-243-6667
Visiting Nurse Association of America	800-426-2547

GriefNet on the Internet

Well, everyone can master grief 'cept he that has it.

William Shakespeare

⇒ **Overview**

We've all heard about the information highway. Well, now you can surf or skate the internet highway for death and dying resources with GriefNet. GriefNet is a program from Rivendell Resources, a nonprofit corporation providing information to professional and lay persons dealing with bereavement, grief, and major loss. GriefNet maintains a free-access Internet referral and support network. They also offer personalized referral services. GriefNet provides:

1. comprehensive support resource listings around the world.
2. a directory of professionals providing services in related areas.
3. an annotated bibliography of grief and major loss resources.
4. an on-line store of books, tapes, videos, and other grief supplies.
5. a set of electronic discussion groups where anyone may discuss specific grief and loss-related topics.
6. crisis assessment with resource referrals.
7. information on ADEC, the Association for Death Education and Counseling.

GriefNet's loss resource listings include general bereavement support; crisis lines; bereaved parents' support; resources for children, adolescents, and young adults; widowed persons' support; hospices; resources for those who have lost someone due to suicide or homicide; resources for both professional and lay caregivers; media resources with reviews; chronic illness and physical loss resources; classes, conferences, workshops, and educational opportunities; natural and human catastrophe resources; topical articles; and even poetry.

GriefNet has nine on-line discussion groups (also called mailing lists) and more are developing as needed. They are (1) *griefnet-announce*, a low-volume list with updated information about GriefNet; (2) *grief-chat*, a general discussion list for persons interested in any aspect of grief, bereavement, and major loss; (3) *grief-widowed*, a list for widowed persons; (4) *grief-training*, an open list for persons interested in discussing training or training people to assist the bereaved; (5) *grief-parents*, a moderated list for bereaved parents; (6) *adult-sibs*, a moderated list for adults and older adolescents who have had a sibling die; (7) *kids-to-kids*, a moderated list for children who have had a loved one die or other major loss; (8) *adult-parents*, a list for anyone who has lost a parent at any stage of life; and (9) *adec-chat*, a closed list for ADEC members.

I highly support GriefNet. For additional information, use these contact points for reaching GriefNet. (1) email: griefnet@griefnet.org, (2) point a web browser to http://rivendell.org or a gopher client to gopher.rivendell org, phone: 313-761-1960, (3) Address: GriefNet, P. O. Box 3272, Ann Arbor, MI 48106-3272, or (4) phone: 313-761-1960.

⇒ **Debriefing**

(1) How might these discussion settings be helpful in ways more traditional "live" support groups might not? (2) What might be some of the pros and cons of such settings? (3) What issues of confidentiality might arise with such internet connections? Explain

NAMES Project AIDS Memorial Quilt

The story that those who died of AIDS tells,
except for the purest of good fortune,
could have been our very own story.

⇒ **Overview**

The purpose of this activity is to go and view *The NAMES Project AIDS Memorial Quilt*. The Quilt was started in San Francisco in 1987 by founder Cleve Jones and friends who wanted to demonstrate remembrance to the over 1,000 AIDS victims in San Francisco at that time. They wanted a way of expressing the unending grief they felt as friends and loved ones of those who had died of this horrible disease. Today the Quilt is a national endeavor, by those who have lost loved ones to AIDS, to "remember their names."

The 26,000 memorial quilt panels that make up The AIDS Memorial Quilt are made by friends, family, and loved ones to commemorate a life of someone who has died of AIDS. Portions of the Quilt are on display worldwide to encourage visitors to better understand and respond to the AIDS pandemic, to provide a positive means of expression for those grieving the death of a loved one, and to raise funds for people living with HIV/AIDS. See the articles which follow.

This exercise provides an excellent opportunity to see firsthand how grieving people, reacting to an epidemic, respond in kindness, love, and with meaningful ritual, observance, and remembrance. This activity is particularly noteworthy as the Quilt brings many people from very diverse backgrounds together to grieve over their deceased loved ones who all share one thing in common: They all died of AIDS.

Please note this may be a profound experience for you, so be prepared. The reason so many volunteers will be present is because many volunteers will be called upon to provide extra emotional support for those viewing the quilt panels. My own experience with the AIDS Quilt is that a surprisingly high number of those viewing the Quilt find themselves in need of extra emotional support, so please be aware of this.

⇒ **Directions and Debriefing**

The Quilt has inspired people to become involved in their own community's response to this epidemic. Since the first display in Washington, D. C. in 1987, there have been over 1,000 displays of the quilt. Approximately 200 times a year, the Quilt or portions of the Quilt are displayed throughout the country. At any given time there are many displays occurring. For a schedule of display locations and times near you, contact the NAMES Project Foundation in San Francisco at 415-882-5500 or Fax 415-882-6200. The foundation produces a handy brochure on "How to Make a Quilt Panel," using traditional mid-western American sewing and quilting bee techniques. This would also be a good project.

After viewing the Quilt, write up a short reaction paper. Discuss your thoughts, feelings, and observations about how others demonstrated their grief and sadness while viewing the Quilt. Comment on some of the positive messages found in many of the quilt panels. Take snapshots of some of your favorite panels and bring them to show in class.

A Stitch in Time Heals Time! The AIDS Memorial Quilt

For an extra-credit project, Ellen, a student in my death and dying class here at Santa Rosa Junior College, went and visited the AIDS Memorial Quilt on display nearby. She couldn't understand why there were so many tissue boxes around until she began reading and viewing some of the 350 quilt panels lovingly made by survivors of the AIDS pandemic. She was particularly moved by a song found on a quilt panel for a young guy in his 30s named Scott Slutsky. His magical song is called *Indian Summer*, and it's filled with love and feeling. (Used here with Names Project permission)

"Who was I kidding as I lay there short of breath/Making peace with the living and the imminence of death/And reprieved I wondered can I say it's been enough/Then the anger surges longing urges me to stay/

No-Oh I'm not ready, There's too much love left unthreshed/No-Oh wait awhile, Indian summer's green and golden/

Days slip by in a cascade rushing out come rain come sun/ And I am exulting in the spectrum of run/ There's my sweet Elena laughing, silly, ebony-haired/ And my brilliant Rachel dancing, singing, unaware/

All the forms of beauty appear to cluster within reach/From the museum galleries to the waves on lighthouse beach/ Biking down a steep hill I feel like I could lose control/ Fuck the neighbors, honey, blast that kick-ass rock n' roll/

There is love in the time of cholera and AIDS/ And I'm showered by it, powered by it every day/ And if I never find that lasting dream of romantic bliss/ Just say that I was happy and left you with a kiss/

No-Oh I'm not ready, There's too much love left unthreshed/ No-Oh Wait awhile, Indian summer's green and golden/"

When Ellen left this moving memorial display she understood why so many tissue boxes were around and why so many people were using them.

What is the AIDS Memorial Quilt all about? In June of 1987, Cleve Jones, founder of the Quilt, wanted to find a way to show the public the hurt, suffering, and grief San Franciscans were experien-

cing from the more than 1000 AIDS-related deaths in that city alone. Using the old fashioned sewing, quilting bees, and fine needlework traditions of the midwestern pioneers, Jones vowed "to take all of our individual experiences, and stitch them together to make something that has strength and beauty." From this community effort the AIDS Memorial Quilt began.

Word of this unique project spread like a midwest prairie fire. The project became a lightning rod for similar quilting efforts throughout the United States. The quilt put a face on AIDS through the names stitched into each loving quilt panel. Since 1987, the NAMES Project AIDS Memorial Quilt has grown from a neighborhood cause to an international symbol and memorial of awareness, love, care, and hope. There are over 38,000 individual fabric panels, each measuring three by six feet, in the overall Quilt. Though the panels are lovingly created in sorrow, the message is the hope that all of us will be moved to participate in the fight against this cruel killer disease.

On October 11, 1987, the Quilt was displayed in its entirety for the first time on the Capitol Mall in Washington, D. C. Over 2,000 panels were laid out at dawn, and a solemn litany of those remembered in the Quilt began. Names were read one by one in memorial. Since then the Quilt has been displayed in as many far-reaching places as the epidemic itself. There have been more than 1,000 displays! The project has raised over $1.5 million dollars for AIDS service organizations around the country. The mission of the NAMES Project is to (1) increase public awareness of AIDS and HIV prevention, (2) offer a creative form of expression for all whose lives have been affected by HIV and AIDS and to preserve the memory of those who have died as a result of the disease, and (3) encourage support and the raising of funds for people living with HIV and their loved ones.

The Quilt has inspired people to respond to the AIDS epidemic. If you would like to get more information about sharing the quilt, call The NAMES Project Foundation at 415-882-5500, fax 415-882-6200 or write to 310 Townsend Street, Suite 310, San Francisco CA 94107. The project has a wonderfully simple "How to make a quilt panel" brochure which you can use to memorialize and remember a loved one who has died in your life. Order one now.

"No-Oh Wait awhile, Indian summer's green and golden." I would have liked to have met Scott and heard this so young a man sing his song in person.

Remembering through Quilting!
How To Create a Quilt Panel

Last time we discussed the history of the NAMES Project AIDS Memorial Quilt. Now I would like to discuss how to create a quilt panel. You don't have to be an artist, a seamstress, or tailor. You just have to think creatively and lovingly when you create your quilt panel. The guidelines that follow are based on NAMES Project guidelines and my own experience making many panels over the years.

All kinds of people have created and submitted quilt panels to the Memorial Quilt. They come in thousands of different colors, styles, and fashions. It makes no difference if you sew, paint, or paste on a photograph. The point to remember is any remembrance is appropriate. It is up to you. How you choose to create your panel is a private and personal matter. You are however, encouraged to use the time-tested traditions of the old-fashioned sewing and quilting bees. You do this by creating your panel among friends, family, co-workers, and loved ones. The NAMES Project makes the following suggestions for creating your memorial panel.

A. **Design.** When you design your panel be sure to (1) include the name of your friend or loved one you wish to remember, (2) add in details such as dates of birth and death and hometown, and (3) limit each panel to just one person.

B. **Materials.** (1) Keep in mind that the Quilt is folded and unfolded many times during displays throughout the world, so durability is crucial. (2) Use of medium-weight, non-stretch fabric such as a cotton duck or poplin seems to work best. (3) The design may be vertical or horizontal, but the finished, hemmed panel must be 3 feet by 6 feet (90 cm x 180 cm) exactly! Those are the rules. When you cut the fabric, be sure and leave an extra 2-3 inches on each side for a hem. If you can't hem it yourself, project staff will. An extra touch is to add batting to the panel, to help keep it clean and maintain fabric shape when it is laid out among the thousands of other panels on the ground in those magical faraway places where the Quilt has become an inspiration to millions.

C. **Construction Techniques.** (1) Appliqué. Sew fabric letters and other small mementos onto the background. Glue rarely holds for long, so a stronger hold such as sewing is recommended. (2) Paint. Brush on good quality textile paint or color-fast dye, or use an indelible ink pen. Use paints which absorb deep into the fabric and don't "layer" as that type of paint tends to flake off. (3) Stencil. Trace a design onto the fabric with a pencil or other marker, lift the stencil, then use a brush to apply textile paint, indelible ink, or other such marker. (4) Collage. Make sure that whatever materials you choose to add to your panel won't tear the fabric (avoid glass and sequins), and stay away from very bulky objects. (5) Photos. The guidelines seem to indicate that the best way to include a photo or letters is to photocopy them onto iron-on transfers, iron them onto 100% cotton fabric, and then sew that fabric onto the panel. You may also place that photo inside clear plastic vinyl and then sew it onto the panel (off center so it avoids the fold mark).

D. **Write a letter.** In many ways this is the most important part. Take some time and write a one- or two-page typed letter that talks about the person you just remembered in your Quilt panel. What was your relationship to him or her? How would they have like to have been remembered? What was a favorite memory you had of this person? What was noteworthy about them? Be sure, if possible, to attach a photograph of the person memorialized.

E. **Packaging and Sending.** When done pack up everything very carefully and lovingly and send it all to the address below. I recommend making two identical panels. One to send to the NAMES Project and one to keep for yourself. When sending your quilt panel to the NAMES Project, you will need to fill out a "panelmaker information card." You can secure this and other necessary "quilt-making" material by writing to the NAMES Project Foundation at 310 Townsend Street, Suite 310, San Francisco, CA 94107. And for gosh sakes make a contribution. The NAMES Project Foundation depends on the support of panelmakers to preserve the Quilt and keep it on display. A gift of any amount is welcome. Gifts of $250 or more will be acknowledged in the AIDS Memorial Quilt Annual Report.

This can be a very grueling and emotionally charged project. So when you're done, light a candle, take a walk along the beach, meditate, or have a large slice of carrot cake. Whatever release you give yourself you've earned it. As you can see there is something to be said for the old-fashioned sewing and quilting bees of the old midwest!

There Must Be Something More I Can Do Than Just Send a Card!

He who binds to himself a joy
Does the winged life destroy.
But he who kisses the joy as it flies
Lives in eternity's sunrise.

William Blake

⇒ **Overview**

Hearing that someone we knew, liked, and loved has died leaves many of us immobilized. Oftentimes we just don't know what to do, what to say, or even how to act. This exercise will assist you in responding more appropriately and helpfully next time a loss occurs.

⇒ **Directions and Debriefing**

Review the situations in the exercise "Assisting in Someone's Grief" on page 84, and determine what you might do other than just send a sympathy card. What might be of real help and use to the bereaved? What would you want? What might <u>really</u> be helpful? Take some time and develop some good ideas. What follows are common responses for acknowledging the death of someone close to us. Use these to stimulate your thinking about what you could do. (1) List and explain your strategies in the blanks below. (2) What will you do next time? (3) Discuss what you have learned from this exercise.

1. Attend wake	14. _____
2. Attend funeral	15. _____
3. Send flowers	16. _____
4. Send charitable donation	17. _____
5. Send sympathy card	18. _____
6. Visit bereaved	19. _____
7. Invite bereaved to home or meal	20. _____
8. Offer help with household chores	21. _____
9. Provide baby-sitting	22. _____
10. Write condolence letter	23. _____
11. Plant a tree in memory	24. _____
12. Provide financial assistance	25. _____
13. Prepare and deliver food	26. _____

Writing a Condolence Letter

Dost thou love life?
Then do not squander time,
for that's the stuff life is made of.

Benjamin Franklin

⇒ **Overview**

Writing a condolence letter which is caring can be an emotional and trying experience. Difficult as it may be, there are some rules which can make it easier to do. Leonard and Hillary Zunin[129] (1991) reviewed and analyzed thousands of condolence letters. They analyzed the structure of these letters and developed seven important elements for writing a clear, sympathetic, and practical condolence letter.

These rules are (1) Acknowledge the loss. Mention the person's name, how you learned of the loss, and your immediate feelings (shock, sadness, dismay, etc.). (2) Express your sympathy. Share sorrow in an honest and sincere fashion. Show care and understanding of how difficult you know the situation is. Use the words "died" and "death" in your comments. (3) Note special qualities of the deceased. Reflect upon the qualities you valued most in the person who has died and share these in the letter. These may be specific attributes, personality characteristics, or other qualities. Such comments show the bereaved their loved one was appreciated by others. (4) Recount a memory about the deceased. Memories of the deceased are a most valued asset. There can never be too many. The bereaved often have difficulty keeping such memories in the forefront during the early days of their loss. Your sharing of such memories, therefore, is helpful as well as thoughtful. Humorous reflections are most useful. (5) Note special qualities of the bereaved. Grieving people need to be reminded of their personal strengths and other positive qualities, characteristics which will help them through their difficult period. By reminding them of these qualities you have observed in them, you will encourage them to use them now during this difficult period. (6) Offer assistance. Offering help need not be part of a condolence letter, but if help is offered, it should be specific. An open-ended offer of help places the burden for determining what that help should be on the bereaved. They have enough burdens already. Making an offer to do something specific and following through is most welcome. (7) Close with a thoughtful word or phrase. Final words in a condolence letter are especially useful. They should reflect your true feelings. Flowery or elaborate phrases do not help. Honest expressions of your thoughts and feelings convey best to the bereaved.

⇒ **Directions and Debriefing**

For this exercise pretend a close college friend has lost his mother in a traffic accident. Assume you know the mother and family fairly well. Write a condolence letter which conveys the elements discussed above. This practice letter will be invaluable to you when the time arrives for such a letter to be sent in earnest to a bereaved friend, colleague, or family member. (1) What was most difficult for you in writing your condolence letter? (2) Would you want to receive such a letter had someone you loved died? (3) How might you compose a letter concerning loss of a pet? (4) What types of concrete help or assistance should you discuss in your condolence letter? (5) What were the merits of this exercise? demerits?

Immortality

Do not stand at my grave and weep;
I am not there. I do not sleep.
I am a thousand winds that blow.
I am the diamond glints on snow.

Clare Harner Lyon

⇒ **Overview**

What does it mean to be immortal? Does it mean living forever?   Besides various religious, spiritual, philosophical, biological, psychological, and other biophysical ideas, immortality is also associated with leaving behind a legacy. There are the Nobel prizes, named after Alfred Nobel, the discoverer of dynamite, and Joe Robbie Stadium where the 1995 Super Bowl was played in Miami. There is the Rockefeller Foundation and great books like *Gone with the Wind*.   And, of course, there is Trump Tower, named after controversial billionaire Donald Trump.   Everything from performing service in one's community to having children are all legacies, all forms of immortality.

⇒ **Directions and Debriefing**

For this exercise discuss how our beliefs contribute to our sense of immortality. List some of the various legacies people have left behind. Be sure to look at history. (1) List some of the different "philosophical" legacies. What kinds of monuments of immortality remain standing today? (2) How do you want to be remembered? (3) What will be your legacy? List some of the legacies you would like to leave behind. (4) What would your legacy be if you had a choice? List some of the different "philosophical" legacies people leave behind when they die. (5) What legacies will your family leave to you? Be prepared to discuss your responses in class.

Immortality of a Thousand Years!

Oh snail,
climb Mt. Fuji,
but slowly, slowly!

Issa

⇒ **Overview**

Some years ago I was invited to visit, with a friend of mine, his great-great-grandmother Helene who was about to turn 100 years old. I was rather excited. I had never met anyone who was actually a century old! When we arrived at the nursing home, my friend and I quietly entered her room. Helene was asleep. He gently nudged her. She woke rather peacefully and soon recognized her nephew. Her first comment was: "Oh God, am I still alive yet?" One of the great challenges of life is accepting one's very own death, a problem Helene apparently did not have. But what if the age-old desire to live forever were possible? What issues, problems, and dilemmas might arise from that Pandora's Box possibility? Often the wish for immortality is nothing more than not making the most of the present. Are you making the most of your present life?

⇒ **Directions**

For this exercise[130] divide into two groups. One group will pretend to be people who were granted immortality one thousand years ago. The other group will consist of people who are mortal and have a normal lifespan. The mortal group is faced with the choice of whether to allow science to produce a new drug that would grant them immortality. Interview members of the first group by asking the following questions.

1. How does it feel to live forever?

2. Do you wish you could die?

3. What changes have you lived through in the last thousand years?

4. Are you bored or lonely?

5. How valuable is each day when you do not have limits on your time?

⇒ **Debriefing**

(1) Discuss your reflections from this exercise. (2) Would you want to live forever? (3) If not, for how long would you want to live? If you would want to live forever, why? What would be the advantages? (4) Does long life assure a good life, a quality life?

Notes: _____

_____

_____

_____

When I'm Dead and Back!

If death did not exist, it would be necessary to invent it!

J. B. Milhaud

⇒ **Overview**

Sometimes we are so wrapped up in our denial of death and in our fears of death that we often forget to ponder our thoughts about what, in fact, happens to us <u>after</u> death. Many cultures believe in reincarnation. In the study of Buddhism, for example, great discussion may be found regarding reincarnation and the eventual goal of reaching nirvana or that perfect state of heaven. Let your mind go and imagine for awhile what the options might be if reincarnation were your fate. I had a college professor who once told us in class he was going to come back as a 1939 Edsel Ford. We could never figure that guy out!

⇒ **Directions and Debriefing**

In what form would you return if reincarnation were our destiny after our death? Take your time and choose your reincarnation carefully. What would you like to be? Would you be a colorful tree? a cloud? one of God's creatures, big or small? When done, discuss your reincarnation below. Discuss your thoughts about immortality. Express your feelings about how this exercise sparked your thoughts and interest in your mortality and afterlife. (1) How did philosophical, spiritual or religious values, and thoughts enter into your thinking? (2) Were there fantasies and unfulfilled dimensions to your choices? (3) Among those people you love and care for, how might you wish for them to return? (4) Do your choices reflect upon your current life? (5) What form might a reincarnation take if it were meant as a punishment? (6) Do you believe in reincarnation? Explain. (7) Do you believe in ghosts? (8) What in fact are your thoughts about afterlife?

_____

_____

_____

_____

_____

_____

_____

_____

_____

_____

_____

_____

7

Course Organization:

Assessment Tools and Strategies

The Lord is my shepherd; I shall not want.
He maketh me to lie down in green pastures:
he leadeth me beside the still waters. He restoreth
my soul: he leadeth me in the paths of righteousness
for his name's sake. Yea, though I walk through the
valley of the shadow of death, I will fear no evil: for
thou art with me; thy rod and thy staff they comfort
me. Thou preparest a table before me in the presence
of mine enemies: thou anointest my head with oil; my
cup runneth over. Surely goodness and mercy shall
follow me all the days of my life: and I will dwell in
the house of the Lord for ever.

Psalms 23

Chapter 7

Course Organization: Assessment Tools and Strategies

This chapter is a tool-kit and foundation-building chapter. Many of the exercises and activities are designed as strategies for the successful use of this workbook and for the successful completion of a course in death and dying. Rather then restrict some of the enclosed tools to a so-called faculty guide, I felt it more meaningful to allow everyone to have all the "tools." This way the workbook has the additional value of being used as a "stand-alone" independent project, workshop, or self-study program.

The first half of the chapter is comprised of exercises related to assessment and research projects. The "icebreaker" and "course intake assessment" exercises are excellent for starting off your program. The second half is related to guest speaker and field-trip ideas. Enclosed are several types of student evaluation tools--as in grading. There are sample "reaction paper," "essay topics," and "research topic" ideas as well. There are "book report" and "book search" exercises for students to use for either extra-credit or grading purposes. Please note the list of suggested textbooks and suggested readings to use in tandem with this workbook.

A note to you the instructor or facilitator. The study of death and dying can be stressful to both student and instructor alike. It is my belief that students should be assessed early in the semester to determine both awareness level and sensitivity level to issues surrounding death and dying. Several of the exercises provide such background information for you the instructor to take into consideration as you work with and guide your students through this sometimes "nerve-racking" experience. Over the years of teaching my course in death and dying, I have had a few students who found the subject matter disturbing to the point where they had to drop the course and/or seek counseling for unresolved issues related to death and dying. For this reason, I have developed several assessment tools which serve the purpose of providing you the instructor with early warning signs. You will find them in this chapter. For example, I had one student who had two prior suicide attempts. This information came out in her assessment materials. I was able to work with this student to make sure she was aware of community resources to assist her should the course become problematic for her. Additionally, I encourage all students to stay in touch with their feelings and emotions and to not hesitate in letting me know if such emotional issues arise. Exercises in chapter one will provide the sensitization necessary to go forward smoothly. Be candid. I always make a point of sharing my emotions, as appropriate, with students about aspects of the death and dying adventure I still grapple with. My candor provides permission for students to show their candor. For example, I share with students that I sometimes have a bad dream from material covered. Some students also have this same experience. I, therefore, make a point of discussing dreams and how to process them through use of a journal. That is one reason why I have provided space for an "Active Journal Keeping" section in the workbook, and why I provide thorough "debriefing" questions for each exercise. In closing, I remind you that 99% of all students will leave your course happier and better for having taken it. It's that 1% I'm talking about who might have problems.

Use common sense and a nice sprinkling of humor and you'll have mostly fun and no problems. I promise you that!

Date: _____

⇒ **Directions**

In small groups introduce yourselves to each other and discuss the following. Be prepared to return to full class and discuss the following questions in class as time permits and your comfort level allows. Note: It will be interesting to look back at this exercise at the end of the course, for comparison purposes. What changes have occurred?

1. What are some of your <u>fears</u> in taking this course?

_____
_____
_____
_____

2. What are some of your <u>goals</u> in taking this course?

_____
_____
_____
_____

3. During full class discussion, if time allows, I may call upon you to share with the class the following information. So prepare some comments.

   a. Name
   b. Current work or career history
   c. Experiences with death and dying
   d. New to college? Just out of high school?
   e. How many and which college courses are you taking?
   f. What are your college and career goals?
   g. Why are you taking this course?

_____
_____
_____
_____
_____
_____
_____
_____

4. Relate a memory or story surrounding death and dying from your personal experiences. Be as specific as your comfort level allows.

_____

_____

_____

_____

5. Read the poem "When I Grow Old I'll Wear Purple!" and relate it to your life and life in general. (You will find this poem located on workbook page 200.)

_____

_____

_____

_____

6. List a couple of the greatest challenges which you have faced or are currently facing. What is the number one goal in your life?

_____

_____

_____

_____

7. Complete the exercise "What Do You Want To Take Away from This Course?" on page 219 of the workbook. Hand it in next class or as directed by your instructor.

_____

_____

_____

_____

8. Suggest one or more questions that <u>you</u> would like answered concerning death and dying issues. I will do my best to incorporate your question(s) into the course--and hopefully address it.

_____

_____

_____

_____

_____

_____

Icebreaker 2: What Do You Want To Take Away from This Course?

Name: _____

(Out-of-class exercise)

⇒ **Directions**

Every class is unique. Every class is composed of students who have individual needs. Knowing these needs will assist me in attempting to address some of your individual needs in taking this course. In group or for next class answer the following questions as candidly as possible.

1. Is this course part of a staff development or career enhancement program? Does this course have particular relevance to your current employment? If so, let me know so I may attempt to incorporate elements into this course which pertain to you and your employment, as regards death and dying issues.

2. What is it you want to take away from this course?

3. What types of learning techniques do you find most helpful (i.e., videos, lecture, guest speakers, group work, role-play, homework, take home exercises, in-class exercises?)

4. What have instructors done in the past that you have really enjoyed? How can I make this class more enjoyable and helpful for you?

5. What type of grading policy are you most comfortable with? There may be some flexibility in test construction, assignments, etc. I will listen to your comments.

6. What do you expect and want from your instructor/facilitator?

7. Share with me something personal about yourself which has bearing on why you are taking this course in death and dying. (This is optional and will be held in strict confidence, if you wish.)

8. Write one question(s) you would like me to address during our time together in this course that you might be afraid to ask out loud in class or seminar. You may also hand in question(s) anonymously if you would like.

9. Anything else you would like to ask or say?

219

*As for life, it is a battle and a sojourning
in a strange land; but the fame that comes after is oblivion.*

Marcus Antoninus

Name: _____

⇒ **Overview and Directions**

The purpose of this intake assessment is to provide your instructor or facilitator with some personal background on you and on your thoughts, values, perceptions, and experiences regarding death and dying. Though this information will be kept confidential, your responses and questions will be used to develop course content and topics for consideration during group work and throughout the course. Your candor will be appreciated and valued in tailoring a meaningful course for you as well as for the rest of the class. You are free to not respond to any question you feel is too personal.

1. At what age and in what year do you expect to die? What do you suspect your cause of death might be? Discuss.

_____
_____
_____

2. Do you have a legal will, advanced directives, or organ donor card? Explain.

_____
_____
_____

3. Do you have any ethical considerations regarding suicide, euthanasia, abortion, life-support practices, or the death penalty? Explain.

_____
_____
_____

4. Do you have any risk-taking behaviors (smoking, drinking, drugs, unsafe sex, etc.)? Do you engage in any life-threatening or life-endangering behaviors? Explain.

_____
_____

5. Have you ever been on medication for emotional problems, been to or are currently seeing a psychotherapist, or hospitalized for mental illness? Explain.

_____
_____

6. Have you ever attempted suicide or had suicidal thoughts? Explain when this was, what the circumstances were, and if you still harbor these thoughts.

_____

_____

_____

7. How do you want your body disposed of when you die (entombment, cremation, burial, cryonics)? Describe some of your funeral wishes.

_____

_____

_____

8. Is there a time in life when you consider someone's death as being "too early to die"? When is that? Explain.

_____

_____

_____

9. What are some of the considerations you have provided when someone you knew and loved died (flowers, card, food, etc.)? Explain.

_____

_____

_____

10. What are your thoughts about afterlife?

_____

_____

_____

11. What does the "Good Death" mean to you?

_____

_____

_____

12. What is your earliest memory of death?

_____

_____

_____

_____

13. Who has died in your family? What were their ages and your age at the time they died? What were the causes of these deaths?

_____

_____

_____

14. When was the most recent death you experienced? Discuss this experience.

_____

_____

_____

15. What non-death losses have you experienced (loss of job, loss of home, divorce or romance breakup, loss of a friendship, loss of financial security, etc.)?

_____

_____

_____

16. What other questions concerning death, dying, bereavement, grief, or losses in general do you have?

Notes: _____

_____

_____

_____

_____

_____

_____

_____

_____

_____

_____

_____

_____

_____

_____

_____

How admirable,
on seeing lightning,
not to think, life too is brief!

Basho

⇒ **Overview**

There are a surprisingly large number of consumer-oriented books which deal with topics relating to death. The purpose of this exercise is to identify at least 5 to 10 such books from the consumer vantagepoint that "knowledge is power." If you understand and appreciate the importance of self-help books, you will further appreciate the number of self-help books which relate to issues surrounding death and dying in childhood, adolescence, and adulthood. Having an understanding of these resources can be of immense help to you and others you love who might be in need now or in need come the future. This exercise is a wonderful tool for beginning the process of desensitizing one's fears of death and dying.

⇒ **Directions and Debriefing**

Look for 5 to 10 titles which specifically address life-threatening illness, grief, dying, and death. When you find your titles be sure to provide (1) title, (2) name of author(s), (3) publisher, (4) year published (5) number of pages, and (6) a paragraph describing what the topic and purpose of the book are. Example: Return from Cancer by Joan Roberts, published by Random House, (1994), 298 pages. This book examines a cancer diagnosis and how to prepare for cancer treatment and the recovery process. Below are broad topic areas to spark your exploration. Be creative! Choose only books which interest you and could help you.

Consider the following questions and ideas. (1) What did you learn from this exercise? (2) Share your research in group and class. (3) Designate a book search day and highlight your findings and book topics available. (4) Develop a comprehensive further readings booklist. (5) How might these books be useful in death education and counseling situations? (6) Were there particular book topics which you could not find? Which ones? (7) You may wish to follow up this exercise with the "Book Report" exercise on page 224.

1. Disease or Illness Specific Books (Cancer, Leukemia, AIDS, etc.)

2. Grief, Bereavement, and Loss Recovery

3. Death Preparation (Funeral Planning, Estate Planning, Wills, etc.)

4. Managing Life-Threatening Illnesses (Accidents, Violence, Heart Attacks, etc.)

5. Dying and Death with Children and Adolescents (Death of a Pet, etc.)

6. Spiritual and Philosophical Issues surrounding Illness, Dying, and Death

7. Self-Deliverance (Physician-Assisted Suicide or Other Assisted Death Situations, etc.)

8. The Law and Legal Aspects of Death (Advance Directives, Power of Attorney for Health Care, Capital Punishment, and Euthanasia, etc.)

9. Beyond Death (Near-Death-Experiences--NDE, Out-of-Body Experiences--OBE, and Afterlife Teachings)

Book Report

I'm not afraid to die, because I'm a Boy Scout.

10-year-old boy

⇒ **Overview**

There are numerous advice and self-help books on the market and at your local library. Most bookstores and libraries have a sizable section devoted to topics related to death, dying, bereavement, terminal illness, catastrophic illness and disease, hospice care, and even "how-to" books on everything from pain management to suicide. The book *Final Exit* is one such title that comes to mind. Many books are self-help in orientation. These books range from good to bad. Though many of these books have merit, others give advice that is unacceptable to current expertise in the field of death education.

⇒ **Directions**

Choose a book from the topics listed above and critique it based on the following <u>eight</u> factors. Your report is to be typed and double-spaced. Three to five pages should be adequate. Be prepared to present in front of the class according to our discussed timetable. This assignment should be an informative experience for you, one which allows you an opportunity to compile information that you have learned about death and dying. The exercise should teach you to be open-minded, but sharp with critical eye, toward the wealth of advice that is being presented today under the guise of expertise and tried-and-tested help.

⇒ **Criteria for Judging**

1. Evaluation   Did you like the book? Title and Author. Bring book to class.

2. Readability   What was the ease of readability and author's use of jargon?

3. Outline   Present a thumbnail sketch of the book.

4. Author   What is the writer's expertise in the topic area?

5. Recommend   Recommend the book to others to read? (Grade? A - F)

6. Likes   What did you enjoy most about the book?

7. Dislikes   What did you find most annoying about the book?

8. Relevant   Relate book to your textbook, lectures, and other class activities.

⇒ **Debriefing Questions**

Use the following questions and ideas for this exercise. (1) Share your book review and report in group and/or in class. (2) Bring in a copy of the book you reviewed and pass it around. (3) Bring in a list of suggested books for particular topics in death education. (4) Designate a "Book Review Day." Use this opportunity to bring in and report on various topics such as self-help books for those dealing with infant deaths, loss of pets, parent losses, murder, suicide, widows, accidents, etc. Choose a topic which interests you.

Research Topics in Death Education

What's this thing with death these days? It's been done!

George Burns

⇒ **Directions**

The following topics are to be used for extra credit, research papers and other class presentations. You should seek advice from your instructor or facilitator prior to beginning any of these projects. You should develop a good solid outline showing how you intend to pursue your research using these broad topic areas. Submit your research topic and outline to your instructor for consideration.

Abortion
Accident Proneness
Accidental Death
Aggression & Violence
Aging
AIDS
Assassination
Autopsies
Bullfighting
Burial Rites
Cemeteries
Chemical and Biological Warfare
Class and Cultural Differences in Life
Courage & Death
Death and Mysticism
Death Customs
Death Fantasies
Death of a Culture
Death of the Soldier
Differences in Culture
Donation of Body Parts
Dynamics of Prayer & Supplication
Embalming
Epitaphs & Eulogies
Ethics and Medical Experimentation
Euphemisms for Death
Expectancy
Facing Surgery
Factors in Life Expectancy
Fear of Death
Genocide
Geriatric Wards
Heroic Measures in Medicine
Holocaust Experience
Physician-Assisted Suicide

Images of Death
Infant Mortality
Infanticide
Isolation and Alienation
Last Words of the Dying
Legal Rights of the Dying and Dead
Life Review
LSD Therapy with Dying
Martyrdom
Mass Hysteria
Murder & Violence
Myths of Death, Rebirth, Resurrection
Natural Disasters
Out-of-Body Experiences
Pediatric Death and Dying
Perception of Time
Personality Factors in Facing Death
Population and Ecological Control
Poverty and Death
Psychopathologies of Aging
Racial Segregation of Death and Dying
Reincarnation
Resistance to Torture by War Prisoners
Science Fiction and Time Machines
Samurai
Sudden Infant Death Syndrome
Suicide
Survival in Extreme Environments
Symbols for Death
Uncertainty of Dying
Use of Medicine and Pain Killers
Voodooism, Magical Rites, Occultism
Youth and Death
Human Sacrifice
Euthanasia

*He took out his trachea, put a finger over
the hole in his throat, and thanked each
of us nurses. Then he died.*

An American Nurse in Vietnam
The Women Who Served
Segment: *"No Time For Tear"*
Turner Broadcasting, 1994

⇒ **Overview**

The essay format is an excellent tool for helping students demonstrate their knowledge, growth, and development in the important area of death education. The following directions and essay selections provide an opportunity to demonstrate knowledge level skills in two important and broad overlapping areas of death education. Each of the following essays should be evaluated/graded and returned by the instructor or facilitator. Students should also prepare to discuss each essay in group or class.

⇒ **Directions**

The following essays will allow you to showcase and bring together your learning and growth to date. But first, what is a good essay all about? The purpose of an essay is to gauge your ability to demonstrate <u>knowledge</u> (use and recall of your new learning), <u>comprehension</u> (interpret, paraphrase or restate information), <u>application</u> (your ability to apply new concepts in new situations), <u>analysis</u> (use of logic and critical thinking), <u>synthesis</u> (your ability to combine ideas and create innovative applications), and <u>evaluation</u> (to make judgments).

As you write, you should be referring to what you have learned. There is a tendency among essay writers in death education to approach their essay from a "touchy, feely, feel-good" perspective. Though understandable and acceptable in part, you must primarily demonstrate <u>what</u> you have learned by making reference to technical learning. Show concrete learning from lectures, readings, group-work, speakers, and from independent study and field-work. Define your terms or provide a glossary in the back of your essay. A good essay demonstrates your technical and personal growth in death education and as such can easily be evaluated or graded well. This, therefore, is a more difficult task than you might think. Prepare early and thoroughly to meet these goals. (1) Use the space below to explain which of the following essay topics you intend to write about and why.

_____

_____

_____

_____

_____

_____

_____

_____

⇒ **Essay Topic 1: The Ethics of Dying in a Technological Age**

Death and dying involve issues of medical ethics. These issues have become prominent with advances in biomedical technology. Modern techniques of cardiopulmonary resuscitation, genetic testing, and organ transplantation, for example, make possible life-sustaining interventions that were unavailable only a few years ago. Such technologies present us with difficult questions about how to use them. In circumstances where sophisticated and innovative medical technologies have the power to dramatically alter the course of dying and to challenge the traditional definition of death, the Hippocratic obligation to keep people alive can lead to confusing consequences. Coming to terms with these consequences and arriving at a satisfactory guide to behavior means grappling with fundamental ethical principles involving autonomy, beneficence, and justice.

Write an essay discussing medical ethics and dying in a technological age. Weave into your essay a discussion of any four of the following seven components.

1. Ethical principles of autonomy, beneficence, and justice as they apply to medical ethics
2. Factors affecting truth-telling in cases involving terminal illness
3. Patients' rights to self-determination and informed consent
4. Consequences of withholding truth from the point of view of both patient and physician
5. Ethical issues involved in euthanasia
6. How competency affects decisions to withhold treatment from infants or comatose patients
7. Emotional, physical, and ethical components of organ transplantation.

⇒ **Essay Topic 2: What to Do, When Asked to Help**

When someone you know and love experiences a death, sending a sympathy card or flowers is the easy way out. What is really needed is to reach out in some concrete and helpful manner. Often we are paralyzed from helping others simply because we don't know how to lessen the pain and suffering of someone in need. This is true of many situations involving death and dying. The following essay topic provides you an opportunity to demonstrate what you have learned in your studies. How will you be helpful the next time tragedy hits and you are asked to help?

Your good friend's partner, a woman of 31 years, has developed a terminal illness and is expected to die within the next six months. Your friend's partner also has a 10-year-old girl, and he has asked you what and how he should tell the child about her mother's condition and eventual death. He himself has many other questions regarding being a caregiver and facing a life-threatening illness and death. Your response should be broken down into an issues-oriented helpful approach. Suggest specific strategies for the father to consider. The following elements are to be woven into your essay.

1. Demonstrate a clear and concise understanding of key information as found in your readings, guest speakers, group work, independent study, and field trips.
2. Personalize your essay by showing a sense of you in your writing.
3. Use and discuss several critical concepts in your essay (i.e., hospice).
4. The essay should demonstrate economy of words and be 4-6 typed and double-spaced pages.
5. Define technical terms and concepts at the end of the essay with a glossary (i.e., chemotherapy).

Course Reaction Paper

It's better to be over the hill than under it!

Eda LeShan

⇒ **Overview**

The purpose of this "Course Reaction Paper" is to bring a sense of closure to the subject matter covered in this course. In essence your goal is to take the many threads of knowledge concerning issues surrounding dying and death and loss and grief and weave them into a tapestry of knowledge which might serve and last you a lifetime.

⇒ **Directions**

Review what you have learned this semester and organize this new knowledge into the following two categories. They are (1) Personal Growth and (2) Professional Growth. For each category address what your growth has been.

For example, in the personal growth category you might discuss how you (a) overcame some of your death fears, (b) came to terms with your own inevitable death, (c) came to terms with past losses in your life, (d) are now more able to work with those you love and care about should they have a terminal illness, and (e) have developed new or enhanced spiritual and philosophical values. In the professional growth category you might discuss how you (a) now have a better understanding of different methods of burial and ritual; (b) have a deeper appreciation of professional caregivers, such as nurses, social workers, and hospice workers; (c) have a better understanding of terminal care options; and (d) have developed opinions about such controversial topics as physician-assisted suicide, euthanasia, and organ transplantation. Feel free to develop other subcategories under these two.

It is most important that you realize that any good and lively discussion must be supported by examples from your readings, class and group work, field trips, speakers, and media usage.

Ideally, your paper will be no more than several pages (please) long, double-spaced, and typed. The paper will be returned so you may include it within your workbook. Good luck and have some fun.

Notes: _____

_____

_____

_____

_____

_____

_____

Death is not the enemy;
living in constant fear of it, is.

Norman Cousins

⇒ **Overview**

The following death education textbooks are recommended for use with *Days of Grieving, Days of Healing*. Many of these textbooks served as a reference point for the development of this workbook, for which the author is most grateful. The list is alphabetized by first author name on each textbook. Additionally, a selection of other excellent readings is also provided for your growth and development. Enjoy them.

Aiken, L. (1994). *Dying, Death, and Bereavement* (3rd ed.). Boston: Allyn & Bacon.

Barrow, G. (1996). *Aging, the Individual, and Society* (6th ed.). New York: West.

Corr, C., Nabe, C., and Corr, D. (1994). *Death and Dying Life and Living.* Pacific Grove, CA: Brooks/Cole.

DeSelder, L. and Strickland, A. (1996). *The Last Dance* (4th ed.). Mountain View, CA: Mayfield.

Fulton, G. and Metress, E. (1995). *Perspectives on Death and Dying.* Boston: Jones and Bartlett.

Hooyman, N. and Kiyak, H. (1993). *Social Gerontology* (3rd ed.). Boston: Allyn & Bacon.

Kalish, R. (1985). *Death, Grief, and Caring Relationships* (2nd ed.). Monterey, CA: Brooks/Cole.

Kastenbaum, R. (1995). *Death, Society, and Human Experience.* Boston: Allyn & Bacon.

Leming, M. and Dickinson, G. (1994). *Understanding Dying, Death, and Bereavement* (3rd ed.). New York: Harcourt Brace.

Oaks, J. and Ezell, G. (1993). *Dying and Death* (2nd ed.). Scottsdale, AZ: Gorsuch Scarisbrick.

⇒ **Other Selected Readings:**

Corless, I., Germino, B., and Pittman, M. (Eds.). (1994). *Dying, Death, and Bereavement.* Boston: Jones and Bartlett.
Corless, I., Germino, B., and Pittman, M. (Eds.). (1995). *A Challenge for Living.* Boston: Jones and Bartlett.
DeSpelder, L. and Strickland, A. (Eds.). (1995). *The Path Ahead* Mountain View: CA: Mayfield.
Dickinson, G., Leming, M., Mermann, A. (Eds.). (1996). *Annual Editions: Dying, Death, and Bereavement* (3rd ed.). Guilford, CT: Duskin Publishing Group/Brown & Benchmark Publishers.
Doore, G. (Ed.). (1990). *What Survives?* Los Angeles: Jeremy P. Tarcher, Inc.
Harvey, J. (1996). *Embracing Their Memory.* Boston: Allyn & Bacon.
James, J. and Cherry, F. (1988). *The Grief Recovery Handbook.* New York: Harper & Row.
Kastenbaum, R. (1994). *Defining Acts: Aging as Drama.* New York: Baywood.
Larson, D. (1993). *The Helper's Journey.* Champaign, IL: Research Press.
Levine, S. (1987). *Healing into Life and Death.* New York: Anchor Books/Doubleday Publishers.
Levine, S. (1989). *Who Dies?* New York: Anchor Books.
Nuland, S. (1994). *How We Die.* New York: Alfred A. Knopf, Inc.
Rando, T. (Ed.). (1986). *Parental Loss of a Child.* Champaign, IL: Research Press.
Shneidman, E. (1995). *Voices of Death.* New York: Kodansha America.
Walsh, F. and McGoldrick, M. (Eds.). (1991). *Living Beyond Loss.* New York: W. W. Norton & Company.
Williamson, J. & Shneidman, E. (1995). *Death: Current Perspectives* (4th ed.) Mountain View, CA: Mayfield.
Worden, J. (1991). *Grief Counseling & Grief Therapy* (2nd ed.). New York: Springer.

Textbook Review

*A man's dying is more the survivors'
affair than his own.*

Thomas Mann

⇒ **Overview and Directions**

To best utilize your textbook you must first become familiar with what it has to offer. One way to do this is to review your entire textbook briefly. In small group thumb through the text, paying special attention to the photographs, graphs, and overall layout. Think about your own life and how it might relate to these images. Be prepared to discuss the following in group and class.

1. What aspects of the textbook interested you most?

_____

_____

2. What thoughts and feelings were provoked?

_____

_____

3. In which areas of death and dying do you find you have little information?

_____

_____

4. In which areas of death education do you find yourself being more knowledgeable or having more information?

_____

_____

5. In which areas would you like to learn more and have more information?

_____

_____

6. After examining and discussing photographs and other visual aids in the text, select two or three images that elicit the most significant impact. Are there one or two images that everyone in your group can agree on?

_____

_____

7. What other resources does the textbook offer? Where are they found? Describe.

_____

_____

Often the test of courage
is not to die but to live.

Conte Vittoria Alfieri

⇒ **Overview and Directions**

My personal review of death education courses taught at the college level has shown the following list of guest speakers and field trips were most frequently used. I've added a couple of others which have proven to be of interest to my classes. You may wish to work with your instructor in arranging some of these guest speakers and field trips. Field trips and guest speakers are not always applicable to all teaching situations. Work with your instructor or facilitator, who will know best.

1. Funeral Home Field Trip

2. City or County Morgue Field Trip

3. Cemetery Field Trip

4. Crematorium Field Trip

5. Home Hospice Agency

6. HIV/AIDS Panel

7. Biomedicine and Ethics

8. Program on Aging

9. War & Post-Traumatic Shock Syndrome - Vietnam Vet

10. Death and Dying in Children and Youth

11. Suicide Prevention

12. Beyond Death, After Life - Religion-Philosophy

13. Law and Death - Probate Attorney

14. Para-Psychology and the After Life - Psychic

15. Violence and Murder - Forensic Psychologist, Police Sciences

16. Psychiatric Clinical Issues of Death and Dying

17. Environmental Death

18. Hospital Chaplaincy Services

19. Organ Procurement Center

20. Support Groups - Advocacy Groups (i.e., MADD, Parents of Murdered Children)

Coroner's Office Field Trip

Even in death you pay taxes, less the Crowner take his due!

Old English saying

⇒ **Overview**

The term *coroner* actually derives from the old English word *crowner*. The term is close to a thousand years old. The Latin word for crown is *corona*, thus one can readily see where the term coroner derives from. Crowners were appointed by the Crown of England as agents to collect and seize revenues from murderers and persons who committed suicide. They often were sent to determine cause of death, again, so as to determine revenues. In the United States most coroners are elected officials, often sheriffs. The following page shows the major causes of death which must be reported to a coroner under California law. Most states have similar laws governing a coroner's inquest into suspicious deaths. You might ask your local county or city coroner's office about its specific laws and regulations.

The task of the coroner is to simply determine the cause of death in cases which are either unknown, unclear, unnatural, or suspicious in origin. Coroners who are also medical doctors are known as *medical examiners*. In cases where the coroner is not a physician, they employ a physician trained in *forensic pathology*. A *coroner's inquest* determines cause of death. The primary tool used to assist in the inquest is the autopsy. An *autopsy* is a *postmortem*--after death--examination of the body. The term "autopsy" derives from the Latin "to see for oneself." Through inspection and dissection the cause of death will hopefully be determined. Autopsies are on the decline due to increasing accuracy of physicians and hospitals now to determine cause of death. In cases of death which are suspicious and controversial a medical specialist known as a *death investigator* may also be used. It should be kept in mind that an autopsy may be conducted even when there is no suspicion of foul play or negligence. Oftentimes it is conducted when there is something to be learned to enhance medical research and progress.

One of the more interesting, though challenging, field trips, is a tour of a city or county "morgue"--more appropriately called "coroner's office." Many coroners routinely provide tours for the purpose of educating students and professionals in allied health fields, including students of death education. The tour can be arranged to include as much as may be appropriate for you and your brave classmates, not to mention your gutsy instructor. As a class, draw up a thorough set of questions before your visit. Don't expect to see an actual autopsy, though. There are often many legal restrictions to viewing autopsies, not to mention the liabilities when the faint-of-heart pass out on the floor. Just kidding. In all my years of conducting tours of coroner's offices, I've never had a student faint. That's a bit of myth perpetuated by television. In fact, most students were surprised how unstressful, professional, and interesting the tour was. You may simply have to settle on viewing the autopsy room with its vast array of instrumentation. A lively discussion is assured when you all return to class. These support materials follow: "Deaths Reportable to the Coroner" and a list of suggested "Coroner's Office Questions." A copy of a death certificate may be found elsewhere in your workbook. Be sure to complete your debriefing questions at the end of this exercise and activity.

Coroner's Office Reportable Deaths*

⇒ **Overview**

The following are the major causes of death which must be reported to the coroner in California. Most states in America are similar regarding a coroner's inquest into suspicious deaths. You should ask your local, county, or city coroner about your state's specific regulations.

1. No physician in attendance

2. Medical attendance less than 24 hours

3. Wherein the deceased has not been attended by a physician in the last 20 days prior to death

4. Physician unable to state the cause of death (unwillingness does not apply)

5. Known or suspected homicide

6. Known or suspected suicide

7. Involving any criminal action or suspicion of a criminal act

8. Related to or following known or suspected self-induced or criminal abortion

9. Associated with known or alleged rape or crime against nature

10. Following accident/injury (primary or contributory, occurring immediately or at some remote time)

11. Drowning, fire, hanging, gunshot, stabbing, cutting, starvation, exposure, acute alcoholism, drug addiction, strangulation, or aspiration

12. Accidental poisoning (food, chemical, drug, therapeutic agents)

13. Occupational diseases or occupational hazards

14. Known or suspected contagious disease, constituting a public hazard

15. All deaths in operating rooms

16. All deaths where a patient has not fully recovered from an anesthetic, whether in surgery, recovery room, or elsewhere

17. All deaths in which the patient is comatose throughout the period of physician's attendance, whether at home or at hospital

18. In prison or while under sentence

19. All solitary deaths (unattended by physician or other person in the period preceding death)

20. Where the suspected cause of death is Sudden Infant Death Syndrome (SIDS)

21. All deaths in state hospitals

*Source: Section 27491, Government Code, State of California

233

Coroner's Office Field Trip Questions

⇒ **Directions**

The following are the top 50 questions students in my death and dying courses have most frequently asked over the years. These questions have been gathered from years of taking students on tours to a coroner's office. You may wish to use these questions as a guide should you utilize such a field trip or presentation in your program. These questions are also useful as a script to help guide your guest presenter as well.

1. How many autopsies are done each year in your office?

2. What types of autopsies are performed each year? What does the law state about when an autopsy must be performed?

3. Under what circumstances are autopsies required? What is their purpose?

4. What actually is an autopsy? Can you describe one?

5. Who actually performs an autopsy?

6. What kinds of specialists and experts are used in autopsies at your office?

7. What is forensic medicine? What is a forensic pathologist?

8. What is the difference between a coroner and a medical examiner?

9. Do you have a copy of a death certificate to review? What is their purpose?

10. Do you use death investigators? If so, could you explain their function?

11. Are there other types of specialized criminalists you work with in cases of suspicious death?

12. What are some of the more interesting cases you have worked on?

13. Can you explain some of the tests conducted during an autopsy (bacteriological, toxicological)?

14. What are some of the more recent developments in forensic medicine which the coroner's office is utilizing? Does your office use DNA experts?

15. For what reasons is the coroner's office sometimes called to a murder or accident scene? Why can't an ambulance just come and take the body to the hospital?

16. What are some of the stranger cases you have seen while employed in the coroner's office?

17. Can insurance companies insist on an autopsy before paying out a claim, for example, if they suspect a suicide?

18. Can you explain what tools and materials are used in an autopsy room?

19. How did you come about choosing a career in the coroner's office?

20. What happens if no one claims a body after an autopsy?

21. What is a "pauper's grave?" How do you handle "unclaimed remains?"

22. What kind of care is taken with a body that has been autopsied?

23. During an autopsy, are organs taken out and not returned to the body?

24. Are contagious diseases a problem with the deceased during an autopsy?

25. What is the longest you've kept a body?

26. How do you keep bodies from decomposing?

27. What is the most number of autopsies you've performed in a day?

28. Is permission needed from next-of-kin before performing an autopsy?

29. I have heard of a case where they used a forensic anthropologist in an autopsy. Why was that?

30. What type of staff is employed here in this office?

31. How do you handle situations where a loved one must come to the morgue and identify a body?

32. How do you handle death notifications?

33. Do you like your job? What do you like most about the job? What do you like least?

34. Could you describe what a regular day's work entails?

35. Is there a high burnout rate and turnover in your job?

36. With so many deaths to deal with, many of them tragic, how do you develop coping skills? How does one take care of oneself emotionally in what I would imagine is a high-stress job?

37. What are some of the functions of the death certificate? What aspect of a death certificate is the coroner's office involved with?

38. Have you had many cases where a body was exhumed and an autopsy performed? If so, what are some of the reasons for doing this?

39. How much does it cost to run this coroner's office each year?

40. What procedures and protections do you use to protect yourselves from illness and disease and to preserve the dignity of the diseased?

41. How does your office work with the organ procurement unit in this region of the country?

42. What types of organs seem to be in demand these days? What types of organs are most commonly removed or harvested in this facility? Which organs and tissues can be donated?

43. What is the Uniform Anatomical Gift Act and how does it work?

44. If police arrive on the scene and find a critically injured person who is carrying a donor card, how is this complicated process of organ removal accomplished? Can you share a recent example of how this situation is coordinated? How are next-of-kin and those awaiting donors brought together in a timely fashion?

45. Are there laws regarding the sale or taking of tissue and organs from cadavers and living persons?

46. Does the coroner's office have any say in what happens to so-called "John or Jane Doe" cases (unknown and unclaimed bodies) in terms of organ donations and use of the body for medical science and research?

47. I've heard the expression "psychological autopsy." What is that?

48. What are some of the stereotypes regarding working in the coroner's office? How do you handle people's surprise when you tell them you work in the coroner's office?

49. Is there special training you must have? If so, what types of training and education do you have for your job here in the coroner's office?

50. Have you ever had a body arrive for an autopsy that was not dead? Any strange stories to share?

⇒ **Debriefing**

In closing out this activity consider the following. (1) What were your impressions of the coroner's office field trip or presentation? (2) Is this a job you could perform? (3) What surprised you? (4) What distressed you, if anything? (5) Were any of your anxieties regarding death and dying lessened or heightened afterwards? (6) What thoughts about death and dying arose as a result of contact with the coroner's office? (7) In group or class discuss individual highlights. Use the following space or the Active Journal section of the workbook for any notes you may have.

Notes: _____

_____

_____

_____

_____

_____

_____

_____

_____

_____

_____

Funeral Home Field Trip

The pomp of funerals
has more regard to the vanity of the living
than the honor of the dead.

Francois Duc de La Rochefoucald

Overview

Most funeral homes are honestly run businesses. Funeral directors often get a bad "rap" and are the brunt of much humor, but the fact is they provide a service many of us would care not to do, and for that we should all be grateful. Most funeral homes provide a full range of services which include preparation of the body, transportation, caskets, burial and cremation assistance, viewing, chapel facilities, and documentation assistance. (i.e., death certificates, permits, insurance benefits, obituaries, and other bureaucratic hurdles). The following field trip activity will provide you with valuable understanding. The information you gather and learn will be most useful when you are called upon to make final arrangements for when someone dies.

⇒ Directions and Debriefing

Visit a modern, respected, and well-known funeral home in your community. During your visit ask the following questions.[131] You might submit these questions to the funeral director in advance so as to assure more thorough responses. Be sure to gather any pamphlets, brochures, and other handouts to keep among your resource materials from this course.

1. Many children say what they want to be when they grow up. I would imagine they don't often say a mortician or funeral director. When did you know that you wanted to be a mortician? What prompted you to choose this career rather than that of a firefighter or a physician?

2. Will you tell us about the first time you saw a dead body? How did you feel?

3. What allows you to handle so much exposure to death? How do you cope?

4. How are you perceived by the public? For example, how do children react to your occupation? What about acquaintances, close friends, and relatives?

5. What training did you receive to perform your job well?

6. Did you receive training in grief counseling?

7. Would you describe the embalming process? Is it required by law and, if so, under what circumstances?

8. Can refrigeration substitute for embalming? How do the costs compare?

9. What is the longest period of time you've kept a body before final disposition?

10. Would you say something about body viewing? For example, under what circumstances would you recommend not viewing a body? When do you think body viewing is most beneficial for survivors? What are your feelings about the importance of viewing the body?

11. Should children view a body? Have there been situations when you thought they should not have viewed the body? What were the circumstances?

12. What are cosmetics? Are they required? What do you think are the advantages? Any disadvantages? Can certain lighting be used in place of cosmetics?

13. Making funeral rituals personally meaningful can be valuable for survivors. What requests do people make? How have some people personalized their funerals?

14. What types of choices about one's funeral need to be made at the time of a death? Can you explain "pre-planning" options in funeral arrangements?

15. What are some of the more creative ways of storing and presenting cremated remains (i.e., urns, sculptures and creative pottery)?

16. Could survivors handle all the details of a funeral themselves? How would it be done and what would be the costs?

17. What do you find to be the most difficult deaths? How do you personally cope with these deaths?

18. What are some of the costs in operating a funeral home?

19. Do you think the stereotype of the rich mortician making money from others' pain is sometimes accurate?

20. What kinds of malpractice suits is a mortuary subject to?

21. How does a funeral director build up their clientele and business?

22. Is this a family-owned and managed funeral home? Did you inherit the family business? What is meant by some media stories that "funeral homes are getting corporate and becoming conglomerates?"

⇒ **Matching Exercise**

For the following, match the correct definition in the right column with the term in the left column. You may wish to complete this exercise in conjunction with the "Cemetery Field Trip" exercise on page 239. After you are finished, compare your responses with the correct responses located in endnote 131.

1. ____ casket/coffin	a.	space in a columbarium, mausoleum, or niche wall to hold an urn
2. ____ cemetery property	b.	concrete cover or vault that fits over or covers a casket in a grave
3. ____ columbarium	c.	space in ground in cemetery for burial of human remains
4. ____ crypt	d.	box or chest for burying human remains
5. ____ endowment care trust	e.	place where a grave, crypt, or niche is located
6. ____ entombment	f.	a structure of vaults lined with recesses called "niches" for urns
7. ____ grave	g.	space in a mausoleum or other building to hold cremated human remains
8. ____ grave liner	h.	money collected for the purpose of maintaining cemetery property
9. ____ interment	i.	burial in a tomb above ground
10. ____ inurnment	j.	burial in the ground, inurnment, or entombment
11. ____ mausoleum	k.	the placing of cremated remains in an urn
12. ____ niche	l.	a large structure for above-ground burial, called entombment.
13. ____ prearrangement	m.	arranging for cemetery property in advance, <u>without</u> advance payment
14. ____ preneed planning	n.	arranging for cemetery property in advance, <u>with</u> payment
15. ____ urn	o.	container for holding cremated human remains

Cemetery Field Trip

Here lies one who for medicines would not give
A little gold, and so his life he lost.
I fancy now he'd wish again to live,
Could he but guess how much his funeral cost!

Unknown

⇒ **Overview**

Though ghostly as an activity, you can learn much about your personal fears and concerns of death through a visit to a local cemetery. Most modern cemeteries have staff who are "full-service" professionals. Services include lawn burial, cremation and niches (for the cremains), crypt entombment, memorial chapels, before-need arrangements and endowment care, and an assortment of grave markers and urns.

⇒ **Directions and Debriefing**

Visit a local but modern cemetery organization and ask some of the following 15 questions. Bring back to class some of the varied brochures describing services and costs. See if you might cost out a burial for yourself that meets your likes and needs. (1) What were your experiences from this visit? (2) How do you want your remains disposed of? Burial? Cremation? (3) Could you work at a cemetery? Why or why not? (4) What would you want written on your gravestone if all that was allowed was one sentence?

1. How do you figure out spacing needs for burials?

2. Explain costs for the different types of burials and dispositions of remains.

3. How do the crypt, niches, and crematorium operate?

4. Is your profession a good career? What personal traits are needed for your job?

5. What are some of the more interesting stories you recall from working here?

6. Explain "cremated remains." How long does it take to cremate a body? What are some of the mechanics and problems associated with cremation? Does everything burn? If not, what do you do?

7. Who pays for care and upkeep of the grounds?

8. What is meant by "in perpetuity"?

9. How do you handle different religions and cultures? Do you have a chapel?

10. How long are remains entitled to "their space in the ground"?

11. What are some of the laws regarding cemeteries?

12. Do you recommend advanced planning? If so, how might this be accomplished?

13. Is there a cemetery section on grounds for different religions, such as Jewish?

14. What is meant by cryonics? Do you provide these services?

15. What types of safeguards are used to assure that one person's remains are not mixed up or confused with another person's remains?

Shed no tear! O shed no tear!
The flower will bloom another year.
Weep no more! O weep no more!
Young buds sleep in the root's white core.

John Keats

⇒ **Overview**

Upon death many issues must be dealt with in a timely fashion. The disposition of the body is usually first. But all the earthly material needs must then be handled as well. The process of administering and executing these matters is referred to as *probate*, a term deriving from the Latin word *proba*re, to prove. This means the legitimacy of last wishes and the last will of the deceased must be proved to the satisfaction of the law. Under American law such post-death duties are carried out by the decedent's personal representative. These repre-sentatives are called either an *executor* (male) or *executrix* (female), if actually named in the will, or called an *administrator* if appointed by the court.

Estate and probate planning are important aspects of any death education program. There are many aspects to probate and estate planning to understand if one is to be sure one's wishes will be carried out when one dies. Simply having a will to give personal property and other estate assets away is no guarantee this will happen. It is always wise to have some guidance from an attorney. The following activity will make you all the wiser as pertains to probate and estate planning.

⇒ **Directions**

This activity involves inviting a probate attorney to class or interviewing a probate attorney at his or her offices. The following questions[132] are designed to inform students about the activities an attorney specializing in estate planning and probate would conduct. The attorney interviewed should be prepared to respond to questions about dying intestate, probate, estate and inheritance taxes, durable power of attorney, education, and personal experience.

⇒ **Questions**

1. We've read about a number of different kinds of wills in our readings and lectures. Some of us have made wills, but statistically, 7 out of 10 people die intestate. Perhaps some of us have not made a will because we have little property to leave our friends and loved ones and so we believe that wills are for others and not for us. Would you describe the average person for whom you draw up a formally executed will? For instance, what is his or her age and socioeconomic status?

2. What is contained in a typical will, with respect to both materials and nonmaterial considerations? Besides the distribution of the testator's property, what are the benefits of drawing up a will? Is there an emotional value for the testator and his survivors?

3. Under what circumstances would a mutual will or a conditional will be executed? What

240

about a holographic or nuncupative will? When would it be appropriate to have one of these types of wills?

4. What occurs in this state when a person dies without having a will? In other words, what are the laws of succession? Let's take a hypothetical case. Suppose a middle-aged corporation officer with two grown children divorces his wife to marry another woman. Then he adopts the new wife's two children from her previous marriage. The next year he dies of a heart attack, intestate. How would his estate be divided? For instance, would the line of succession go from his present spouse to the four children? What about the former wife he was married to for more than 20 years? If a former spouse is not included in the laws of succession, does she or he have any recourse? How would a court determine the distribution of property in such cases?

5. In turning to the subject of probate, would you describe the legal procedures that occur when a client dies? What actions do you take? Under what circumstances might you be named as executor? What does an executor or executrix do? What is the cost of probate and is there any way to reasonably avoid it? Are there any pitfalls in trying to avoid probate?

6. With respect to estate and inheritance taxes, would you briefly describe each and how they differ. What exactly is taxed? How might one reduce tax burdens?

7. Are you familiar with living wills or natural death directives? Have you been asked to prepare any? Under what circumstances do you find them to be valuable? Do you believe that having a living will may result in an individual experiencing a "better" death? Is the living will legally enforceable? Are individuals truly able to exercise choice about life support? What are some problems of living wills and similar measures?

8. What are some of your comments regarding advanced directives and durable power of attorney for health care and legal affairs?

9. What was the most complicated or difficult will you prepared? Why?

10. As a professional, how do you cope with loss when one of your clients dies? Would you describe any particularly difficult experiences related to issues of loss?

11. In your experience, does law school prepare attorneys for dealing with survivors? One might imagine a course entitled "Survivors 102" being of some use. If there is some law school preparation, how is the topic of death dealt with? Has this aspect of your work ever been a problem to you?

⇒ **Debriefing**

(1) What is the importance, in your own words, of having an understanding of probate and estate planning? (2) Discuss what might happen if you died without a legal will. (3) What are some advantages of having your affairs in order for your survivors? (4) Put together a timeline for completing your will. (5) See the exercise "Using NOLO Press's WillMaker" found on page 122. Use this software on your computer and complete a will and other advance directives.

Post-Test

"I've always thought it was eerie. He expired the same day as his Visa card."

And sweet is death who puts an end to pain.

Alfred, Lord Tennyson

⇒ **Overview**

The purpose of this post-test is to gauge how much your *personal level of information* about some of the major issues in death education has increased since you first took the same pre-test version at the beginning of this course, workshop, or seminar. You have learned much, I'm sure, about many of the major themes in death education. Now, let's see how much more confident and knowledgeable you have, in fact, become. Remember, there are some blank spaces at the end should your instructor or facilitator wish additional item statements be included in this post-test. Be sure to write the same ones in, if any, as found on the pre-test. Compare your post-test score with your pre-test score. Were you pleased with your growth? You may wish to compare your findings in small group. What were your strengths and weaknesses? Develop a new list of growth areas to work on for the future. Commit yourself to further growth by reading additional books suggested by your instructor or facilitator.

⇒ **Directions**

Using the following five point scale indicate your level of agreement or disagreement with each statement. Total your score for each statement and divide by the total number of statements (40). This is your knowledge level score.

Strongly Disagree	Disagree	Neutral	Agree	Strongly Agree
1	2	3	4	5

_____ 1. I am not uneasy thinking about death.

_____ 2. I feel able to discuss issues of death, dying, and bereavement with myself and others.

_____ 3. I feel able to face and accept my own death.

_____ 4. It is important to prepare for death in myself and with others I love.

_____ 5. I am knowledgeable in helping others face issues surrounding death.

_____ 6. I understand reasons for suicide.

_____ 7. I could actively help someone who is feeling suicidal.

_____ 8. I would be able to work with someone who is terminally ill.

I understand the function and utilization of the following:

9. _____ Hospital resources   11. _____ Spiritual resources
10. _____ Chaplaincy services   12. _____ Funeral homes

243

13. _____ Nursing homes		16. _____ Cemeteries	
14. _____ Coroner's office		17. _____ Hospice programs	
15. _____ Probate attorney		18. _____ Rituals	

_____ 19. I understand many of the various community self-help and support programs available for people dealing with dying, death, grief, and bereavement.

_____ 20. I am knowledgeable about the issues of patient biomedical ethics.

_____ 21. I am knowledgeable about organ donor programs and transplantation programs.

_____ 22. I am knowledgeable concerning issues about "the right to die," advance directives, living wills, and patient self-determination.

_____ 23. I understand what my particular fears of death are.

_____ 24. I understand how culture in general and my culture in particular responds to death with rituals.

_____ 25. I could hold discussions with a dying person.

_____ 26. I understand how AIDS is transmitted and other facts about AIDS.

_____ 27. I could be helpful in assessing how serious a suicide threat is.

_____ 28. I understand issues of death due to violence and natural disaster.

_____ 29. I would be helpful to someone who has lost a pet.

_____ 30. I could plan a funeral.

_____ 31. I could assist someone who is grieving a death.

_____ 32. I am able to discuss death with children.

_____ 33. I know how to write a condolence letter and how to choose and write a sympathy card.

_____ 34. I understand how our society views death and how the media portrays death.

_____ 35. I understand what an "out-of-body" experience is.

_____ 36. I have an understanding of afterlife issues.

_____ 37. I have developed philosophical and/or spiritual values.

_____ 38. I understand some of the processes of dying.

_____ 39. I understand some of the processes of mourning.

_____ 40. I am familiar with issues surrounding aging as it relates to death and dying.

_____ 41. _____

_____ 42. _____

_____ 43. _____

_____ 44. _____

Appendixes

1. Active Journal Keeping Notes

2. Endnotes

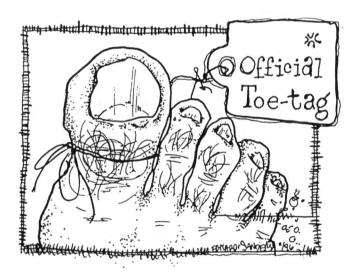

Active Journal Keeping

For certain is death for the born
And certain is birth for the dead;
Therefore over the inevitable
Thou shouldst not grieve.

Bhagavad Gita

⇒ **Overview**

Make photocopies of the following pages and keep them in your Active Journal. As the name suggests an Active Journal--or AJ--is one which is used *actively* in conjunction with your text readings, lectures, activities, and exercises. Journals and diaries are ageless and timeless tools for communicating with oneself, thus sorting out the day's traumas, events, experiences, and circumstances. They are as relevant as they were at the time of the great Egyptian pharaohs. They are what I call written dreams. Whereas sleep and dreams "knit up the unraveled sleeve of care" of the past day's events, to quote Shakespeare, so does the dialogue between oneself and a journal accomplish the same.

In terms of purpose, Active Journal Keeping provides (1) a method for personal reflection and non-threatening communication and feedback; (2) a way of processing anxiety-producing thoughts; (3) a method of identifying confusion, questions, feelings, and puzzling thoughts; (4) a gauge for noting growth, change, directions, insights, learning, and new discoveries; and (5) a technique for reinforcing concepts and knowledge associated with classroom and textbook learning. It is a wonderful tool for exploring death and dying--and for moving on with your life!

⇒ **Directions and Debriefing**

The AJ is your confidential tool, and as such should be utilized regularly with utmost candor, thoughtfulness, and effort. There is no formal format or ritual to follow. The extent of positive results will hinge, however, on nothing less then your best effort at learning, growing, and self-actualizing. After all it is your journal, thus it is you. Use your AJ daily and whenever possible.

Questions for you to consider at course's end include (1) Was the journal useful? (2) Was the journal difficult to maintain? (3) Will you continue to keep a journal? (4) What kinds of changes might you make to maximize the AJ for you? (5) Were there any noteworthy changes and growth in you from keeping your AJ? Best wishes. To help commit yourself, set your own ground rules, then date and sign your name. Add new pages as needed.

I, _____, will maintain my Active Journal by writing entries in my AJ daily for at least one month before changing how frequently I will write in it. Date _____ (30 days later). The frequency of my journal keeping will be _____

_____

_____

_____

Active Journal Keeping

(Note: Make photo copies before using!)

Endnotes

1. Kochanek K. D. & Hudson, B. L. (1995). Advance report of final mortality statistics, 1992. *Monthly Vital Statistics Report*; Vol. 43 No 6, suppl. Hyattsville, Maryland: National Center for Health Statistics, pp. 18-19, Tables 3 and 4.

2. Cutler, R. G. (1976). Evolution of longevity in primates. *Journal of Human Evolution, 5,* 169-202 and Kochanek K. D. & Hudson, B. L. (1995). Advance report of final mortality statistics, 1992. *Monthly Vital Statistics Report*; Vol. 43 No. 6, suppl. Hyattsville, Maryland: National Center for Health Statistics, p. 1.

3. Phillips, D. P. (1975). Deathday and birthday: An unexpected connection. In K. W. C. Kammeyer (Ed.), *Population studies* (2nd ed.). Skokie, IL: Rand McNally and Phillips, D. P., and Feldman, K. A. (1973). A dip in deaths before ceremonial occasions: Some new relationships between social integration and mortality. *American Sociological Review*, pages 38, 678-696.

4. Aiken, L. R. (1994). *Dying, Death and Bereavement.* Boston: Allyn & Bacon, pp. 33-34.

5. In 1992 life expectancy at <u>birth</u> reached 75.8 years for all Americans on average. The figures are 79.8 for white women, 73.9 for black females, 73.2 for white males and 65.0 for black males. See Kochanek K. D. and Hudson, B. L. (1995). Advance report of final mortality statistics, 1992. *Monthly vital statistics report*; Vol. 43, No. 6, suppl. Hyattsville, Maryland: National Center for Health Statistics, p. 1.

6. Leming, M. R. (1979-1980). Religion and death: A test of Homan's thesis. *Omega*, pages 10 (4), 347 364.

7. Gallup Poll. (1991). *Fear of Dying.* The Gallup Poll.

8. Templer, A. (1972). *Journal of General Psychology,* pages 82, 1167-1972. Reprinted with permission of the Helen Dwight Reid Educational Foundation. Published by Heldref Publications, 1319 Eighteenth St., NW, Washington DC 20036-1802. © 1972. Note: Answers are 1T, 2F, 3F, 4T, 5F, 6F, 7F, 8T, 9T, 10T, 11T, 12T, 13T, 14T, 15F. If your responses were similar to 10 or more of the 15 scale items above, your anxiety level may be considered unusually high.

9. For further information see Kearl, M. C. (1989). *Endings: A Sociology of Death and Dying.* London: Oxford University Press, and Kastenbaum, R. J. (1992). *The Psychology of Death,* (2nd ed.). New York: Springer Publishing Company.

10. The author wishes to acknowledge Dr. Joseph Simons, my colleague at Santa Rosa Junior College, for sharing this humorous story with me.

11. Hall, G. S. (1904). *Adolescence: Its Psychology and Its Relations to Physiology, Anthropology, Sociology, Sex, Crime, Religion, and Education* (Vols. I and 2). New York: Appleton.

12. Nagy, M. H. (1948/1969). The child's theories concerning death. In H. Feifel (Ed.). *The Meaning of Death.* New York: McGraw-Hill. Reprinted from *Journal of Genetic Psychology*, pages 73, 3-27.

13. See Kastenbaum's very capable chapter 8, Death in the World of Children, for further discussion. In

Kastenbaum, R. (1995). *Death, Society, and Human Experience*. Boston: Allyn & Bacon, pp. 189-221.

14. Wenestam, C. G., & Wass, H. (1987). Swedish and U. S. children's thinking about death: A qualitative study and cross-cultural comparison. *Death Studies*, 11: 99-122.

15. Kastenbaum, R. (1995). *Death, Society, and Human Experience*. Boston: Allyn & Bacon, p. 194.

16. Adapted from: DeSpelder, L. and Strickland, A . (1992). *The Last Dance* (3rd Ed.). Mountain View, CA: Mayfield. Used by permission.

17. Excerpted from: Michael Talbot. (1986) *The Bog*. New York: William Morrow, pp. 192-194. Used by permission.

18. I am indebted to Carleen Madsen, Facilitator, "Just for Kids," a support group for children and youth dealing with death and dying. The program is part of Home Hospice of Soma County (Santa Rosa, California). This exercise was based on a presentation she gave to my death and dying class in April of 1996.

19. Things to remember about these ten tips: (1) Children look to adults, especially adults in their own family, for guidance. Nice as it might be to hope all will be gathered from a child's time in school, this is not the case. Parents must communicate and discuss issues surrounding death and dying. Tell i t honest, tell i t the way it is. Kids know when you are lying. For example, when i t comes to explaining to a young child why a body died, you might say it was broken, worn out, tired, or old. Children understand discussions where simple basic words are used. (2) Involve children in the sickness and dying stages early on. It is important for them to learn how life really is, that is, often a series of sequential stages from health, to sickness, to dying, to death. (3) Don't wait until there is a crisis of death and dying to explain death to children. Introduce the topic early on, keeping in mind the developmental nature of children. (4) The best way to explain the facts is by being a supportive listener and by asking a child to describe what it is he or she thinks has happened or is happening with someone who is dying or is dead. Verify with a child what he or she thinks they heard you say. This feedback loop is important. (5) Be clear and don't use euphemisms when talking directly about death. "We lost grandma," may only make the child wonder if you might lose him or her too! Call i t like i t is! (6) Children can process information of a stressful nature in manageable "bits and pieces." You would never expect a child to go from simple math to algebra in one sitting, and so it is equally true of discussions on death and dying. Share meaningful but manageable information on the subject and have the child report back what he or she is hearing. Correct children when errors in thinking pop up. (7) When i t comes to God or other spirituality issues, choose your words carefully. Share your spiritual values and beliefs, but the fact is we will not know until we die what actually happens; let children know this, too. Let children also know what you believe are your beliefs. This is what faith is all about, isn't it? Children may not feel very good about a god "that took daddy," so watch your use of fairy tales, metaphors, and euphemisms. (8) Children, like most of us learn best by OJT--on-the-job training. Involve children in the rituals of loss and remembrance. If you go and visit a grave from time-to-time, take the children with you. It is important they learn early on ways of processing grief and loss and of remembering those loved but now dead. (9) Providing children with books appropriate to their age, letting them draw, paint, do puzzles, play with clay, etc., are all good therapeutic methods of encouraging children to handle and manage the anxiety and stress associated with loss. (10) Develop an understanding of resources and familiarize yourself with a t least some of them. Better yet, keep some resources like community support group listings and books for children and adolescents handy and available when you need them.

20. For a fine discussion of death in childhood games see Opie, I., and Opie, R. (1969). *Children's Games in Street and Playground*. London: Oxford University Press.

21. For a more comprehensive listing of books see the following bibliographies. Benson, H. B. (1988). *The Dying Child: An Annotated Bibliography*. Westport, CT: Greenwood Press; Miller-Lachmann, L. (1992). *Our*

Family, Our Friends, Our World: An Annotated Guide to Significant Multi-cultural Books for Children and Teenagers. New York: R. R. Bowker; Pyles, M. S. (1988). *Death and Dying in Children's and Young People's Literature.* Jefferson, NC: McFarland; and Rudman, M. K., Gagne, K. D. and Bernstein, J. E. (1993) *Books to Help Children Cope with Separation and Loss: An Annotated Bibliography,* (4th ed.). New York: R. R. Bowker.

22. The author wishes to thank Dr. Carla Sofka of the School of Social Welfare at the University of New York at Albany for her assistance in the critique and improvement of this exercise.

23. Hutchins, S. H., (1986). Stillbirth. In T. A. Rando (Ed.) *Parental Loss of a Child,* pp. 129-144. Champaign, IL: Research Press. Adapted by permission.

24. You may also wish to see Bowlby's discussion of "attachment and loss" in Bowlby, J. (1980). *Loss.* New York: Basic Books; Kohlberg's discussion of "moral development," in Kohlberg, L. (1981). *The Philosophy of Moral Devleopment.* New York: Harper & Row; and Ainsworth's discussion of "attachment" in Ainsworth, M. D. S. (1989). Attachments beyond infancy. *American Psychologist,* pp. 44, 709-716.

25. Nagy, M. H. (1948). The child's theories concerning death. *Journal of Genetic Psychology,* pp. 73, 3-27.

26. Erikson, E. (1950). *Childhood and Society.* New York: W.W. Norton.

27. Pulaski, M. A. S. (1980). *Understanding Piaget: An Introduction to Children's Cognitive Development.* New York: Harper & Row.

28. Barrow, Georgia M. (1996). *Aging, the Individual, and Society* (6th ed.). St. Paul, MN: West Publishing, p. 24.

29. Adapted from: Rebelsky, F. G. (1981). Life span development. In L. T. Benjamin, Jr. and K. D. Lowman (Eds.). *Activities Handbook for the Teaching of Psychology* (Vol. 1). Washington, DC: American Psychological Association, pp. 131-132. © 1981 by the American Psychological Association. Adapted with permission.

30. Zimbardo P. (1993). *Psychology and Life* (13th ed.). New York: HarperCollins, pp. 200-201.

31. Barrows, G. M. (1996). *Aging, the Individual, and Society* (6th ed.). St. Paul, MN: West Publishing, p. 6. Other sources used for this exercise include: Norman, M. (1996, February 1). Are people living too long? *The Press Demeocrat.* Sonoma County, California, p. B5; Cole, T. R. (1992). *The Journey of Life: A Cultural History of Aging in America.* Cambridge: Cambridge University Press; and Stern, C. (1996, January 21). Who is old? *Parade,* pp. 4-5.

32. Zimbardo, P., Conrad, E., and Rafter, M. (1992). *Instructor's Resource Kit to Accompany Zimbardo's Psychology and Life* (13th ed.). New York: HarperCollins, pp. 209, 211. A discussion of the *Aging Quiz* follows. The answers to all the statements are false. (1) False. Younger people are more likely to attend church. This does not mean that religious commitment decreased with age. (2) False. In decision-making problems where the choice is between low-risk and high-risk alternatives, older people are as likely as younger people to choose the high-risk alternative. (3) Older people belong to a cohort that experienced the same historical events and environmental conditions. For example, they lived through and were affected by the depression of the 1930s and World War II. Your own age cohort has similarities as a result of the events of your times. Individual differences are just as pronounced among older people as among younger ones. (4) False. Adaptive ability is an aspect of the personality that tends to remain stable over time. Many older people voluntarily change their place of residence after retirement, and they buy personal computers, and compact-disc players. (5) False. There is no general decline in life satisfaction with age. The life satisfaction of individuals as they grow older is, however, more likely to be affected by death or illness of friends and loved ones. (6) False. At any one time about 5% of people over 65 are residing in this type of institution. Some are permanent residents but many

of incurable disease or physical disability. Others are temporary residents who are recovering from an illness or injury. (7) False. The National Institute of Mental Health has concluded that older people are less likely than younger people to suffer from psychopathology. (8) False. Depression is relatively common at any age, but older people are no more likely to have chronic depression than younger people. (9) False. Decrease in cognitive functions is not inevitable. Research suggest that if it occurs among healthy senior citizens, it is a result of lack of practice at intellectual tasks. Intellect is apparently like sex--use it or lose it. (10) False. Researchers have suggested that the brain could continue to function efficiently for 150 or 200 years if it were supported by other bodily systems. (11) Most suicides occur with people under age 45, but the suicide rate for the very elderly is on the rise. (12) Alzheimer's disease affects approximately 10% of people over age 65. The percentage rise to 47.2% for those age 85 or older.

33. Berman, D. M. (1978). Death on the job: Occupational health and safety struggles in the United States. New York: *Monthly Review Press*, pp. 179-180.

34. See Rando, T. A. (1984). *Grief, Dying, and Death.* Champaign, IL: Research Press, pp. 227-250.

35. Oken, D. (1961). What to tell cancer patients. *JAMA*, 175: 1120-1128.

36. Novack, D., Plumer, R., Smith, R. Ochitill, H. Morrow, G. and Bennett, J. (1979). Changes in physician's attitudes toward telling the cancer patient. *JAMA, 241:* 897-900.

37. Branden, N. (1987). *How to Raise Your Self-esteem.* New York: Bantam.

38. Selye, H. (1974). *Stress Without Distress.* New York: New American Library.

39. Zimbardo, P. (1992). *Psychology and Life.* New York: HarperCollins, p. 475.

40. Holmes, T. H., & Rahe, R. H. (1967). The social readjustment rating scale. *Journal of Psychosomatic Research,* 11(2), 213-218.

41. Myers. D. G. (1995). *Psychology.* New York: Worth, p. 575.

42. Selye, H. (1936). A syndrome produced by diverse nocuous agents. *Nature, 138,* 32, and Selye, H. (1976). *The Stress of Life.* New York: McGraw-Hill.

43. Maslach, C. (1982). *Burnout: The Cost of Caring.* Englewood Cliffs, New Jersey: Prentice-Hall, p. 580.

44. Larson, D. (1993). *The Helper's Journey.* Champaign, IL: Research Press.

45. Adapted from: Pines, A. M., & Aronson, E. (1988). *Career Burnout: Causes and Cures.* New York: Free Press, p. 219. Adapted with the permission of The Free Press, an imprint of Simon & Schuster from *Career Burnout: Causes and Cures* by Ayala Pines and Elliot Aronson. Copyright © 1980, 1988 by Ayala Pines, Ph. D. and Elliot Aronson, Ph. D.

46. Silverman, P. (1986). *Widow to Widow.* New York: Springer.

47. Kastenbaum, R. (1995). *Death, Society, and, Human Experience.* Boston: Allyn & Bacon, p. 39.

48. Ibid., p. 41.

49. For a good discussion of death from historical perspectives see Aries, P. (1981). *The Hour of Our Death.* New York: Alfred A. Knopf.

50. Ibid., p. 40.

51. Oaks, J. and Ezell, G. (1993). *Dying and Death: Coping, Caring, Understanding* (2nd Ed.). Scottsdale, AZ: Gorsuch Scarisbrick, pp. 54-57.

52. Corr, C. A., Nabe, C. M., & Corr, D. M. (1994). Death and dying, life and living. Pacific Grove, CA: Brooks/Cole, pp. 105-106.

53. Though it is important to note that Kübler-Ross herself didn't propose a theory that described an orderly predictable progression through stages, it has unfortunately come to be viewed that her theory does in fact do just that.

54. I wish to acknowledge Dr. Carla Sofka of the School of Social Welfare at The State University of New York at Albany for her helpful comments regarding living wills.

55. Emanuel, L. L., and E. J. Emanuel. (1989). The medical directive: a new comprehensive advance care document. *JAMA*, 261: 3288-3293; Emanuel, L. L., and E. J. Emanuel. (1990). The medical directive: A new comprehensive advance care document. *Harvard Medical School Health Letter*, (Supplement), June; and Emanuel, L. (1991). The health care directive: Learning how to draft advance care documents. *JAGS*, 39: 1221-1228.

56. Choice In Dying, (1995). *California Advance Directive Guide*. New York: Choice In Dying.

57. Copyright California Medical Association, 1995. Published with permission of and by arrangement with the California Medical Association. Copies of this form, as well as an accompanying brochure and wallet card, may be obtained from CMA publications at (415) 882-5175.

58. The SUPPORT Principal Investigators. (1995). A controlled trial to improve care for seriously ill hospitalized patients: The study to understand prognoses and preferences for outcomes and risks of treatments (SUPPORT). *Journal of the American Medical Association*, 274(20):1591-1598, and Perlman, D. (1995, November 22). Dying patients' wishes often ignored, study says. *San Francisco Chronicle*, pp. 1, 19.

59. American Hospital Association (1992). A patient bill of rights. Chicago: American Hospital Association. *A Patient's Bill of Rights* was first adopted by the American Hospital association in 1973. This revision was approved by the AHA Board of Trustees on October 21, 1992. Copyrighted © 1992 by the American Hospital Association. One North Franklin, Chicago, IL 60606, (312) 442-2119. Reprinted with permission.

60. Though there are several different versions to be found, my version of "A Dying Person's Bill of Rights" was influenced somewhat by: Donovan, M. and Pierce, S. (1976). *Cancer Care Nursing*. New York: Appleton-Century-Crofts, p. 33.

61. DeSpelder, L. and Strickland, A. (1992). *The Last Dance* (3rd ed.). Mountain View, CA: Mayfield.

62. Glaser, B. G., and Strauss, A. L. (1968). *Time for Dying* . Chicago: Aldine.

63. Kübler-Ross, E. (1969). *On Death and Dying*. New York: MacMillan.

64. Glaser, B. G., and Strauss, A. L. (1966). *Awareness of Dying*. Chicago: Aldine.

65. Trajectories answers are as follows: (1) lingering trajectory, (2) pointed trajectory, (3) danger-period trajectory, (4) crisis trajectory, (5) will-probably-die trajectory, (6) unexpected quick trajectory: suddenly and unexpectedly, and (7) unexpected quick trajectory: rescue.

66. Associated Press. (1995, December 16). 18.5 million infected with AIDS virus. *San Francisco Chronicle*, p. A4. The article reported that the World Health Organization (WHO) presented its new figures as a result of better reporting data. The new figures show a greater spread of HIV by several million over earlier data released in early 1995.

67. Kochanek K. D. & Hudson, B. L. (1995). Advance report of the final mortality statistics, 1992. *Monthly vital statistics report*; Vol. 43, no. 6, suppl. Hyattsville, MD: National Center for Health Statistics, p. 23-24.

68. Answers for <u>Part I: Fact or Fiction About AIDS</u> questions 1-19. (1) F, AIDS is an equal opportunity infector; (2) F, there is no evidence; (3) F, it is recommended you be tested yearly unless you have no sexual contacts. If you have any reason to suspect you might have been infected you should be tested more often; (4) heterosexuals are the primary carriers of the HIV virus worldwide; (5) T; (6) F, the rate of HIV transmission among women is greatly on the rise; (7) T; (8) F, numerous studies of medical staff have found no greater rate of transmission other than by an occasional needle prick from a contaminated needle; (9) F, see above 8; (10) F, no evidence; (11) F, though generally safe, improper use of condoms and condom breakage together with having sexual contact with an infected person can lead to HIV transmission; (12) F, this is a myth. Use of birth control pills does not prevent transmission of the HIV virus; (13) F, no evidence; (14) T, but only prior to 1985. If the source of the blood supply is in question, yes, you could receive HIV transmission. In the United States, however, safeguards are adequate to prevent such an occurrence; (15) F, no evidence, though it is not recommended you use such utensils; (16) F, no evidence, very low risk; (17) F, in the later stages of AIDS the loss of weight and "wasting away syndrome," might be evident. However in the early stages there would be no signs thus the virus might be considered more dangerous; (18) F, the rural and country spread of AIDS is growing at alarming rates; (19) T, there is no cure for AIDS and none in sight. Though with treatment one may live for many years, there appear to be very few long-term survivors. Answers for <u>Part II: Defining AIDS</u> 1-c; 2-a; 3-d; and 4-b. Answers for <u>Part III: Major Routes of HIV Transmission</u> (1) birth or perinatal birth; (2) unprotected; (3) sharing or exchanging; and (4) blood or plasma.

69. Fitts, W., and Ravdin, I. (1953). What Philadelphia physicians tell patients with cancer. *JAMA, 153*: 901-904; Greenwald, H., and Nevitt, M. (1982). Physician attitudes toward communication with cancer patients. *Social Science and Medicine*, 16: 591-594, and Novack, D., Plumer, R., Smith, R., Ochitill, H., Morrow, G., and Bennett, J. (1979). Changes in physician's attitudes toward telling the cancer patient. *JAMA*, 241: 897-900.

70. Oken, D. (1961). What to tell cancer patients. *JAMA, 175*: 1120-1128 & Novack, D., Plumer, R., Smith, R., Ochitill, H., Morrow, G., and Bennett, J. (1979). Changes in physician's attitudes toward telling the cancer patient. *JAMA, 241*: 897-900.

71. Glaser, B., and Strauss, A. (1965). *Awareness of Dying*. Chicago: Aldine.

72. The task force was called the International Work Group on Death and Dying and included Dr. Cicely Saunders who is credited with founding the first modern hospice, St. Christopher's Hospice in London.

73. Kastenbaum, R. (1995). *Death, Society, and Human Experience*. Boston: Allyn & Bacon, pp. 115-118.

74. The author wishes to acknowledge psychology graduate student and friend Damon Jacobs for his helpful ideas in reworking my first draft of this exercise.

75. Wilcox, S., and Sutton, M. (1985). *Understanding Death and Dying: An Interdisciplinary Approach* (3rd ed.). Mountain View, CA: Mayfield.

76. Adapted from DeSpelder, L., and Strickland, A. (1992). *The Last Dance* (3rd ed.). Mountain View, CA: Mayfield. Used with permission.

77. The author wishes to acknowledge Professor Ricardo Joseph of Santa Rosa Junior College, Santa Rosa, CA, for providing some ideas and rough draft materials for this exercise.

78. Opening paragraph adapted from Harvey, J. H. (1996). *Embracing Their Memory: Loss and the Social Psychology of Storytelling*. Boston: Allyn & Bacon, p. 92.

79. This graphical depiction was based on a figure of 25,488 reported homicides in 1992. The weekly figure was drawn by dividing the total by 365 days and multiplying by 7 days to pull a representative weekly total. This is an inference as exact weekly totals are not available.

80. Kochanek K. D., and Hudson, B. L. (1995). Advance report of final mortality statistics, 1992. *Monthly vital statistics report*; Vol. 43, No. 6, suppl. Hyattsville, Maryland: National Center for Health Statistics, Table 6, p.23.

81. Comment by Children's Defense Fund, Washington, D.C., April, 1996.

82. Kastenbaum, R. J. (1995). *Death, Society, and Human Experience*. Boston: Allyn & Bacon, p. 256-257; Kochanek K. D., and Hudson, B. L. (1995). Advance report of final mortality statistics, 1992. *Monthly Vital Statistics Report*; Vol. 43, No. 6, suppl. Hyattsville, Maryland: National Center for Health Statistics; and Holmes, R. M., and Holmes, S. T. (1994). *Murder in America*. Thousand Oaks, CA: Sage.

83. Flood, R. A., & Seager, C. P. (1968). A retrospective examination of psychiatric case records of patients who subsequently committed suicide. *British Journal of Psychiatry*, 114, 433-450.

84. Kochanek K. D. & Hudson, B. L. (1995). Advance report of final mortality statistics, 1992. *Monthly Vital Statistics Report*; Vol. 43 No 6, suppl. Hyattsville, Maryland: National Center for Health Statistics, p. 23 Table 6.

85. Zimbardo, P. G. & Gerrig, R. J. (1996). *Psychology and Life*. New York: HarperCollins, p. 655.

86. LaFromboise, T. (1988, March 30). Suicide prevention. In *Campus Report*, p. 9. Stanford, CA: Stanford University Press.

87. Kochanek K. D. & Hudson, B. L. (1995). Advance report of final mortality statistics, 1992. *Monthly Vital Statistics Report*; Vol. 43, No. 6, suppl. Hyattsville, Maryland: National Center for Health Statistics, p. 23 Table 6.

88. National Center for Health Statistics. (1989). Hyattsville, MD: Public Health Service. In Zimbardo, P. G. & Gerrig, R. J. (1996). *Psychology and Life*. New York: HarperCollins, p. 655.

89. Coleman, L. (1987). *Suicide Clusters*. Winchester, MA: Faber & Faber, and Garland, A. F., & Zigler, E. (1993). Adolescent suicide prevention. *American Psychologist*, 48, 169-182.

90. Associated Press. (1996, January 14). Suicide rate increasing among elderly in U. S. *San Francisco Chronicle*, p. A3.

91. DeSpelder, L. & Strickland, A . (1996).*The Last Dance* (4th Ed.). Mountain View, CA: Mayfield, p. 487.

92. Fish, W. C., & Waldhart-Letzel, E. (1981). Suicide and children. *Death Education* 5: 217-220; Peck, M. (1982). Youth suicide. *Death Education* 6:29-47; Stillion, J. M., McDowell, E. E., & May, J. H. (1989). *Suicide Across the Life Span: Premature Exits*. New York: Hemisphere, p. 95-100. In DeSpelder, L., & Strickland, A.

(1996). *The Last Dance* (4th Ed.). Mountain View, CA: Mayfield, p. 483.

93. Fish, W. C., & Waldhart-Letzel, E. (1981). Suicide and children. *Death Education* 5: 217-220; Peck, M. (1982). Youth suicide. *Death Education* 6:29-47; Stillion, J. M., McDowell, E. E., & May, J. H. (1989). *Suicide Across the Life Span: Premature Exits.* New York: Hemisphere, pp. 95-100. In DeSpelder, L., & Strickland, A. (1996). *The Last Dance* (4th Ed.). Mountain View, CA: Mayfield, p. 483, and Associated Press. (1996, January 14). Suicide rate increasing among elderly in U. S. *San Francisco Chronicle*, p. A3.

94. Capuzzi, D. (1989). *Adolescent Suicide Prevention.* Ann Arbor, MI: ERIC Counseling and Personnel Services Clearinghouse. In Berk, L. E. (1996). *Infants, Children and Adolescents* (2nd Ed.). Boston: Allyn & Bacon, p. 614.

95. Wekstein, L. (1979). *Handbook of Suicidology.* New York: Bunner/Mazel, p. 129.

96. Fremouw, W. J., De Perczel, M., & Ellis, T. E. (1990). *Suicide Risk: Assessment and Response Guidelines.* New York: Pergamon Press; Rosenthal, H. (1988). *Not with My Life I Don't: Preventing Your Suicide and That of Others.* Muncie, IN: Accelerated Development; and Shneidman, E. S., Farberow, N. L., & Litman, R. E. (Eds.). (1970). *The psychology of Suicide.* New York: Science House.

97. The answers are all false The responses represent the most recent knowledge and consensus regarding such statements about suicide. A brief discussion of each follows. (1) Eight out of ten of the people who commit suicide have given some warning beforehand that they were about to do so. Often they have given multiple warnings. (2) Those who commit suicide are not certain that they really want to die. They often take a gamble that someone will save them. The person who overdoses on drugs often calls someone first, in hopes they will be saved. (3) In fact, most suicides occur while an individual is still depressed but after the individual shows some recovery. Often, people who are severely depressed are unable even to gather the energy to put together the means to commit suicide. (4) Most suicides occur during an acute crisis. Once the person gets through the crisis, the desire to commit suicide fades. One researcher tracked down 515 people who had attempted suicide by jumping off the Golden Gate Bridge many years earlier. Fewer than 5% had actually committed suicide in the subsequent decades (Seiden, 1978). (5) Though there appears to be a genetic link for some forms of depression, no major evidence exists for a genetic connection for suicide. There are some family and generational suicidal clusters, but the reasoning is not yet understood. It may have more to due with family value systems as to why various family members commit suicide.(6) Suicide is about equally prevalent at all levels of the socioeconomic spectrum, though higher rates are at both extremes of the spectrum--the very poor and unemployed and the very successful and high-pressured, such as attorneys and executives.(7) Although suicide is linked to depression, relatively few people who commit suicide are truly out of touch with reality. (8) Although depressed people commit suicide at a rate 25 times higher than nondepressed people, many suicides are by those who are chronically ill or elderly. Peace of mind or not becoming a burden are often factors rather than depression. (9) There is no "suicidal type." The reasoning and motive for a suicide are often as varied as those who commit suicide. There are some cluster factors. They include depression, isolation, loneliness, substance abuse, romantic and financial factors. (10) Men do not attempt suicide as often as women do. However men succeed more often in actually committing suicide because they use more lethal means, such as guns. Women attempt suicide more often, but fail, as they use drugs, such as pills rather than guns, thus contributing to the likelihood they will be hospitalized rather than die. Despite fewer attempts, adolescent boys are over four times more likely to succeed at suicide than are adolescent girls. (11) Women are more prone to depression and thus more prone to attempting suicide more often than men. They succeed far less than men, however. (12) The method used in suicide is (60%) firearms, (18%) poison, (15%) hanging or strangulation, and (7%) other. (13) Although suicide rates are generally lower for nonwhites than for whites, there is one startling exception: Among Native American youth, suicide is five times greater than among youth of the general population. (14) Gay and lesbian youth are several times over the national average for suicide attempts and completed suicides. These higher suicide rates undoubtedly reflect the relative lack of social support for a homosexual orientation. (15) After declining for nearly four

257

decades, the suicide rate among elderly Americans climbed nearly 9% between 1980 and 1992. The rates seemed to be increasing in 1993 and 1994. The reasons may include acceptance of suicide and chronic illness. (16) Unfortunately, suicide rates have tripled among adolescents and young adults in the last several decades. College students are at higher risk than their noncollege peers. Suicide is the third leading cause of death for young people between the ages 15-24. (17) Someone with a chronic disease or illness is more prone to commit suicide than someone with a terminal illness. (18) The figure is 250,000 attempts each year. Otherwise the statement is correct. (19) Most people who commit suicide are over the age of 45. However youthful suicide has grown between 200 and 300% between 1960 and 1988. (20) According to the Centers for Disease Control (1995), AIDS moved ahead of suicide as the eighth leading cause of death. Suicide is now ninth. These statistics are for 1992, the last reporting year available.

98. The following sources were used for the *Suicide Knowledge Questionnaire*. Wade, C., & Tavris, C. (1996). *Psychology* (4th Ed.). New York: HarperCollins; Weiten, W. (1995). *Psychology: Themes and Variations* (3rd Ed.). Pacific Grove, CA: Brooks/Cole; Despelder, L. A., & Strickland, A. L. (1996). *The Last Dance* (4th Ed.). Mountain View, CA: Mayfield; Berk, L. E. (1996). *Infants, Children, and Adolescents* (2nd Ed.). Boston: Allyn & Bacon; Zimbardo, P. G., & Gerrig, R. J. (1996). *Psychology and Life* (14th Ed.). New York: HarperCollins; Sternberg, R. J. (1994). *In Search of the Human Mind*. New York: Harcourt Brace; and Seiden, R. (1978). Where are they now? A follow-up study of suicide attempters from the Golden Gate Bridge. *Suicide and Life-Threatening Behavior*, 8: 203-216.

99. Alzheimer's Association (1994). *Alzheimer's Disease: An Overview*. Chicago: Alzheimer's Disease and Related Disorders Association, Inc.

100. Alzheimer's Association (1994). *Especially for the Alzheimer Caregiver*. Chicago: Alzheimer's Disease and Related Disorders Association, Inc.

101. When someone has a mild infection, the condition is referred to as HIV-associated minor cognitive/motor disorder. If the infection is severe, the condition is referred to as HIV-associated Dementia Complex or AIDS-related Dementia Complex (ADC). See Mark, R. (Ed.). (1996). *FOCUS: A Guide to AIDS Research and Counseling*, 2(2), 8; and Moran, F. (1992). *Living with Dementia*. San Francisco: Impact AIDS, Inc., p. 1. Available from 3692-18th St., San Francisco, CA 94110. This material deals with AIDS-related dementia.

102. Alzheimer's Association (1993). *Alzheimer's Disease and Related Disorders: A Description of the Dementias*. Chicago: Alzheimer's Disease and Related Disorders Association, Inc.

103. Alzheimer's Association (1990). *If You Think Someone You Know Has Alzheimer's Disease*. Chicago: Alzheimer's Disease and Related Disorders Association, Inc.

104. The following resources were used in the development of the *Alzheimer and Dementia-Related Diseases and Illnesses Questionnaire*. *Communicating with the Alzheimer Patient; When the Diagnosis is Alzheimer's; If You Have Alzheimer's Disease: What You Should Know, What You Can Do; Caregiving at Home; Alzheimer's Disease and Related Disorders: A Description of the Dementias; If You Think Someone You Know Has Alzheimer's Disease; Financial and Health Care Benefits You May Need; Memory and Aging; Care for Advanced Alzheimer's Disease; Alzheimer's Disease: Services You May Need; Alzheimer's Disease: An Overview; Local Considerations for Alzheimer Patients; Standing By You: Family Support Groups; Directions in Alzheimer's Disease Research; The Alzheimer's Association; Especially for the Alzheimer Caregiver; The Younger Alzheimer Patient; Alzheimer's Disease:* and *Especially for Teenagers*. The above educational brochures by Alzheimer's Association (1990-1994). Chicago: Alzheimer's Disease and Related Disorders Association, Inc.

Additional major resources included Moran, F. (1992). *Living with Dementia*. San Francisco: Impact AIDS,

Inc., Available from 3692-18th St., San Francisco, CA 94110. Mace, N. L., and Rabins, P. V. (1991).*The 36-Hour Day: A Family Guide to Caring for Persons with Alzheimer's Disease and Related Dementing Illnesses*. Baltimore: Johns Hopkins University Press, and Aronson, M. K. (1988). *Understanding Alzheimer's Disease*. New York: Scribners.

105. The correct responses for the "Alzheimer and Dementia-Related Diseases and Illnesses Questionnaire are as follows: (1) False. At this time, there is no single diagnostic test for AD. A complete physical, psychiatric and neurological evacuation by a physician experienced in diagnosing dementing disorders should be obtained when symptoms are noticed. The exam should include a detailed medical history, mental status test, neuropsychological testing, blood work, urinalysis, chest x-ray, electroencephalography (EEG), computerized tomography (CT scan), and electrocardiogram (EKG). Such an evaluation is essential to determine whether the dementia is the result of a treatable illness. When this kind of detailed examination is done, the accuracy of the diagnosis is about 90%. However, the only way to confirm a diagnosis of Alzheimer's disease is through autopsy of the brain tissue at the time of death. (2) False. The label senile dementia often was used in the past to describe an individual 65 years or older with dementia. Senility used to be considered a normal part of aging. Today, physicians recognize that dementia is not a normal part of aging, but the result of an illness such as AD. (3) False. Dementia is more likely to occur as a person gets older. Approximately 10% of people age 65 are affected by AD. This percentage rises to 47.2% for those 85 or older. AD and other dementias can occur in middle age as well. The youngest documented case is that of a 28-year old individual. AD and other dementias can strike those in their 20s, 40s and 50s. (4) False. Dementia is not a disease itself, but a group of symptoms that characterize certain diseases and conditions. Dementia is commonly defined as a decline in intellectual functioning that is severe enough to interfere with the ability to perform routine activities. In addition to being caused by diseases such as AD or Parkinson's, the second most common form of dementia is caused by strokes and other vascular diseases. (5) True. A number of other conditions can cause dementia or dementia-like symptoms: depression, drug reactions, thyroid disease, nutritional deficiencies, brain tumors, head injuries, alcoholism, infections (meningitis, syphilis, AIDS) and hydrocephalus. (6) False. 56% of all dementia is due to AD, whereas 14% are caused by vascular and stroke causes. (7) True. AD and dementia-related diseases are progressive, degenerative diseases that attack the brain. The results are impaired memory, thinking and behavior. AD alone affects 4 million American adults. (8) True. The statement is correct as written. (9) False. The correct medical term is arteriosclerosis. Dementia symptoms can be associated with arteriosclerosis, but only when multiple cerebral infarcts (strokes) have occurred. And when this does happen, the condition is called multi-infarct dementia. (10) True. Though different than AD, this disease shares many of the same characteristics. Huntington's Disease begins with muscle tremors in the face and limbs. Personality changes occur along with depression and memory disturbances. Though this disease can be partially controlled through drug management, there is no treatment available to halt the progression. (11) False. Great headway has been made into the causes of AD and the other dementias over the last 15 years, but the answer is still elusive. Research of significance is now occurring in the fields neuropathology, biochemistry, genetics, virology, toxicology, and other risk factors. (12) True. (13) True. (14) True. (15) True. See #1 above for more detail. (16) False. Recent trends in behavioral management are moving away from the use of drugs and focusing on non-drug management. These methods include better environmental design, patient monitoring systems, organized activities, and programs tailored to individual needs. (17) True. As with any chronic illness or disease, there may be a support group which addresses the particular needs of people with that disease or illness. The support group allows those working with dementia patients to learn about and locate community resources. The ideas shared in the group can also go a long way in preventing caregivers from having to "re-invent the wheel." (18) False. There are many legal options for dementia patients prior to their disease disabling them. The reader is encouraged to look to such legal instruments as "durable power of attorney," "living trusts," "wills," "living wills," "conservatorships," and "guardianships." (19) False. AD, and most of the other dementias, strike equally at men and women, all races, and all socioeconomic groups. (20) False, though it is possible. How quickly AD and the other dementias progress varies. For AD the course of the disease usually progresses an average of eight years from the time the symptoms first appear, although AD has known to last as long as 25 years. From onset of symptoms, the life span of a person with Alzheimer's can range anywhere from three to 20 or more years. The disease is always fatal.

106. Lindemann, E. (1944). The symptomatology and management of acute grief. *American Journal of Psychiatry*, 101, 141-148 and Rando, T. A. (1993). Anticipatory grief. In R. Kastenbaum & B. K. Kastenbaum (Eds.), *Encyclopedia of Death*. New York: Avon, pp. 12-15

107. Rando, T. A. (1992-1993). The increasing prevalence of complicated mourning: The onslaught is just beginning. *Omega, Journal of Death and Dying*, 26, 43-60

108. Kochanek K. D. and Hudson, B.L. (1995). Advance report of final mortality statistics, 1992. *Monthly Vital Statistics Report*; Vol. 43, No. 6, suppl. Hyattsville, Maryland: National Center for Health Statistics. It should be noted that the figures are average totals. Figures vary by sex, race, and other factors. But they do provide a flavor for one's life expectancy.

109. Adapted from Greer, W. R. (1985, June 26). Value of one life? from $8.37 to $10 million. *New York Times*, p. 1. Printed with permission.

110. Mason, M. (1991, May 20). In no time, back on all four feet. *Newsweek*, pp. 61-63.

111. Albert, A., & Bulcroft, K. (1988). Pets, families and the life course, *Journal of Marriage and the Family*, 50, 543--552; Cain, A. O. (1985). Pets as family members. In M. B. Sussman (Ed.), *Pets and the Family*. New York: Haworth Press, pp. 5-10; Cowles, K. U. (1985). The death of a pet: Human responses to the breaking of the bond. In M. B. Sussman (Ed.). *Pets and the Family*. New York: Haworth Press, pp. 135-148; and Cusak, O. (1988). *Pets and Mental Health*. New York: Haworth Press.

112. Keddie, K.M.G. (1977). Pathological mourning after the death of a domestic pet. *British Journal of Psychiatry*, 131, 21-25.

113. Katcher, A. (1982, September-October). Are companion animals good for your health? A review of the evidence. *Aging*, pp. 2-8.

114. McCulloch, M. (1981). The pet as prothesis: Defining criteria for the adjunctive use of companion animals in the treatment of medically ill, depressed outpatients. In B. Fogle (Ed.) *Interrelations Between People and Pets*. Springfield, IL: Charles C. Thomas, pp. 101-123.

115. Corson, S. A., and Corson, E. O. (1980). Pet animals as nonverbal communication mediators in psychotherapy in institutional settings. In S. A. Corson and E. O. Corson (Eds.). *Ethology and Nonverbal Communications in Mental Health*. Elmsford, NY: Pergamon Press, pp. 83-110.

116. Bricke, C. M. (1984). Depression in the nursing rooms: a pilot study using pet-facilitated therapy. In R. R. Anderson and L. A. Hart (Eds.). *The Pet Connection*. Minneapolis: University of Minnesota Press, pp. 407-415; Bustad, L. K., and Hines, L. M. (1982). Placement of animals with the elderly: Benefits and strategies. *California Veterinarian*, 36, 37-44; Cusak, O. (1988). *Pets and Mental Health*. New York: Haworth Press.

117. Levinson, B. M. (1965). Pet psychotherapy: Use of household pets in the treatment of behavior disorder in childhood. *Psychological Reports*, 17, 695-698.

118. Heiman, M. (1965). Psychoanalytic observations on the relationship of pet and man. *Veterinary Medicine/Small Animal Clinician*, 60, 713-718, and Muschel, I. (1984). Pet therapy with terminal cancer patients. *Social Casework*, 65, 451-458.

119. Dickinson, G. (1992). First childhood death experiences. *Omega*, 25(2): 169-182.

120. Cowles, K. U. (1985). The death of a pet: Human responses to the breaking of the bond. In M. B. Sussman (Ed.), *Pets and the Family*. New York: Haworth Press, pp. 135-148.

121. *News and Courier* (1987). Pet's death can be as grievous as person's. Charleston, S.C., March, p. 7A.

122. Worden, J. (1991). *Grief Counseling and Grief Therapy: A Handbook for the Mental Health Practitioner*. New York: Springer.

123. Some of the clinical definitions of the defense mechanisms were taken from Lahey, B. (1995). *Psychology. An Introduction*. Dubuque, IA: Brown & Benchmark, pp. 516-517.

124. Some of the material used was derived from Oaks, J. & Ezell, G. (1993). *Dying and Death: Coping, Caring, Understanding* (2nd. ed.). Scottsdale, AZ.: Gorsuch Scarisbrick, pp. 109-110. They cite Ferguson et al. in Margolis, O. (1981) *Acute Grief*. New York: Columbia University.

125. This exercise was developed after a conversation on GriefNet/Internet with Maryanna L. Fournier for which the author wishes to acknowledge her helpful suggestions.

126. I wish to thank Dr. Carla Sofka, a member of the Association for Gravestone Studies, for sharing this information with me. It is excellent advice.

127. Joseph, Jenny. (1992) "Warning: When I Am An Old Woman I Shall Wear Purple." Watsonville, CA: Paper-Mache Press. From Selected Poems published by Bloodaxe Books, Ltd. Used by permission.

128. Jung, C. G. (1964). *Man and His Symbols*. New York: Doubleday & Company.

129. Adapted from Zunin, L. M. and Zunin, H. S. (1991). *The Art of Condolence*. New York: HarperCollins, 1991.

130. Stanford, G., and Perry, D. (1975). *Death out of the Closet: A Curriculum Guide to Living with Dying*. New York: Bantam, p. 105.

131. Some questions were adapted from DeSpelder, L., and Strickland., A. (1992). *The Last Dance* (3rd ed.). Mountain View, CA: Mayfield. The correct answers to the matching exercise are: 1-d; 2-e; 3-f; 4-g; 5-h; 6-i; 7-c; 8-b; 9-j; 10-k; 11-l; 12-a; 13-m; 14-n and 15-0.

132. Adapted from DeSpelder, L. and Strickland, A. (1992). *The Last Dance* (3rd ed.). Mountain View, CA: Mayfield.

Next Edition Update
Grieving Days, Healing Days

Have a Good Activity That Should Be in This Book?
Send It In And You Will Get Credit In The Next Edition!

To: Dr. J. Davis Mannino
      Post Office Box 14031
      San Francisco, CA 94114-0031
      Fax: (707) 869-0628 or email: psychdavis@aol.com

1. _____   Davis, I think the following needs to be changed in your next edition.

_____

_____

_____

_____

_____

2. _____   Davis, I think an exercise regarding the following needs to be in your next edition.

_____

_____

_____

_____

3. _____   Davis, I have attached a copy of a suggested activity I think should be in the next edition. I understand that by signing my name below I grant permanent and free permission to use the attached exercise and that I am the said author of the exercise. I understand further that the exercise may be modified and that I will be acknowledged as the author of the exercise.

Print Name: _____

Signature: _____

Address: _____

              _____

Phone/Fax/email   _____

To The Readers of This Book

I hope you have found meaning, enjoyment, and real help from using *Grieving Days, Healing Days*. As Epicurus said in the third century b.c.: "The art of living well and the art of dying well are one." Your thoughts and ideas concerning this book are most valuable to me. Your comments will help me craft a better book in future editions.

1. Please describe what you enjoyed and found helpful in *Grieving Days, Healing Days*.

2. How might I improve this book? You tell me.

3. In the space below or in a separate letter, please write any other additional comments you might have.

4. Optional: Please provide your name and address. May I quote you, either in the promotion of this book or in future publishing ventures? ___ Yes ___ No Thank you for your time in this matter.

Dr. J. Davis Mannino
Post Office Box 14031
San Francisco, CA 94114-0031
Fax: (707) 869-0628 or email: psychdavis@aol.com

About the Author

Dr. J. Davis Mannino teaches "death and dying" among other psychology courses in the Behavioral Sciences Department of Santa Rosa Junior College in Santa Rosa, California. He has spent the last 15 years working with death and dying patients in his private clinical practice in San Francisco and in the Russian River area of Sonoma County, California. He is an expert on the mental health aspects of AIDS and authors a "caregiving column" for a local community newspaper. His education includes a Bachelor of Arts, magna cum laude, in Social Sciences from the University of New York at Stony Brook; a Masters in Social Work, summa cum laude, from San Francisco State University; and a Doctorate of Education in Counseling and Educational Psychology from the University of San Francisco. Dr. Mannino has over 16 years experience in San Francisco city government, with his last two major assignments including that of a Managing Supervisor for Child Abuse Investigation and Director, Office of Refugee Affairs. In the latter position he additionally served as Refugee Affairs Liaison to former San Francisco Mayor Dianne Feinstein, currently a California United States Senator. He is most proud of the fact that his office assisted in the meaningful resettlement of nearly 20,000 refugees and political asylum cases to San Francisco.

Davis is a big fan of cats, especially his own 19-pound black-and-white cat named Slyvester, whom he advises should be handled with caution as he is often mistaken for meatloaf.